I0795621

IMAGES
of America

AROUND BLAIR COUNTY

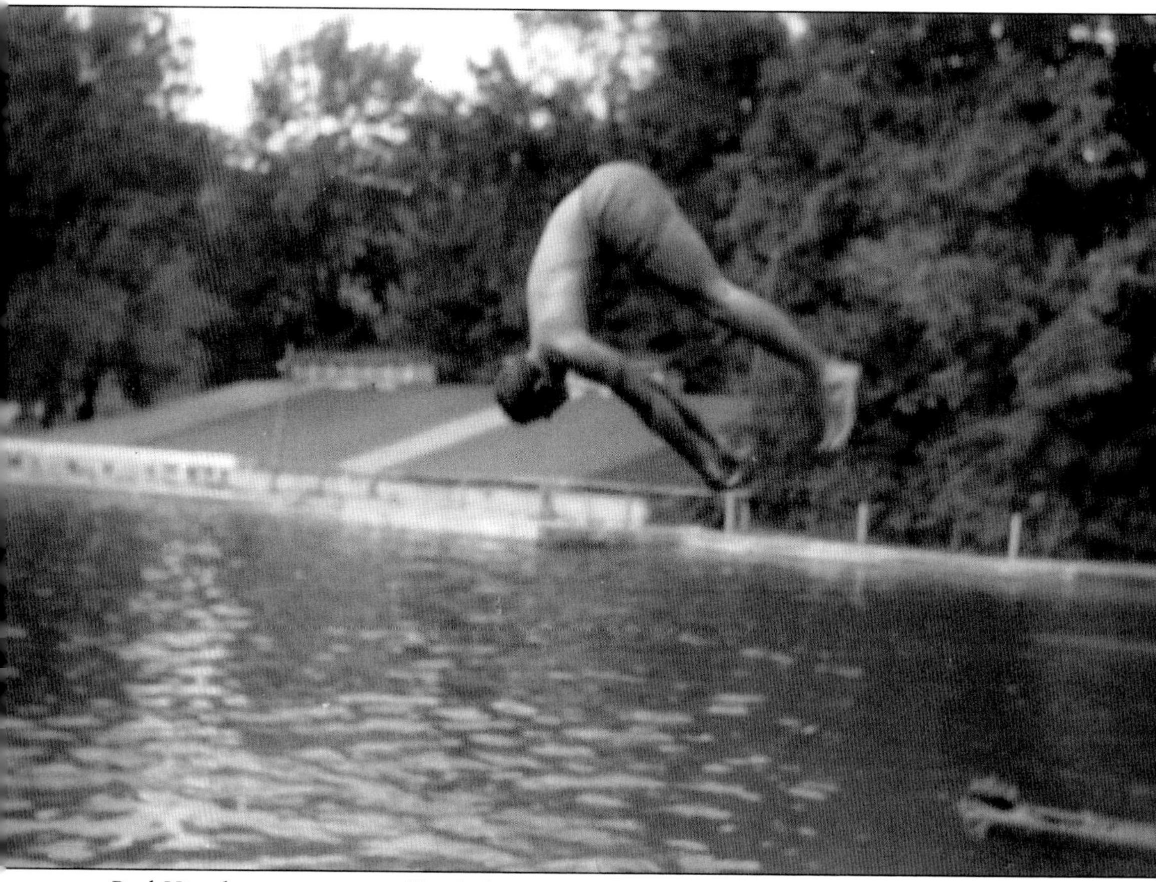

Paul Hite demonstrates a jackknife dive at Mountain Lake in the summer of 1959. There were various dives, including the swan dive from the high-diving board. Youngsters came from various hamlets on bike to swim in the cool Mountain Lake.

IMAGES
of America

AROUND BLAIR COUNTY

Sr. Anne Frances Pulling

ARCADIA
PUBLISHING

ISBN 978-0-7385-1024-8

Published by Arcadia Publishing
Charleston, South Carolina

Printed in the United States of America

Library of Congress Catalog Card Number: 2002102014

For all general information contact Arcadia Publishing at:
Telephone 843-853-2070
Fax 843-853-0044
E-mail sales@arcadiapublishing.com

Visit us on the Internet at www.arcadiapublishing.com

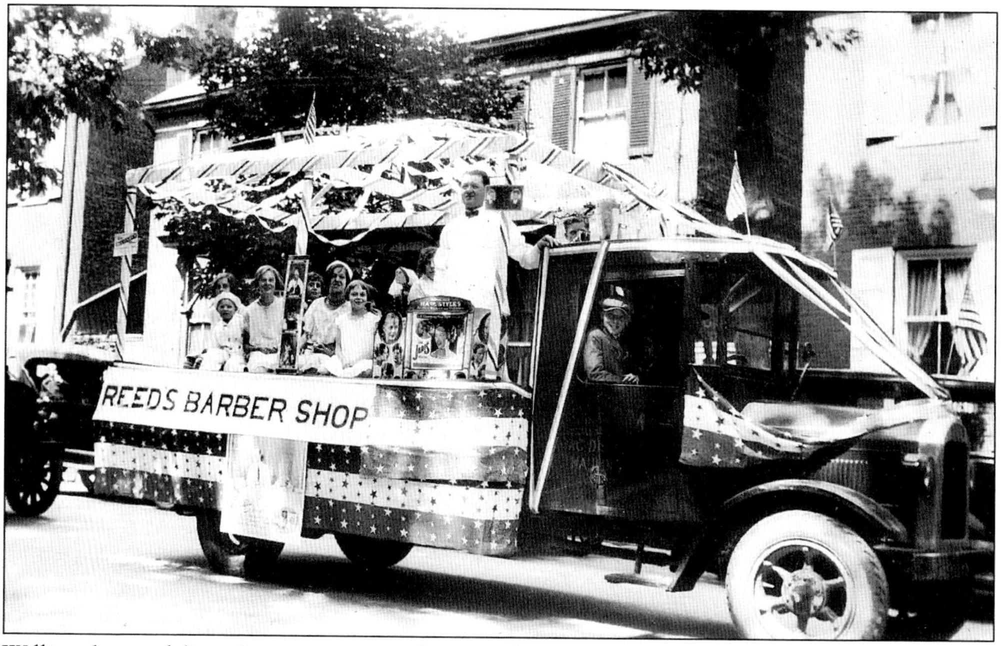

Williamsburg celebrated many events with a parade. The parade of September 1, 1932, featured Reeds Barbershop, a prominent business in Williamsburg at that time. The parade was held in memory of Wilmer Stultz. This native son was the first aviator to fly across the Atlantic Ocean with passengers aboard. Amelia Earhart and Louis Gordon accompanied him from Newfoundland to Wales.

Contents

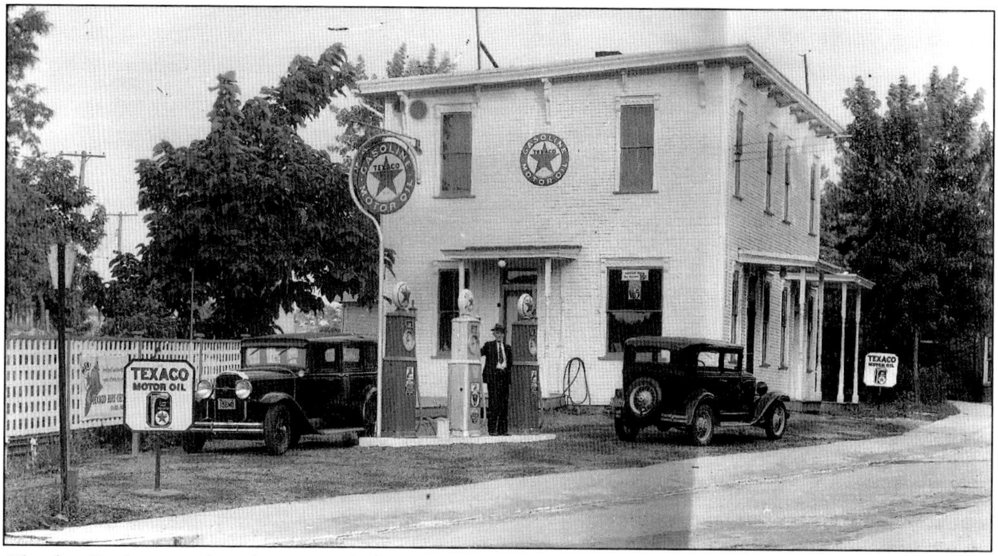

Charles Dick owned and operated this service station in Roaring Spring across the street from Nason Hospital. Established in 1932, the station was among the earliest Texaco dealerships in the area. Texaco later came out with the slogan "You can trust your car to the man who wears the star." Many residents did. In addition to motor oil and gasoline, Charles Dick offered an extensive line of confections.

Acknowledgments

This publication is based on research, records, periodicals, documents, newspapers, and interviews with residents, many of whom graciously supplied information and offered constructive suggestions. A special thank-you goes to Tim Vanscoyoc of the Blair County Historical Society and the Blair County Chamber of Commerce for sharing many photographs and a wealth of knowledge.

Gratitude is extended to the Altoona Mirror; David Snyder of the Cove Herald; Suzanne Ohl and Robert Tennis of Tyrone; Betty and Thomas James of Slinky Inc.; Msgr. Timothy Stine of the Catholic Register; Charles Pillar, manager of the Altoona-Blair County Airport; Sr. Joachim of Garvey Manor; Sr. Evelyn Marie of the Sisters of the Holy Family of Nazareth; the Franciscan Friars of Hollidaysburg; Ferd and Mary Hite of Newry; Brian Meiser of Leighty's Market; Cloyd Neeley and Kathleen Kennedy of Duncansville; Michelle McIntyre, Nevin Albright, and Linda Ricci of Roaring Spring.

A prayerful gratitude goes to all who assisted in any way by supplying photographs, constructive suggestions, and proofreading. I am especially grateful to my own religious community, the Sisters of Mercy of the Dallas Regional Community, for their support and encouragement in this project.

—Sr. Anne Frances Pulling

INTRODUCTION

Blair County, a picturesque area of 530 square miles, is nestled in the foothills of the Allegheny Mountains of western Pennsylvania. History comes alive in its charming hamlets and towns. Its diverse natural resources and exquisite vistas were attractive to the early settlers. The county abounds in lush forests, fertile valleys, and vibrant minerals. The hills of Blair County hold an unlimited supply of iron, lead, and especially limestone. Early in the 20th century, iron furnaces, forges, mills, and quarries sprang up throughout the hamlets. Many are still preserved.

Stephen Franks, a fur trader on the Susquehanna River, established the area's first permanent white settlement and, in 1764, created the first highway in Blair County. Once a Native American trail, it became the Frankstown Road from the Frankstown branch of the Juniata River. The county was named for John Blair (1766–1832), a progressive businessman and an early advocate of a new county. Blair had an intense interest in roads, transportation, and commerce in central and western Pennsylvania. He represented Huntingdon County in the state legislature. Blair County was carved from both Huntingdon and Bedford Counties in 1846. Judge Jeremiah Black presided at the earliest elections. Black later became a Supreme Court justice, attorney general, and secretary of state under Pres. James Buchannan.

The Hollidaysburg Canal System became a transfer point for canal traffic in 1832. Passengers and cargo arrived by boat and were transferred to the Old Portage Railroad, which took them on a series of inclined planes over the Allegheny Mountains. It became a significant transportation center and, later, the seat of Blair County. Duncansville has retained its position as an antiques mecca. Passengers who brought too much cargo for the Old Portage Railroad had to leave some behind, thus giving rise to the secondhand and antique industry. This settlement, once rich in the iron business, derived its name through the flip of a coin. Religious, educational, and cultural needs were met in all the hamlets. Churches of various denominations and schools on all levels dotted the landscapes throughout the settlements.

Morrison's Cove is a canoe-shaped valley formed by three mountains and divided by a watershed. Huge springs are prominent throughout the cove. The largest and loudest spring was located at what became Roaring Spring. Early interest in the cove's fertile land was realized when government officials from Cumberland County hired a surveyor, James Morrison, to make a study of the cove. He realized unusual potential for agriculture, reported back, and then relocated his family to the cove. He settled in what is now Martinsburg, in the center of the cove. This was later the chosen site for the Altoona–Blair County Airport.

The manufacture of iron was the principal business of the county during the 19th century. Much of the coal and coke was sent to Pittsburgh and Johnstown for the steel furnaces. Williamsburg gave the steel industry Charles Schwab. His honored position as president of U.S. Steel and Bethlehem Steel did not deter him from remembering his hometown and humble beginnings. Mount Etna, the oldest and one of the largest furnaces in the county, is preserved in Williamsburg.

Roaring Spring was the site where a physician, with a reputation as a skilled surgeon, turned an old hotel into a prominent hospital that has prospered, thrived, and expanded beyond his wildest dreams. Dr. Albert Nason was superintendent and chief of staff for more than 30 years and held the same position at Mercy Hospital, in Altoona, in its early days. Roaring Spring native Homer Butler was the town lamplighter. Each evening, he climbed his ladder and lit the streetlights. The lamps were cleaned and filled with kerosene twice weekly. A float caused the wick to extinguish itself at midnight, when everyone had to be off the streets. Lamplighters worked in all kinds of weather for the grand sum of $9 a month.

Tyrone took a prominent place in history on several occasions. Fred Waring, a native of Tyrone, was a musical genius who formed the internationally famous Pennsylvanians. He was also a celebrated inventor. Housewives of midcentury remember his Waring blender. Waring always remembered his roots. When Tyrone Hospital was just a dream, Waring brought his orchestra home and gave a concert for its benefit. Early in Tyrone history, George Wilson invented and manufactured his famous Cloverline Salve, which was a remedy for all ills. The Gardner Candy Company initiated the heart-shaped box so prevalent on Valentine's Day.

Branches of the Pennsylvania Railroad reached into many of the small hamlets. When ribbons of steel graced the hinterlands and shrill whistles echoed through secluded mountain settlements, inhabitants welcomed a new contact with the outside world. It meant transportation for citizens and convenient transit for moving commodities to markets. Shipping by rail became an industry in itself. Everything from coal and coke for the steel mills to produce for city markets was transported by rail.

There remain mementos of the historical past in many of these small hamlets. In Duncansville, the Old Canal Inn was established in 1957. It is located on the old canal site, where the Old Portage Railroad and canal boats met. It was here that boats were loaded on the railroad cars for the 36-mile trip over the Allegheny Mountains. The little inn has always been a family project. Its fine food keeps it as popular today as it was a half century ago.

One

Blazing the Trail

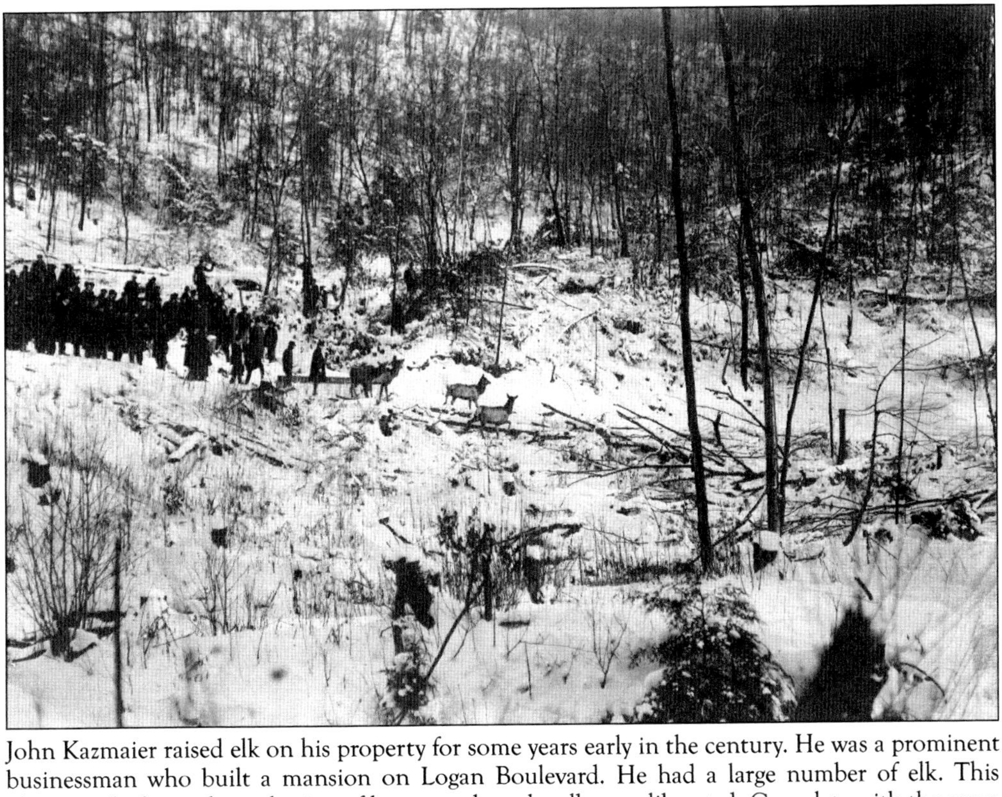

John Kazmaier raised elk on his property for some years early in the century. He was a prominent businessman who built a mansion on Logan Boulevard. He had a large number of elk. This photograph shows the gathering of hunters when the elk were liberated. Complete with the game warden, the party led the elk to pastures on the mountain. Animal tracks in the snow aided the party in tracking the elk.

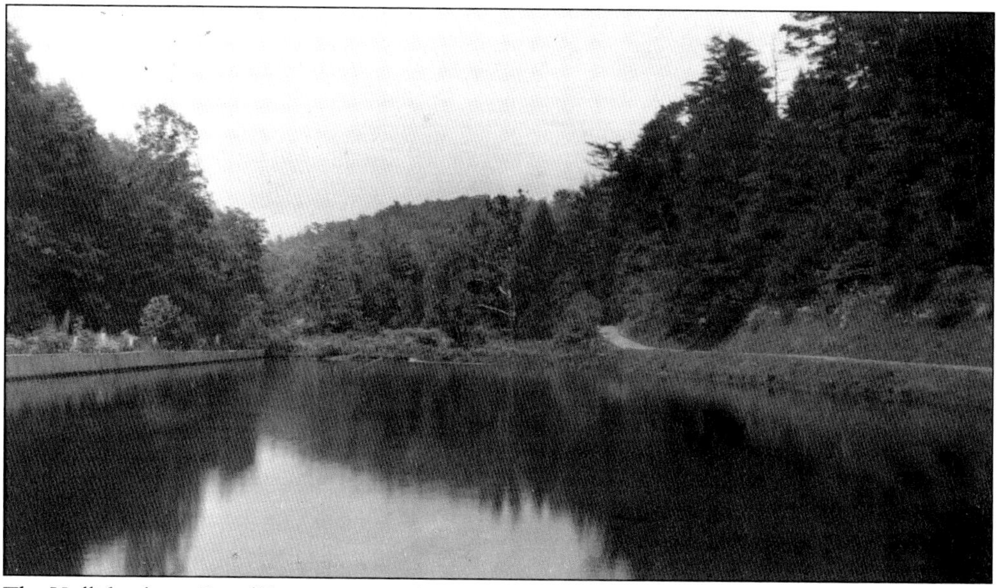

The Hollidaysburg Canal Basin site was determined by Sen. Thomas Jackson. It was 1,695 by 120 feet along South Juniata Street. The upper basin was 1,000 by 120 feet along Bedford Street in Gaysport (the present south side of Hollidaysburg). It was formed by damming the waters in the Beaver Dam branch of the Juniata River. The water level was regulated in 1839, when the Eastern Reservoir, south of Hollidaysburg, was constructed. Five hundred acres of valley farmland were flooded to create the reservoir.

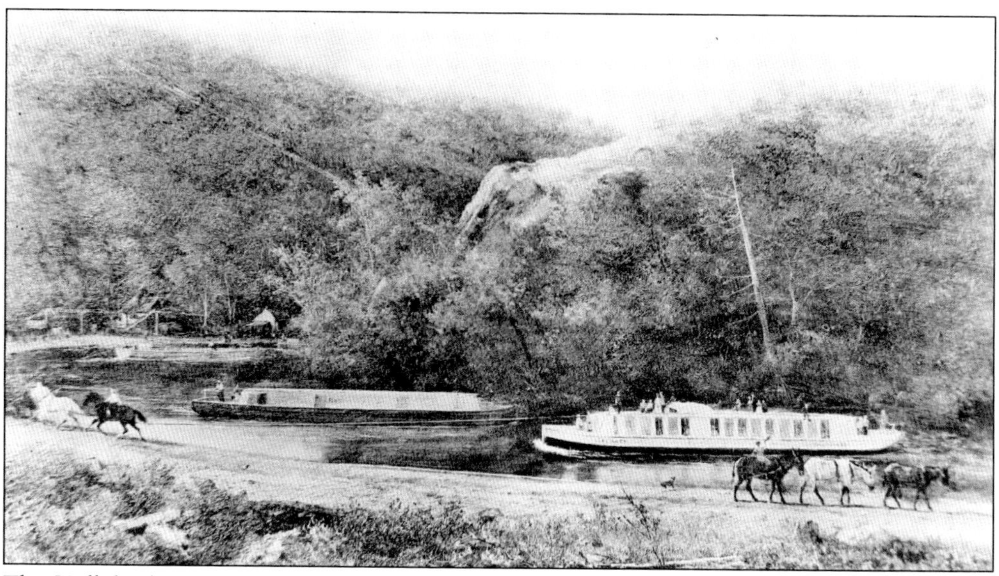

The Hollidaysburg Canal System served as a transfer point for canal traffic. It was here that passengers and cargo from the canal boats were loaded on to the railroad cars for the lift up on a series of 10 inclined planes over the rugged Allegheny Mountains. In 1834, the canal basin became a busy inland port offering seaport services. This included boat repair, chandlery supplies, inns, taverns, and shipping wharfs where cargo was transferred. During the busiest months, canal boats arrived and departed every 20 minutes.

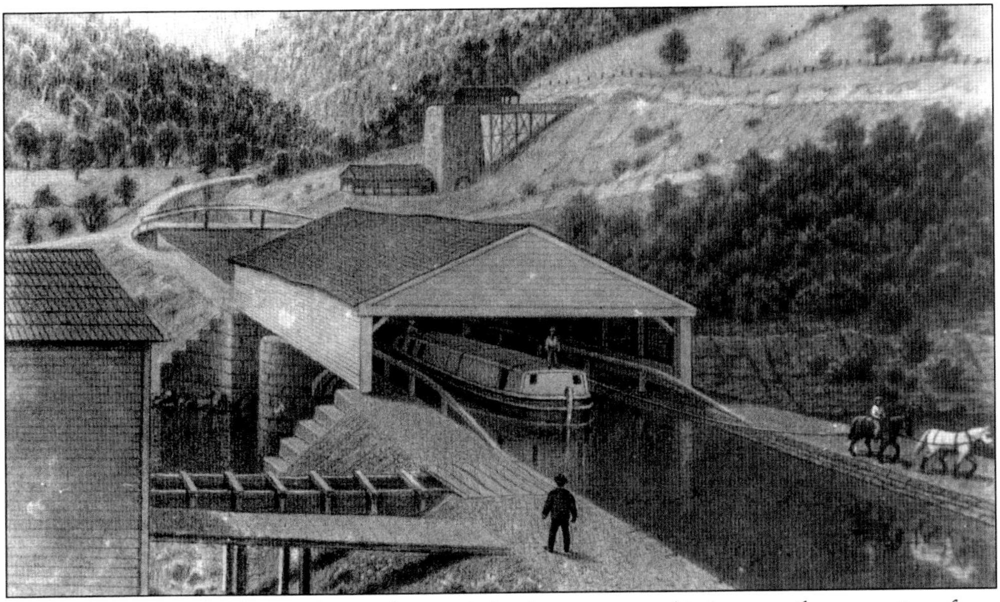

The Main Line Canal was designed as a hybrid system combining a rail connection from Philadelphia to Columbia on the Susquehanna River with canal passage to Hollidaysburg via the Juniata River Valley. It was built in 1826 to link Philadelphia and Pittsburgh. Westward expansion was feasible until it reached the mountain barrier. The Old Portage Railroad connected the canal basin of the Juniata River at Hollidaysburg in the east with the Connemaugh River Canal Basin near Johnstown in the west.

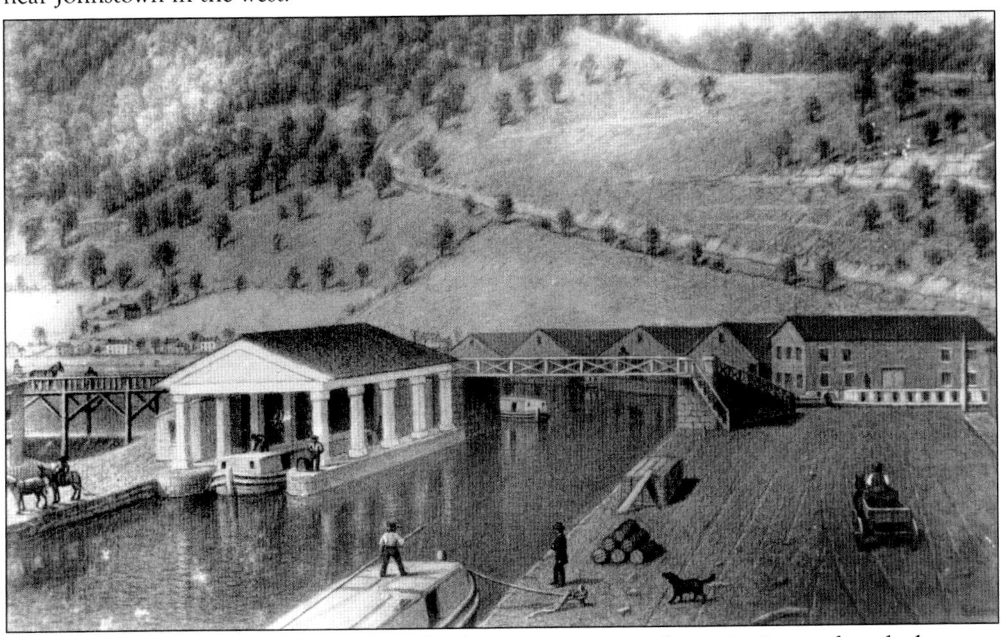

The canal basin expanded to include both construction and repair. Loss of trade between New York and the west spurred the construction of both the canal system and the Old Portage Railroad. Basin-based commercial operations included a leather tannery, boatman's tavern, a gristmill, and several shipping offices and warehouses. Boats were floated into the Connemaugh River at Johnstown for the final leg of their journey to Pittsburgh.

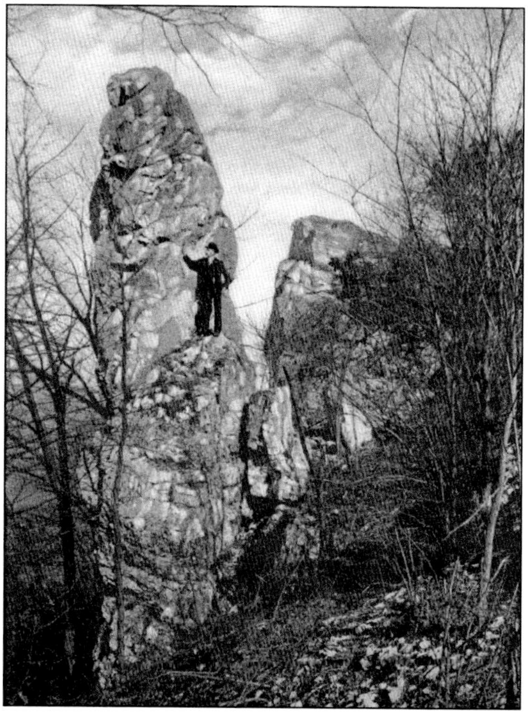

The Chimney Rocks are strange, tall, imposing formations of limestone that border the Juniata River. They initially served as a lookout for Native Americans. The largest one contained 120 perches. The rocks were used for signaling warriors who were watching in the valley below. Hollidaysburg has been guarded through the centuries by these silent sentinels, a natural wonder of Blair County. The Chimney Rocks can be viewed in clear weather from William Penn Highway and by moonlight on clear nights.

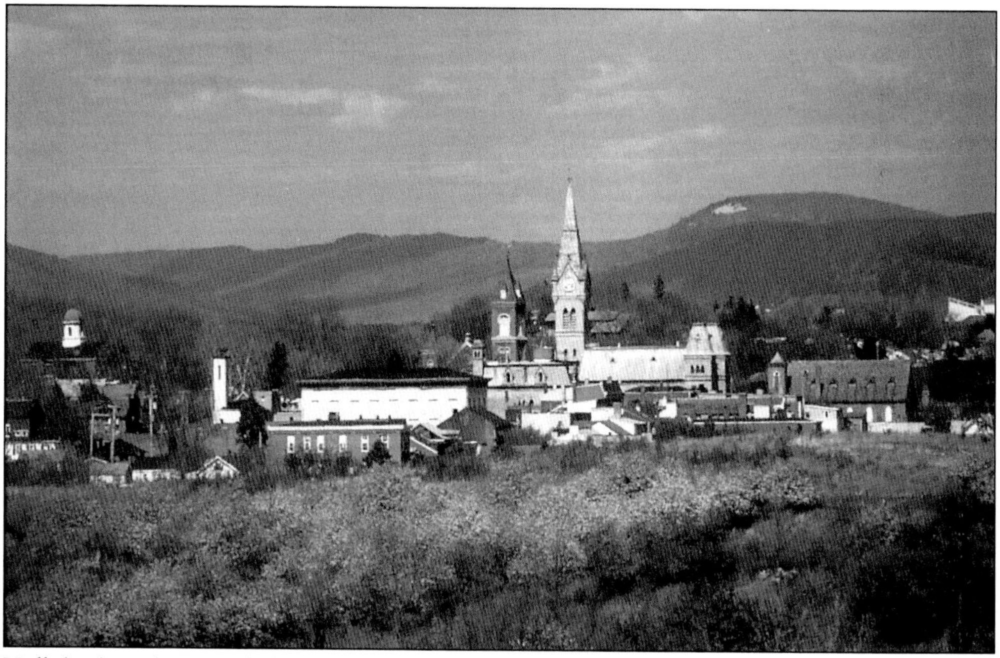

Hollidaysburg has a rich heritage. The spires of the courthouse dominate the landscape. The Mountain House was originally constructed at the junction of the Old Portage Railroad and the Hollidaysburg branch of the Pennsylvania Railroad known as the wye switches. The Mountain House was the scene of many local functions. When the Old Portage Railroad was abandoned, the building was razed and transported by train to Cresson, where it was assembled in its original form. It became Cresson's Mountain House.

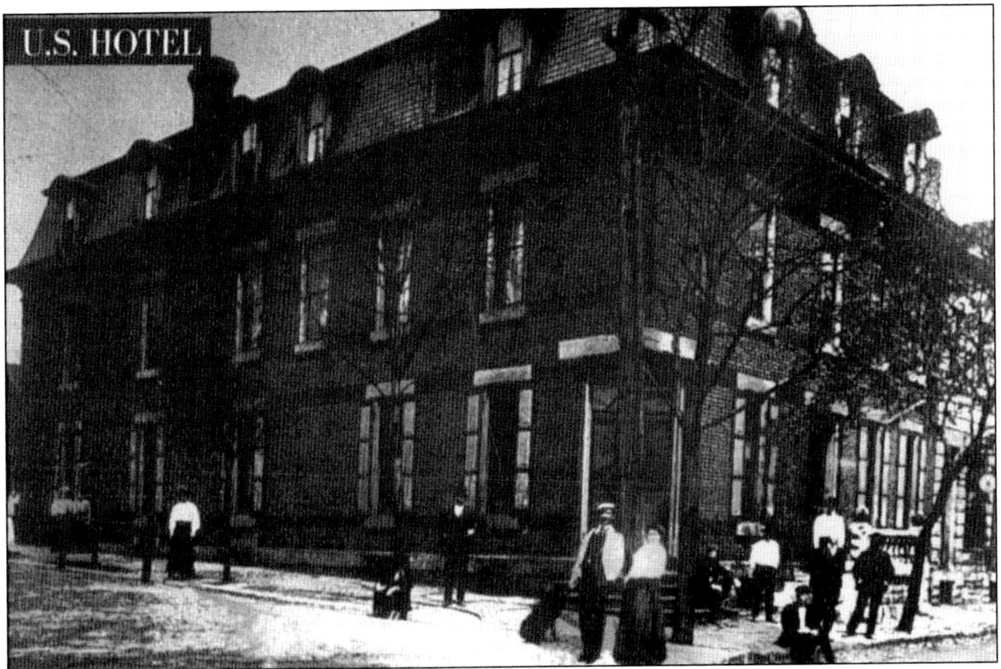

The U.S. Hotel was built by John Dougherty in 1835 to accommodate travelers on the canals and the Old Portage Railroad. Hollidaysburg boasted 14 daily canal boat lines, and the Juniata River Basin was the center of warehouses for shippers and traders. Hotel rooms were always full. In 1871, a fire destroyed the hotel. In 1886, Bavarian-born Engelbert Gromiller rebuilt the U.S. Hotel. It was dubbed the "best $1.50 a day house in the borough."

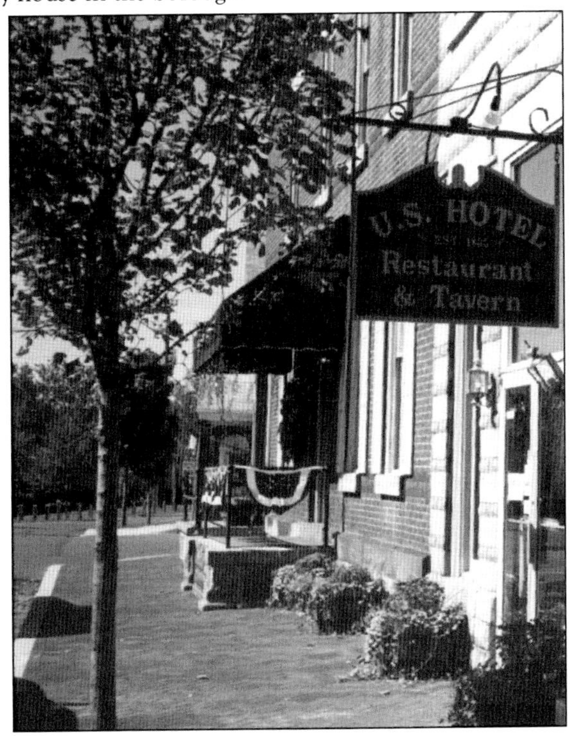

Englebert Gromiller was a brewmaster who installed a brewery beside the U.S. Hotel. In 1905, a cut-block barroom was added to the brick structure. The hotel boasts such original relics as a hand-carved mahogany backbar, stained-glass windows, and a brass foot rail, under which flows a still active water-trough spittoon. The hotel changed hands several times. The grandeur of this establishment has never diminished. The historic U.S. Hotel is still famous for its reputation as the best fine-dining house in the borough.

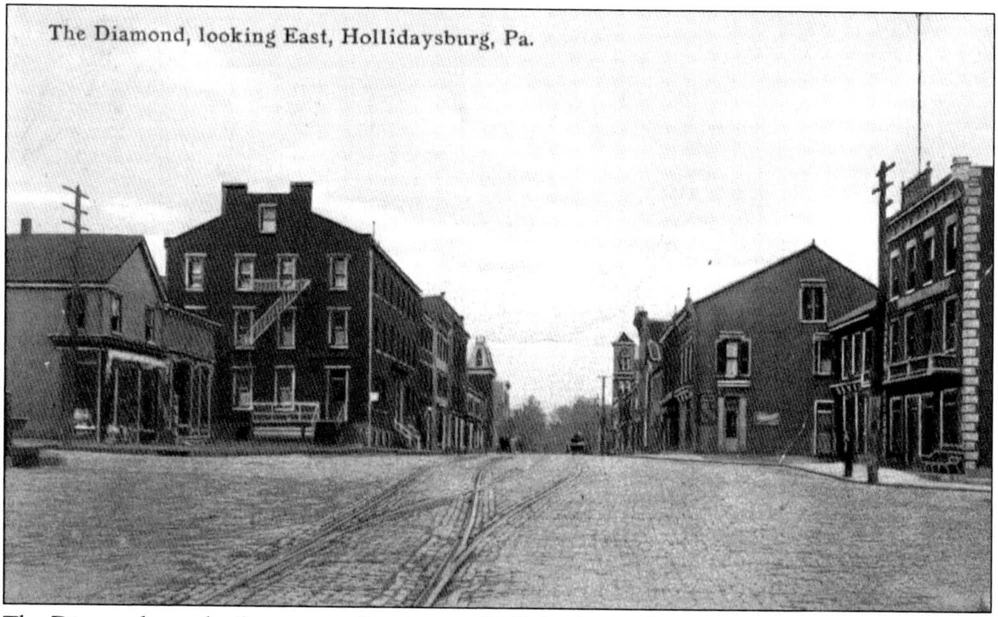

The Diamond was the first scene of activity in Hollidaysburg when pioneer Adam Holliday built a home here on the Juniata River in 1768. The town was laid out by surveyor Patrick Cassidy and, in 1836, became a borough. This 1896 photograph shows the American House on the left and Treese's Drug Store on the right. The American House, a first-class hostel, provided luxurious accommodations to travelers. The courthouse is on the extreme left. Note the trolley tracks along Allegheny Street.

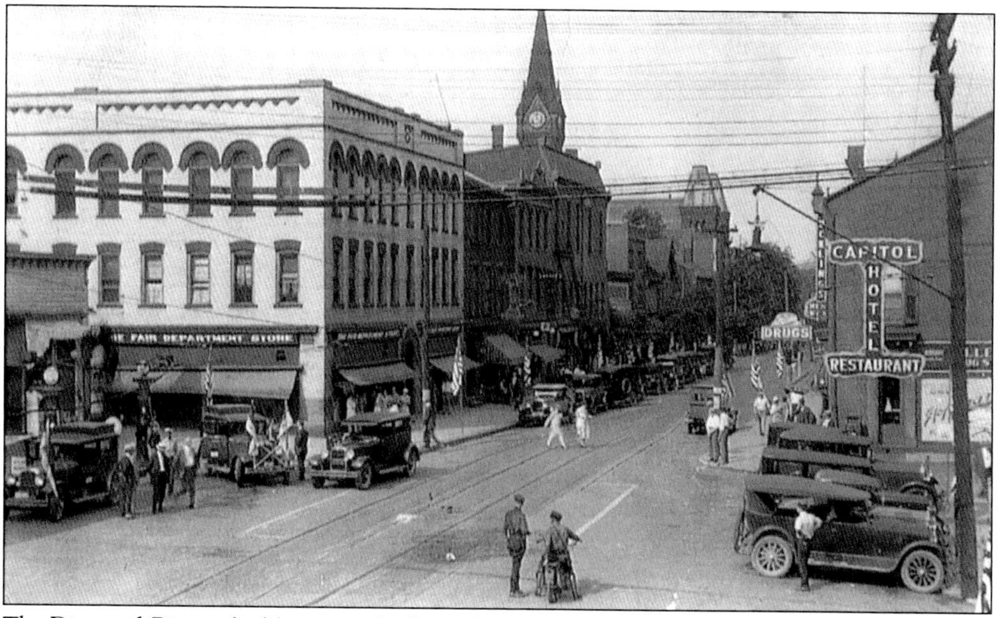

The Diamond District had become a beehive of activity by 1925. The Fair Department Store (left), owned by William Krelitz, had replaced the American House. The Capitol Hotel (right) was a prominent haven for visitors to the courthouse. Note the traffic light on the left corner and the Model T carrying American flags, turning on to Allegheny Street. Today, the Diamond District provides visitors a charming streetscape, selective shops, and distinctive dining opportunities.

The St. Mary's Roman Catholic parish was established in Hollidaysburg in 1841. Located on the corner of Clark and Church Streets, the original church was dedicated on St. Patrick's Day 1844. Three years later, there were 700 members in the congregation. The convent, school, rectory, and church later formed a complex at St. Mary's. This is the oldest standing church in the borough.

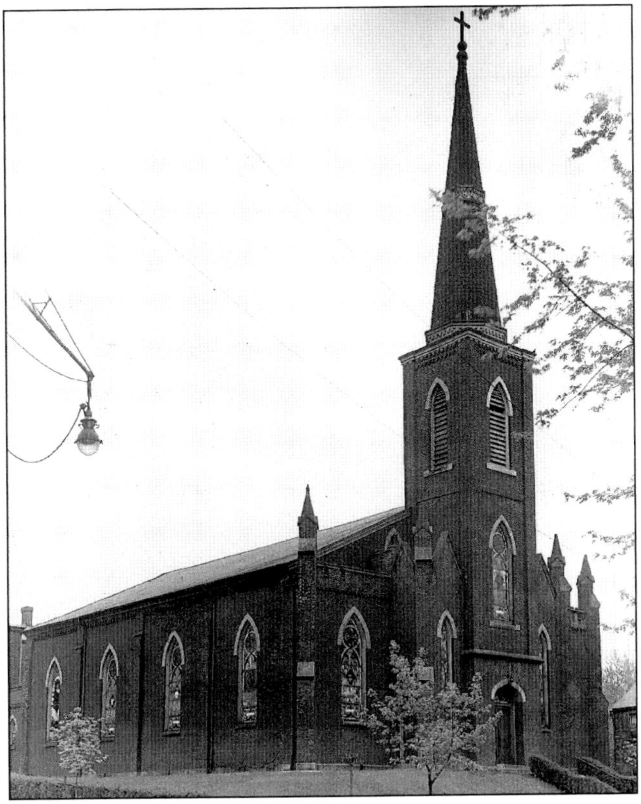

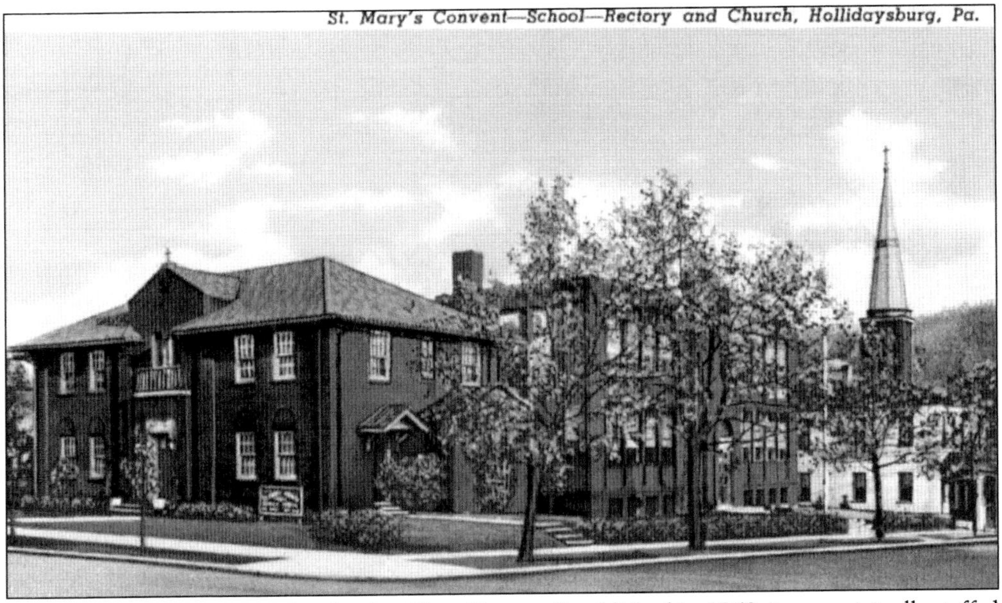

St. Mary's Convent—School—Rectory and Church, Hollidaysburg, Pa.

St. Mary's was the first parish school in Blair County. Established in 1853, it was originally staffed by the Sisters of Mercy of Pittsburgh. Sr. Elizabeth Strange, a pioneer who came from Ireland with the first Sisters of Mercy to the United States, was among the faculty. The original convent and school was the old St. James Hotel. Young ladies were trained in social graces and pursued classes in music, fine arts, courtesy, and etiquette in keeping with the custom of finishing schools.

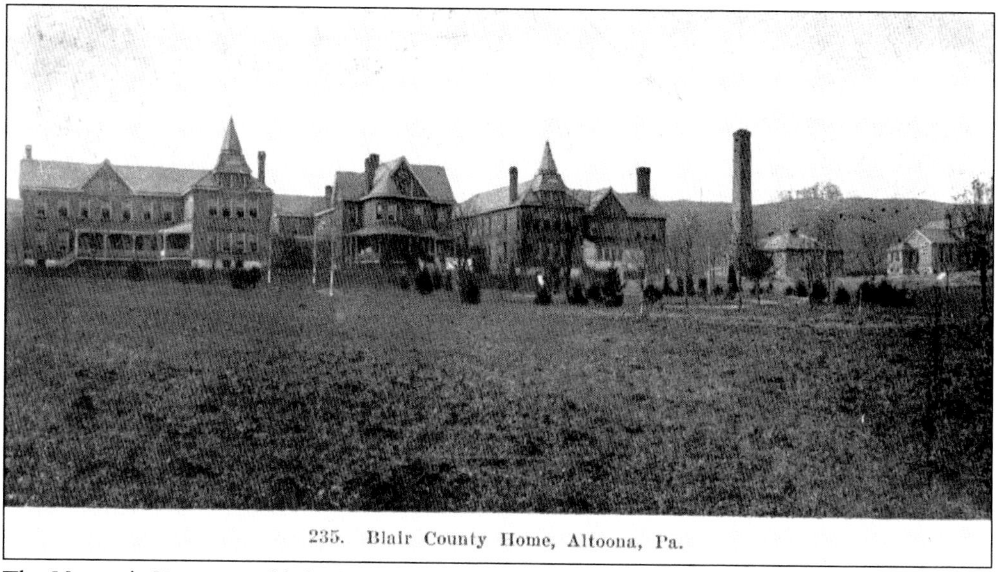

The Veteran's Home, established in 1904, was originally a poorhouse. The first residents were admitted in January 1906. It was under the jurisdiction of the directors of the poor until 1938, when that title was abolished. In 1941, it came under the Department of Welfare as a state mental institution until it closed in 1970. In 1977, it was transferred to military affairs. The hospital evolved into 326 acres to accommodate its 514 veterans. The facility is divided into nursing and personal care. Medical, clinical, nursing, and rehabilitative services are available to all residents.

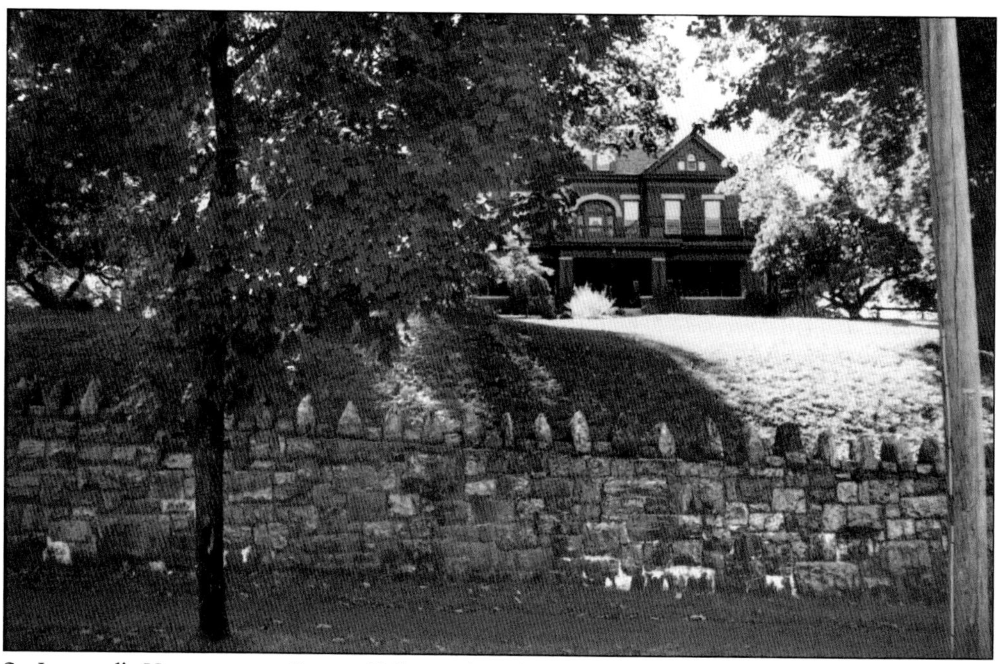

St. Leonard's Home crowns Sunset Hill. Purchased in 1946 by Leonard Miller, the property was presented to Bishop Richard T. Guilfoyle as a possible home for the aged. The Sisters of the Holy Family of Nazareth staffed the facility. Remodeling and additions to the former home of Peter Duncan were completed and, in 1947, St. Leonard's opened.

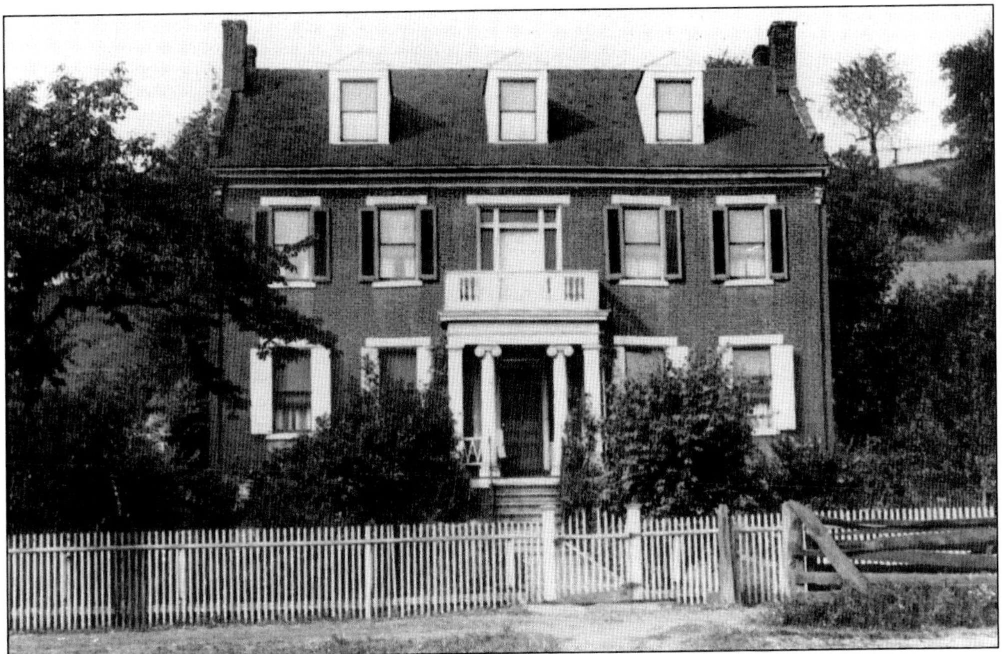

The Jackson Inn was built by Sen. Thomas Jackson in the 1830s. Jackson was instrumental in the location of the Juniata Division of the Main Line Canal. The 16-room Federal-style house, located on the corner of Newry and Allegheny Streets, contained fireplaces of Italian marble. In 1840, Catherine Jackson married Jacob Mattern. In 1901, an orchard was planted. This was the site of the prominent Mattern Orchards.

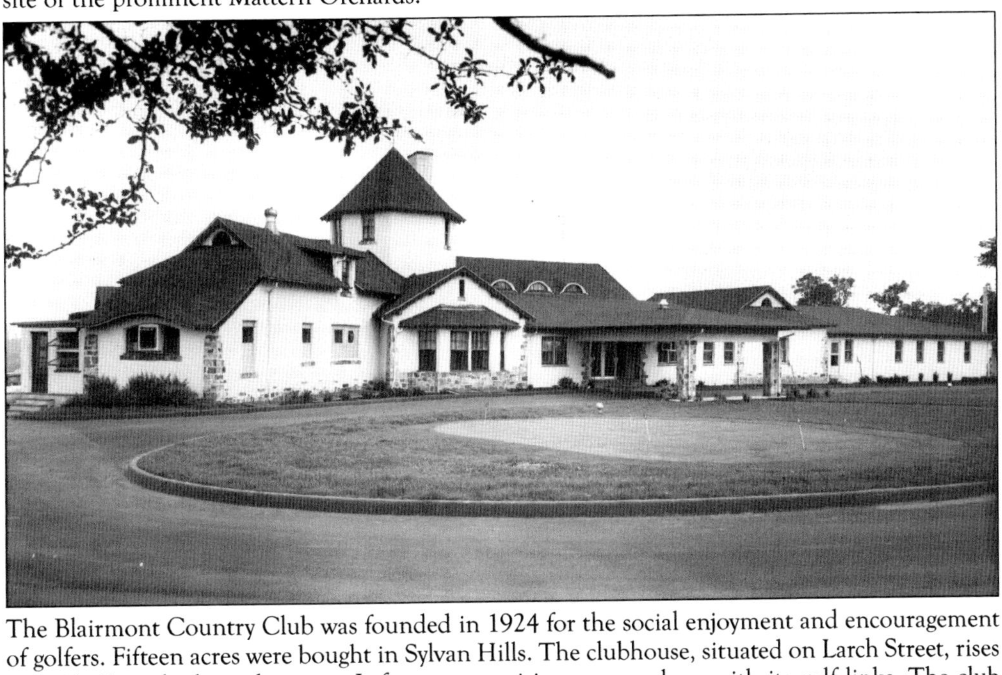

The Blairmont Country Club was founded in 1924 for the social enjoyment and encouragement of golfers. Fifteen acres were bought in Sylvan Hills. The clubhouse, situated on Larch Street, rises on a bluff overlooking the town. It features exquisite scenery along with its golf links. The club has been reestablished to provide an environment where business and social activities mingle. The interior reflects the original design.

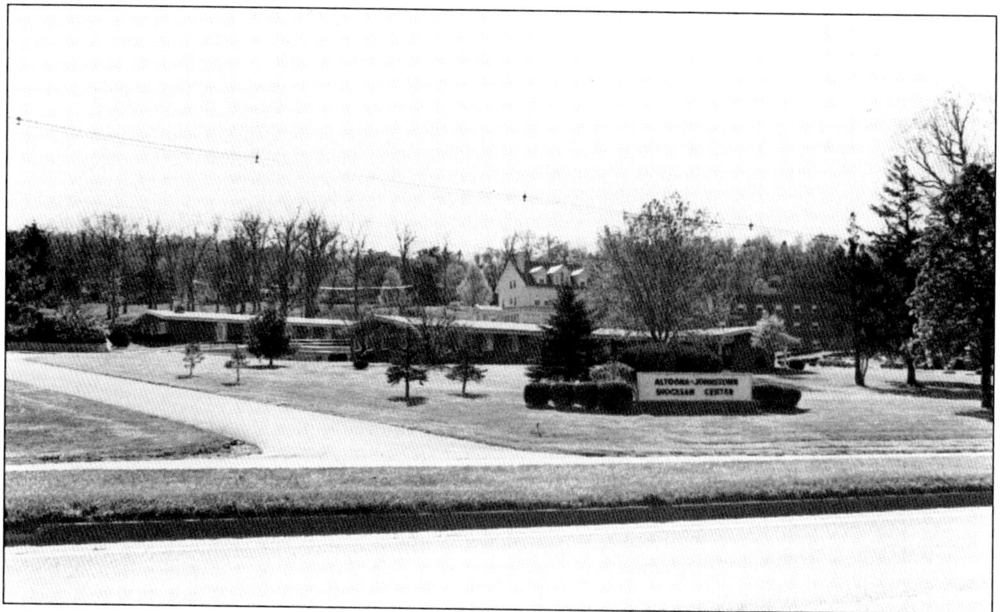

John Kazmaier built a white mansion along Logan Boulevard in 1906. In 1950, the Sisters of the Holy Family of Nazareth purchased the 15-room estate as a rest home for their community members, who also staffed Mercy Hospital. The sisters enjoyed this mountain dwelling for one decade. Its disadvantages began to outweigh its advantages. The aging mansion needed costly repairs, and its location was deemed unfeasible. It was sold to the Diocese of Altoona-Johnstown in 1960. The mansion rises in the center background.

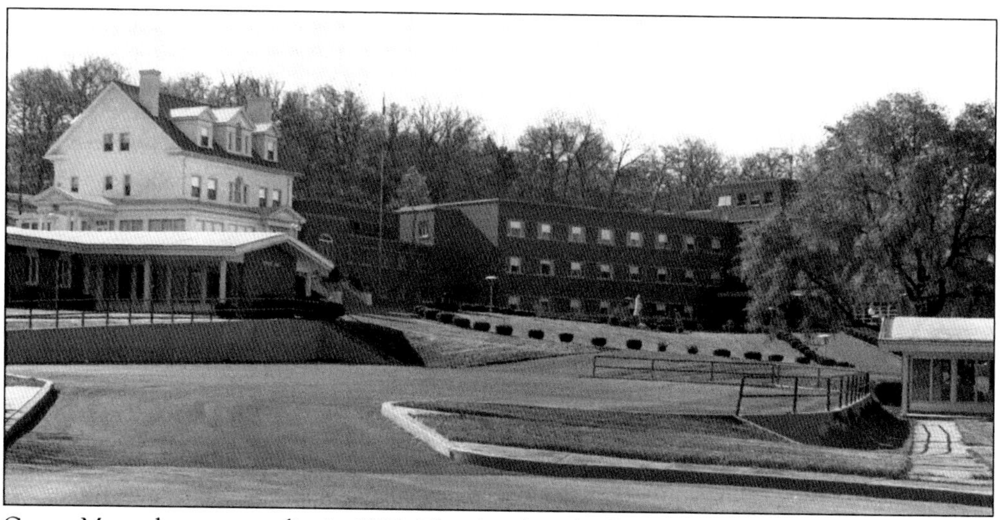

Garvey Manor became a reality in 1963. The abandoned villa, in its next lifetime, would witness Roman Catholic diocesan offices relocate from the city. In 1963, ground was broken for a diocesan nursing home that would be staffed by the Carmelite Sisters of the Aged and Infirm. It was named in honor of the first bishop of the diocese, Eugene Garvey, and the old renovated estate became a convent. The mansion dwarfs Building B, which houses the educational and tribunal offices. The walkway takes one into Garvey Manor. The chancery (Building A) is in the right foreground.

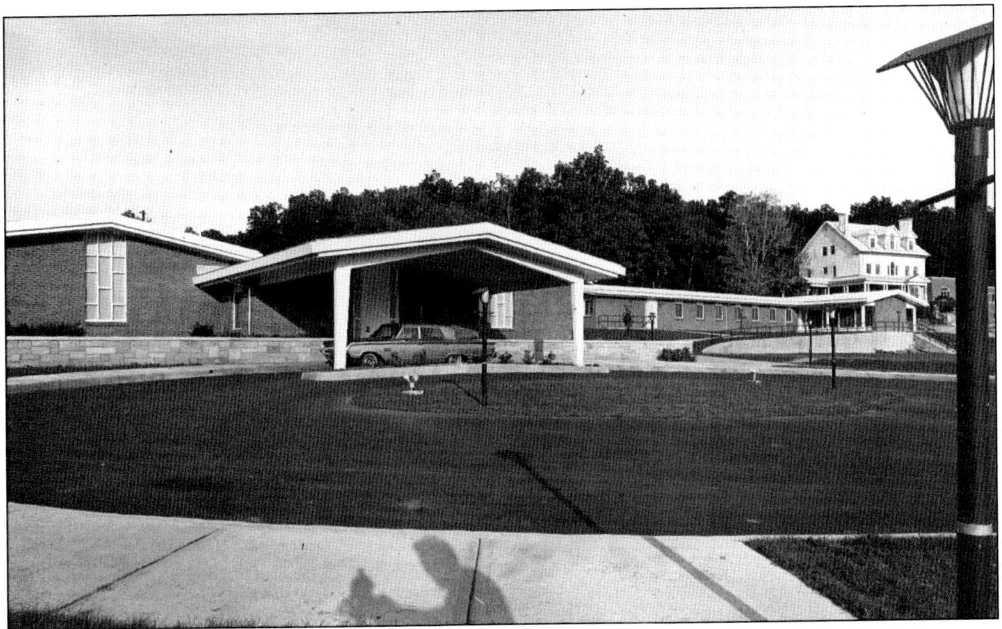

Building C, of the Roman Catholic diocesan complex, houses the office of the local diocesan newspaper, the *Register.* Other offices in the complex include those of the missions, adult formation, liturgy, deaconate, and stewardship. Building B, the Kazamier estate (now a convent), and Garvey Manor are on the right.

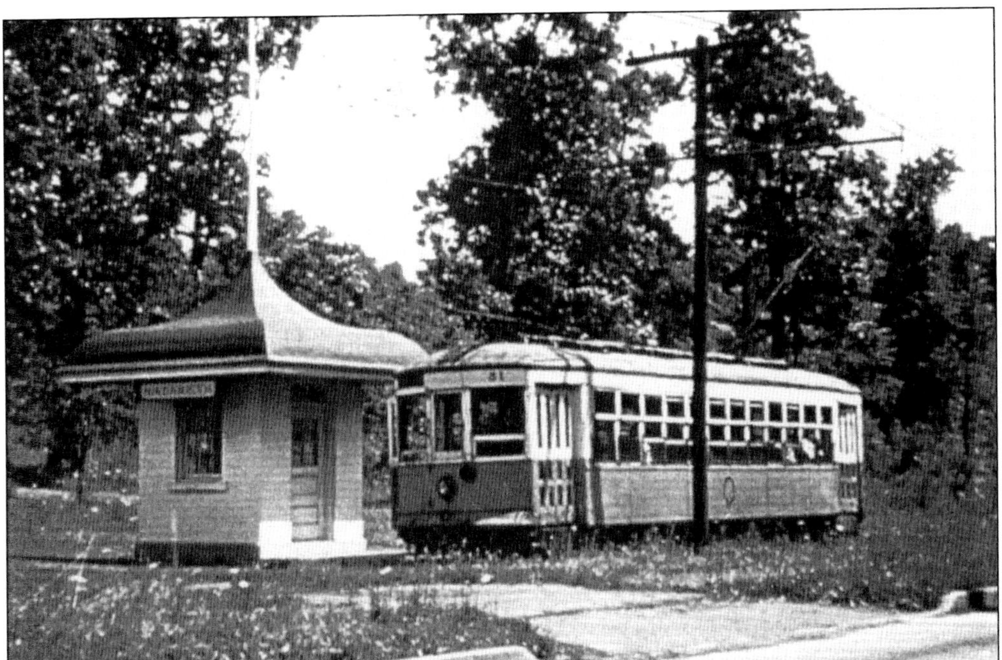

The tracks of the Logan Valley Electric Railway extended from Altoona to Hollidaysburg. Located along Logan Boulevard, this site is known as Nazareth Stop. It was named during the decade when the Sisters of Nazareth occupied the Kazmaier mansion. The trolley was discontinued in 1954.

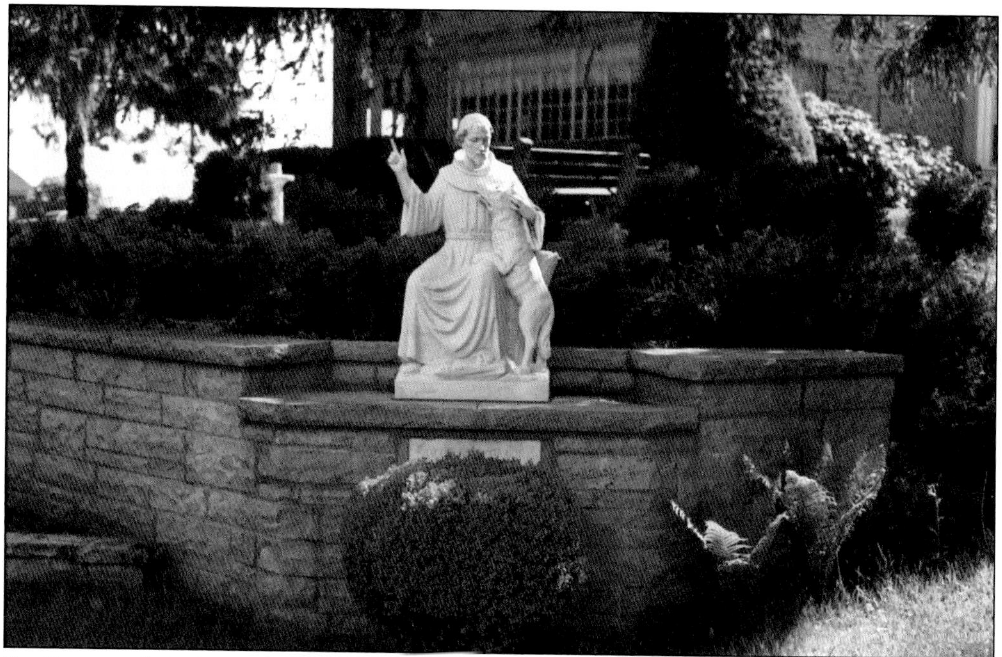

St. Francis of Assisi with the wolf dominates the landscape at St. Bernardine's Monastery. In 1908, Italian-speaking priests were needed in the diocese. Two members of the Loretto Franciscan Community initially responded. They established a mission dedicated to parish work among immigrants. With the sanction of the bishop and the blessings of Sacred Heart Province in Loretto, Immaculate Conception Province was formed on July 22, 1920. The priory is in the background.

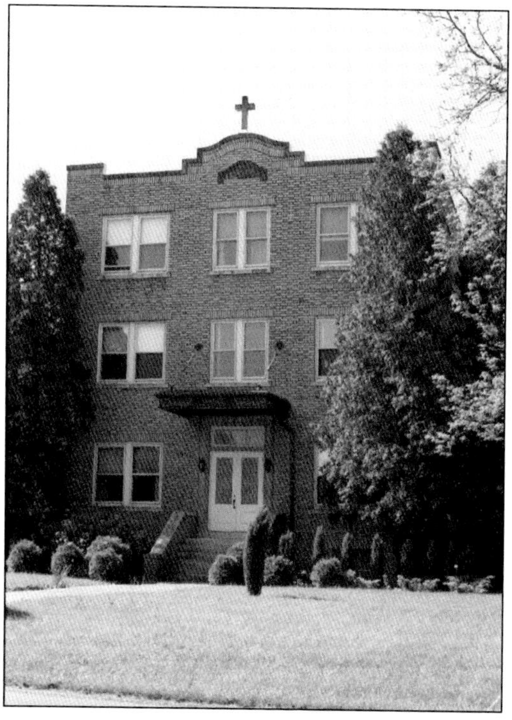

St. Bernardine's Monastery was constructed in 1928. A decade earlier, a tract of land three miles south of Altoona was purchased by the Franciscans. Surrounded by exquisite rolling hills with Kladder Station close by, it was the ideal location for a monastery. This would become the headquarters of Immaculate Conception Province. An old homestead on the property served as the friary until the monastery was finished.

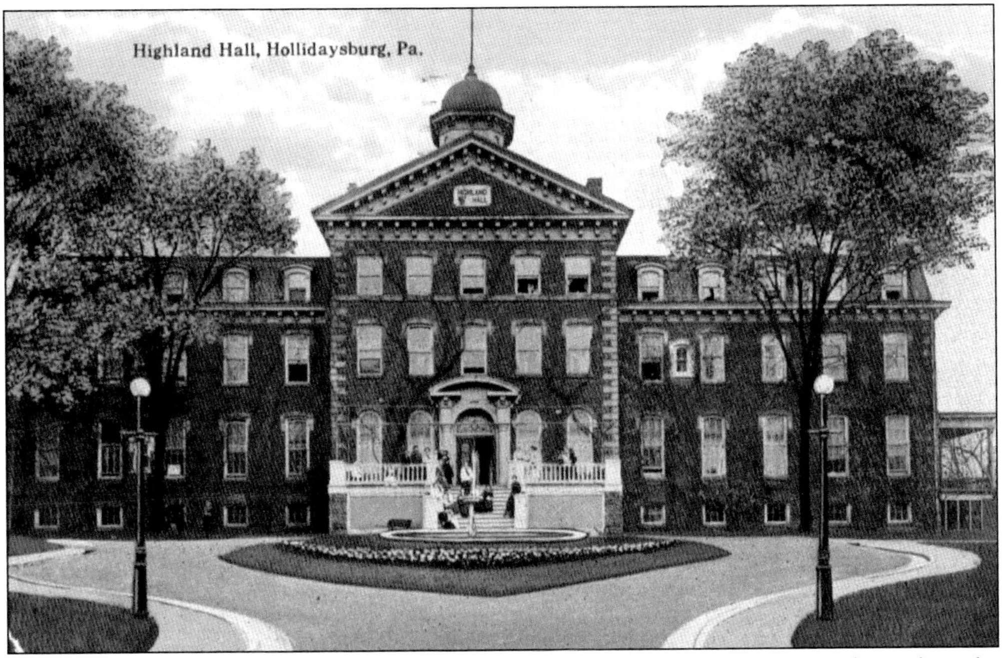

Highland Hall was constructed of stone quarried on the grounds in 1876. It was located on the commons of the Seminary. Originally called the Seminary, it catered to the general population until 1910, when it became a select school for girls. Highland Hall was famous far and wide as a select school. In later years, it was occupied at various times by soldiers, a navy radio training school, the Franciscans, and (in more recent years) the courthouse.

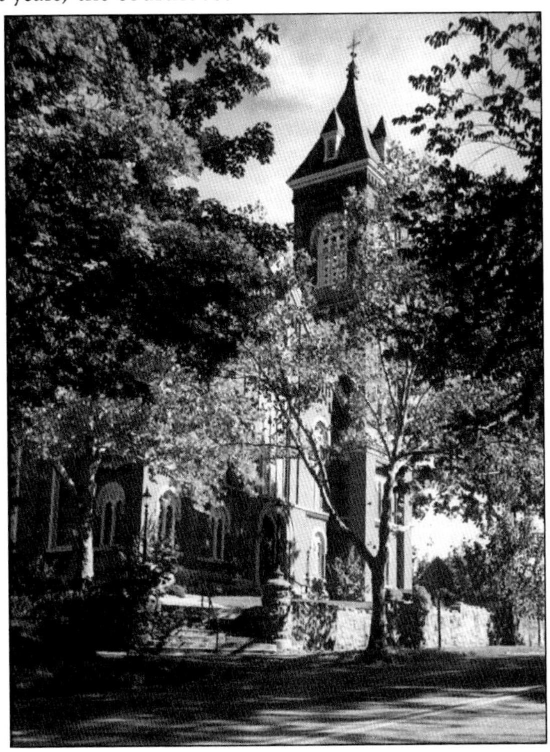

The Methodist Episcopal congregation was formed in 1756. The first church was erected on Walnut and Penn Streets in 1788. Hollidaysburg gained prominence when the Old Portage Railroad connected with the Pennsylvania Canal System. The town became a hub of activity. Blair County was formed on February 16, 1846. The first session of court was held in the Methodist Episcopal church in 1846. A stone building adjacent to the church served as a jail.

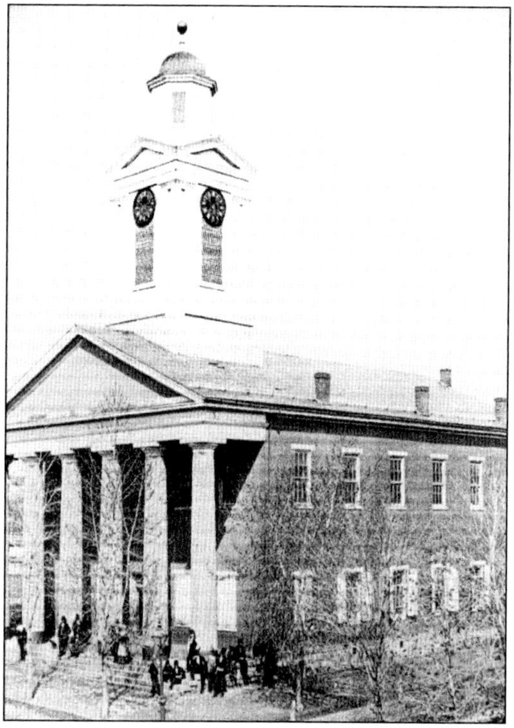

The original courthouse was constructed in 1846 on Allegheny Street. It was built by Daniel K. Reamy and served for nearly three decades, until increased business in the county necessitated the construction of more adequate quarters. In the mid-1870s, the building was razed to make way for a larger courthouse on the same site. A new prison, located between Mulberry and Blair Streets, was constructed from 1868 to 1869.

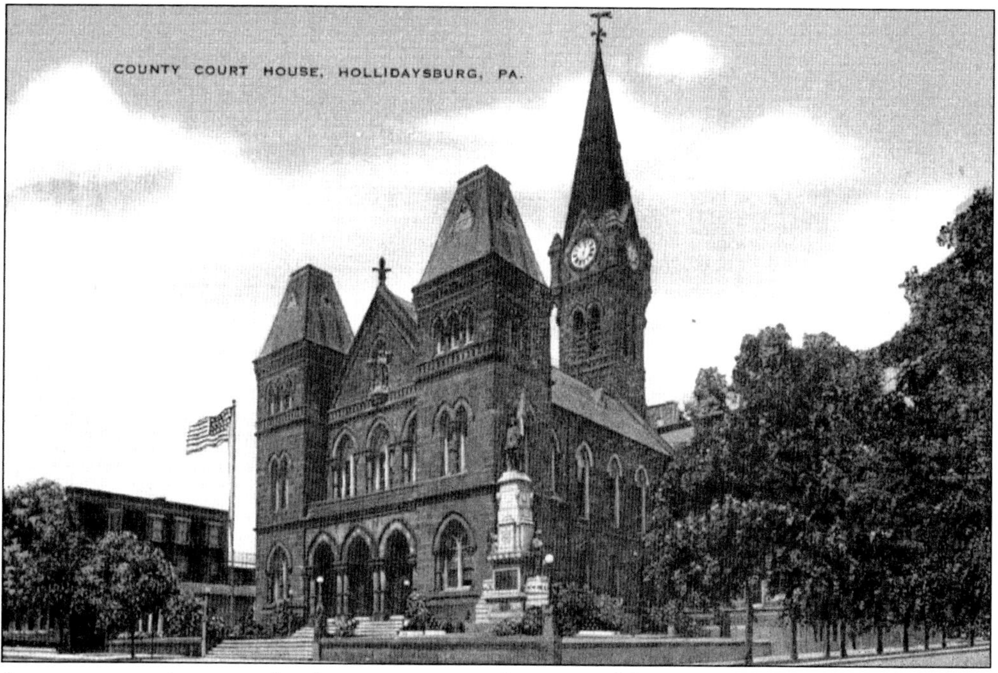

A contract was drawn up for the construction of a new and larger courthouse on the same site as the original building. The new courthouse was erected in 1875 on Allegheny Street. Its clock tower became almost a lighthouse to the settlers. The huge tower rises above the ground and takes a prestigious place in an already spectacular landscape. Additions were necessary through the years.

The Soldiers and Sailors Monument represents all branches of military service. It was erected by the commissioners of Blair County as a tribute to those men who served defending our country. It was unveiled on June 11, 1896, and was rededicated a century later. The monument rises 33 feet in front of the courthouse.

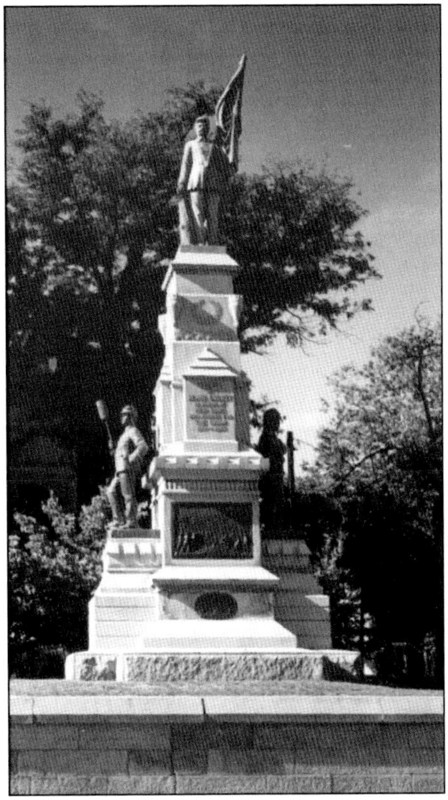

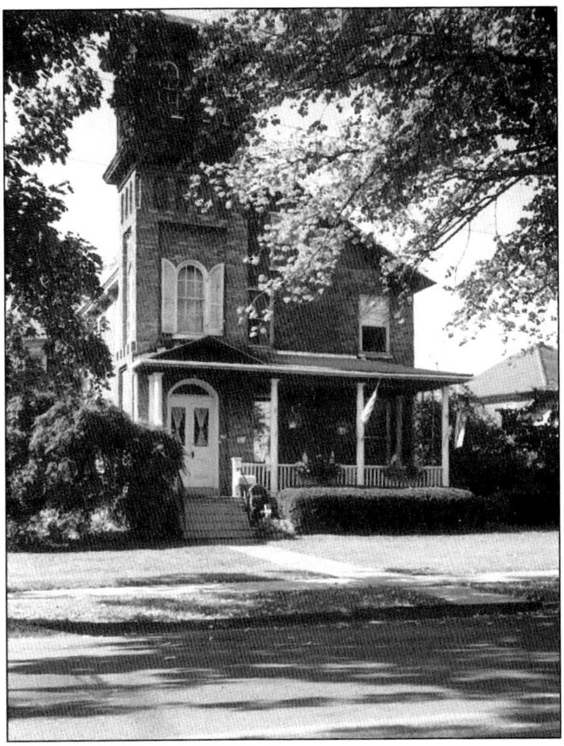

Capt. A.M. Lloyd's home was distinguished by a third-story tower. Located beside the railroad on Newry Street, it was the forerunner of our signal system today. A bell was rung in the tower to signal the arrival and departure of trains, in either direction, on a single track. Lloyd's tower kept the railroad operating smoothly.

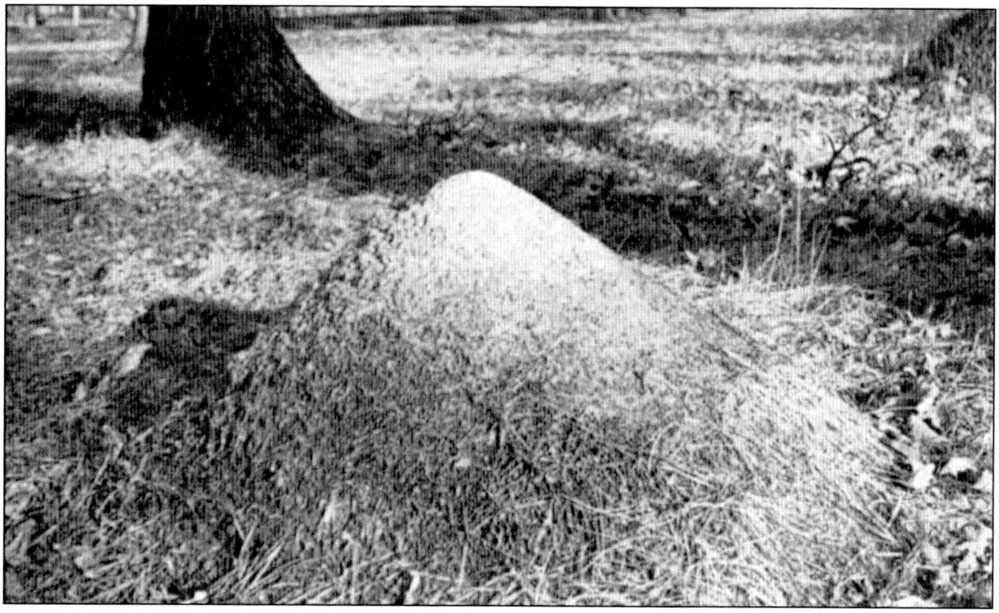

The world-famous anthills were located along Logan Boulevard in Hollidaysburg. It was the route of the trolley. In 1896, scientists from all over the country came to study the habits of the ants and witness this strange scenario. The section was almost designated a state park in order to preserve the anthills. A park did not materialize, and a real estate development took over the area—anthills and all. The ants had to find new quarters.

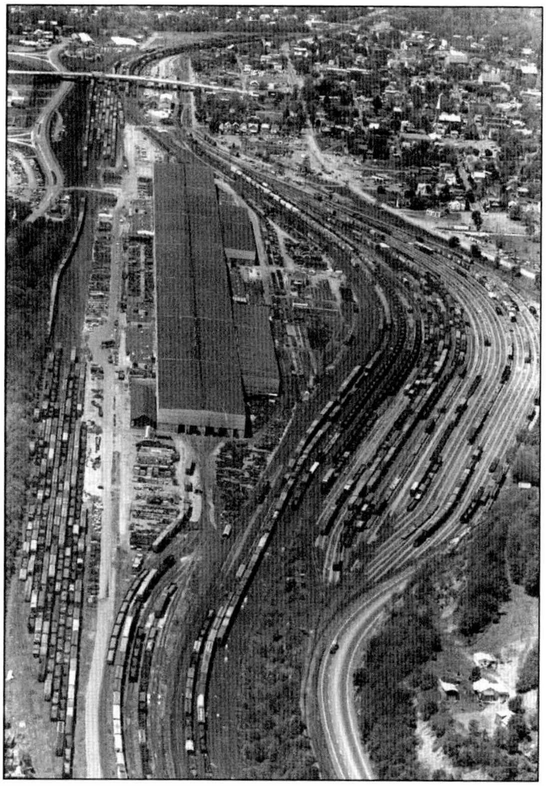

Samuel Rea shops bear the name of the Hollidaysburg native who was president of the Bedford-Hollidaysburg Railroad, which paved the way for industrialization of the area. In April 1909, under his direction, the first railroad car (No. 460) made its initial trip from Bedford to Hollidaysburg. Rea was vice president of the Pennsylvania Railroad from 1913 until 1925. He later served as chairman of the Morrison's Cove branch of the railroad.

Canoe Creek is a 958-acre park that lies nestled in the foothills of the Allegheny Mountains. Limestone was discovered here in 1899. The picturesque park abounds in geological lime formations and was dedicated in 1979. The panoramic vista of rolling hills is breathtaking as one crests the hill approaching the entrance. Canoe Creek features a lake that provides year-round fishing and includes a popular swimming area. The park has several old quarry operations. The Blair Limestone Company was active here.

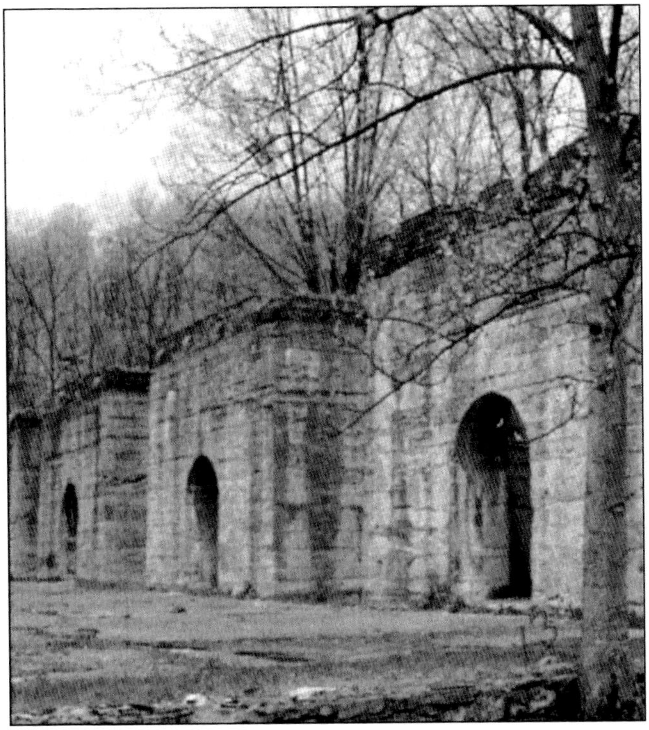

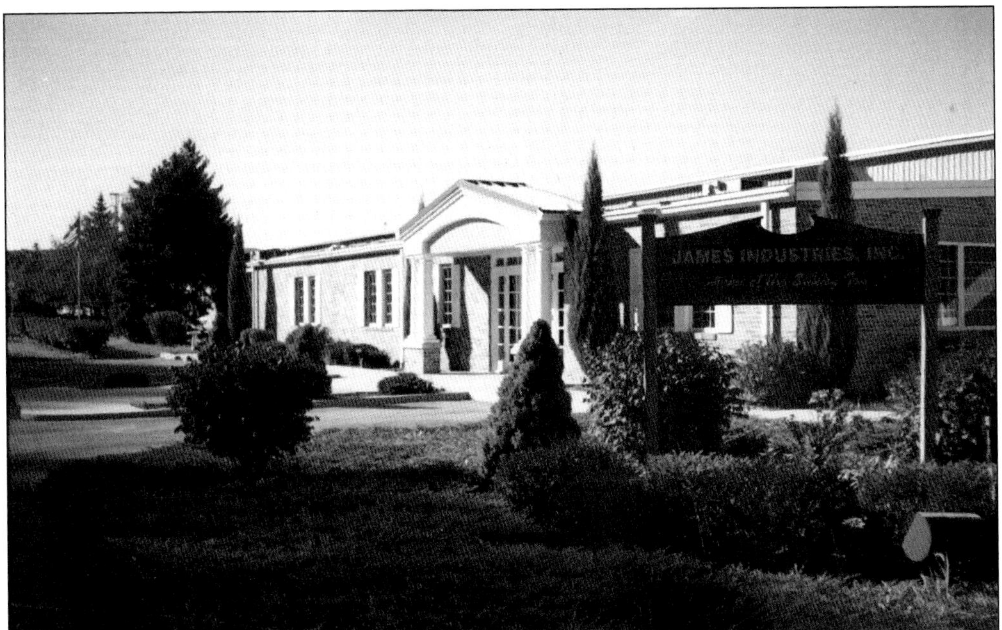

Slinky is at home in Hollidaysburg. The toy is sold on nearly every continent around the world. In 1943, while working in Philadelphia's shipyard, Richard James, a native of Altoona, encountered a mishap when a torsion spring fell and tumbled end over end across the floor. Convinced it was material for a toy, he took it home, and his wife, Betty, named it Slinky. By 1945, Gimble's Department Store sold 400 of them. A factory was established, and Slinky was the hit of the 1946 American Toy Fair in New York City.

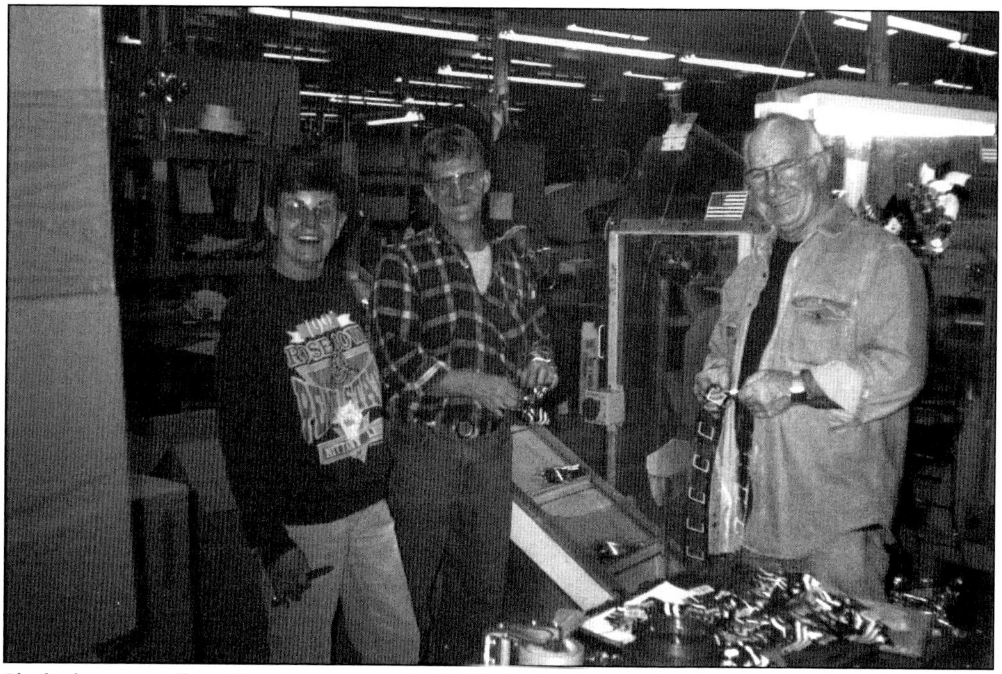

Slinky became a flourishing enterprise. In 1960, Richard James bowed out. Left with six children and a thriving business, Betty James relocated to Hollidaysburg. Slinky became one of the first toys advertised on television with its own jingle. The original Slinky contained 80 feet of wire. The toy has universal appeal because of its simplicity. It is still made in machines designed and engineered by its founder. Many new Slinky-related items have been added to the James Industry line of toys. In this photograph, Halla Maidi, Bill Kung, and George Gill work the pinwheel machine.

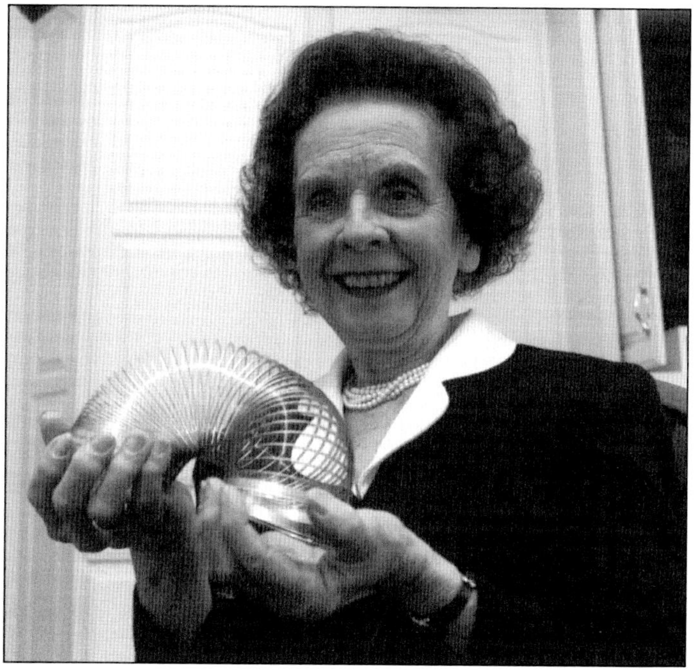

Altoona native Betty James, a graduate of Penn State University, managed the Slinky business for many years. Her eldest son, Tom, served as sales manager. Today, Slinky is made of both wire and plastic with color added. In 1997, a Slinky postage stamp was issued. A year later, Betty James received her doctorate degree from St. Francis University in Loretto. In 2001, she was inducted into the Toy Industry Hall of Fame in New York on par with Walt Disney.

Two

THE FLIP OF A COIN

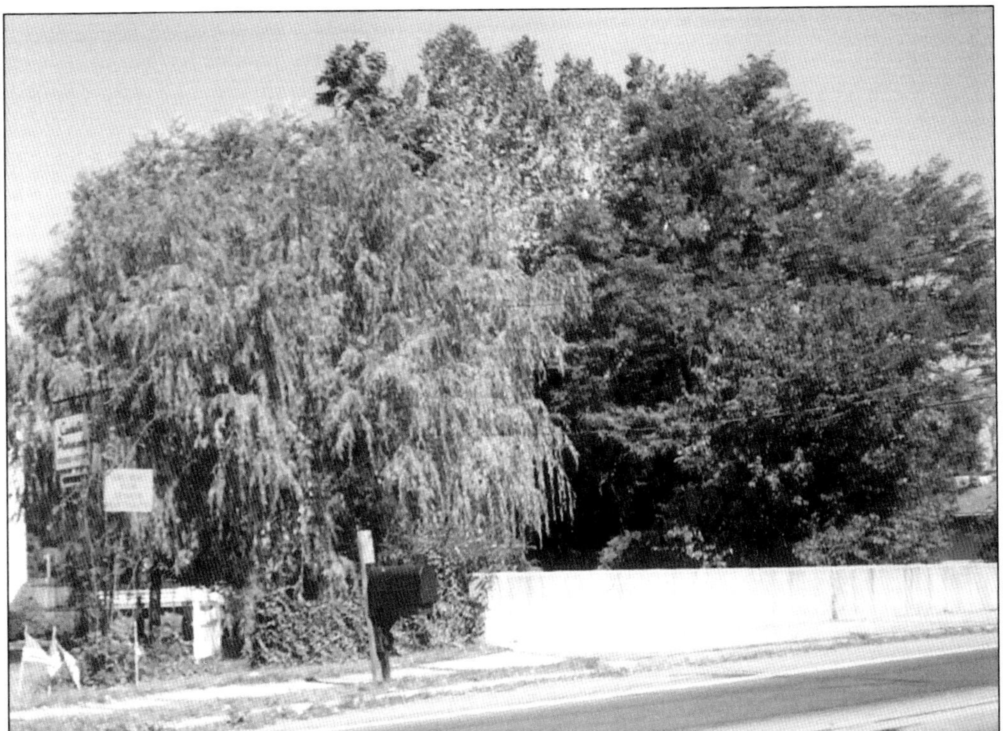

A bridge that gave Duncansville its name still spans Blair Creek. Built in 1933, this bridge replaced an historic wooden bridge and later a single-lane iron bridge. In 1836, Samuel Duncan owned land west of the creek and Jacob Walters owned land on the east. This led to confusion and rivalry among settlers. The men agreed to solve the difficulty by flipping a coin. They met on the historic wooden bridge and, in the presence of large groups from both sides, they tossed the coin. Duncan won! This site is located between Tenth and Eleventh Streets.

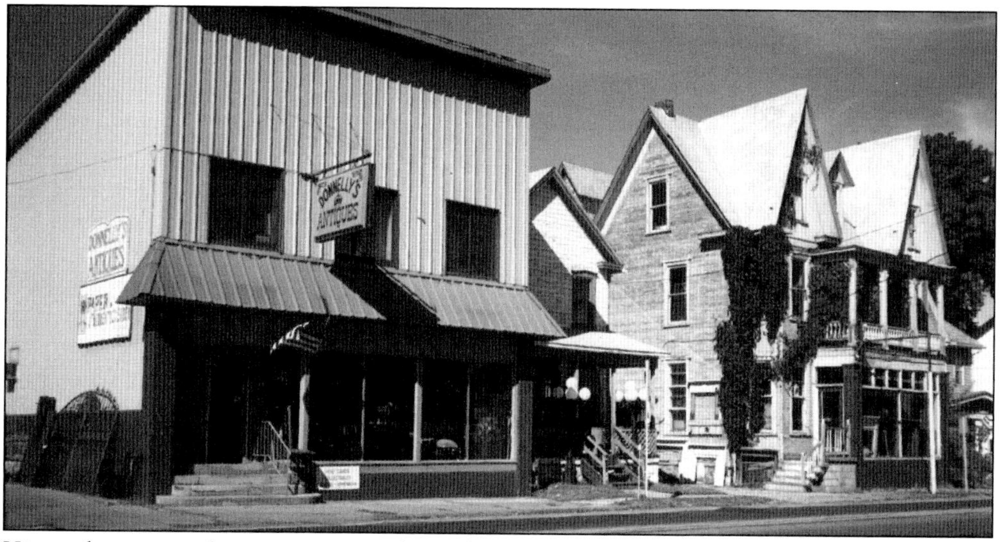

History lives on in the many antique shops that dot the main route through Duncansville. The town became an antiques mecca because of its location at the foot of the Allegheny Mountains, where the last link of the statewide canal system connected. Canal boats brought passengers and cargo to this site, where they transferred to the inclined planes and were carried over the mountains to Johnstown. Their belongings did not always accompany them. Passengers often had to leave furniture and other items behind.

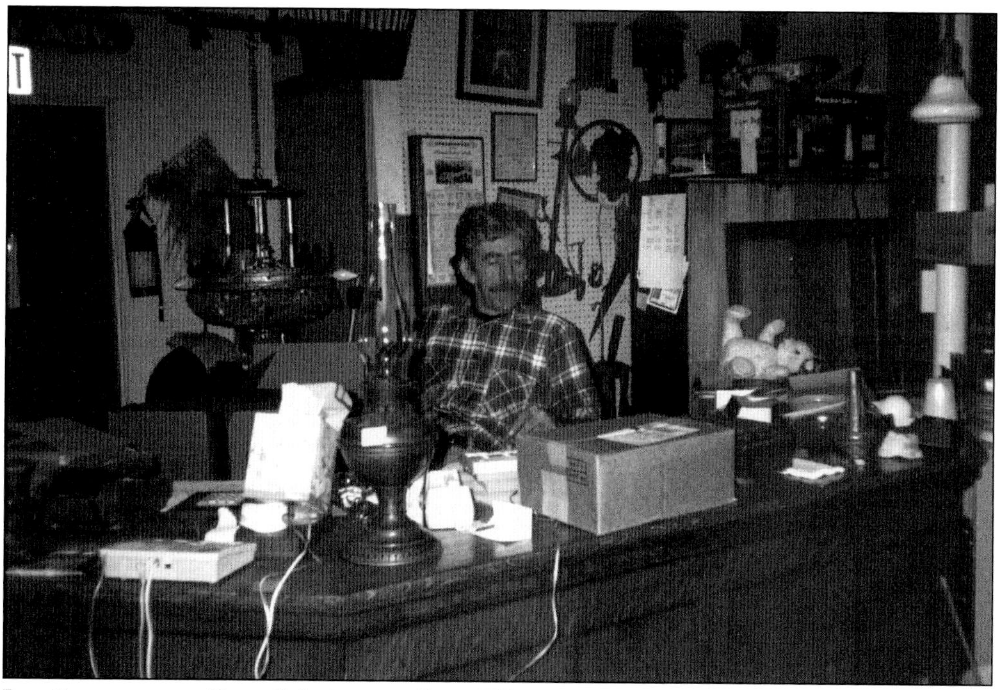

Ron Estep manages Donnelly's Antique Shop. When cargo was too heavy, large, or cumbersome (furniture especially), it was left along the way, thus creating secondhand stores that later became antique shops. Today, the town boasts of many such shops, including the Allegheny Trade Company, Creekside Antiques, Dave's Sports Collectibles, Paper Americana, Duncansville Antique Depot, and Remember When. Duncansville also featured Piccadilly Center.

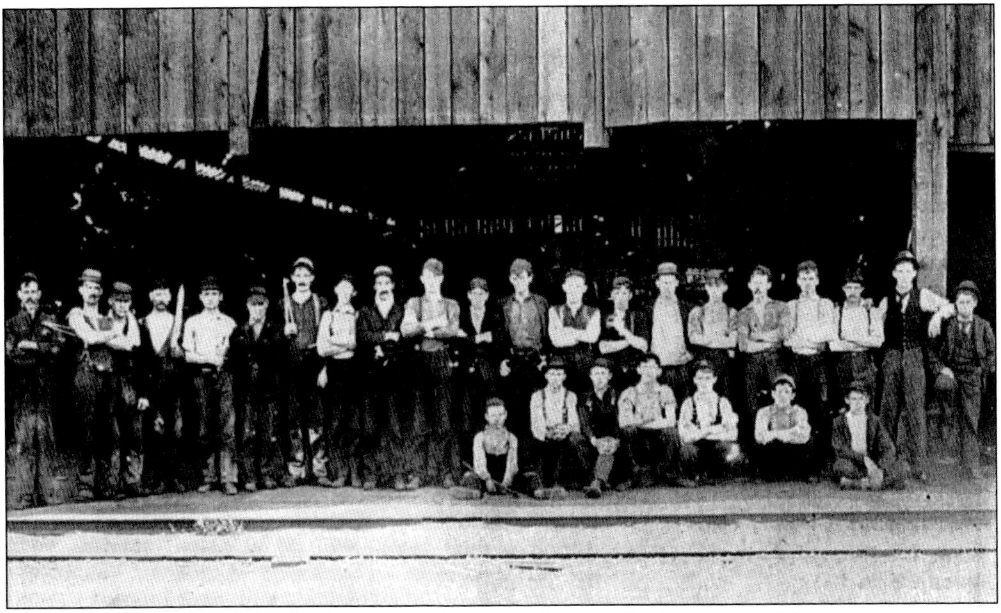

The iron industry was very prominent in Duncansville. The buildings stood between Fourteenth and Sixteenth Streets along the south side of Third Avenue. Once called Irontown, Duncansville was designated a borough on March 4, 1891. Forges, iron mills, and foundries became prominent among its industries. Due to its proximity to the Old Portage Railroad, Duncansville always retained its reputation as the antique capital of the county.

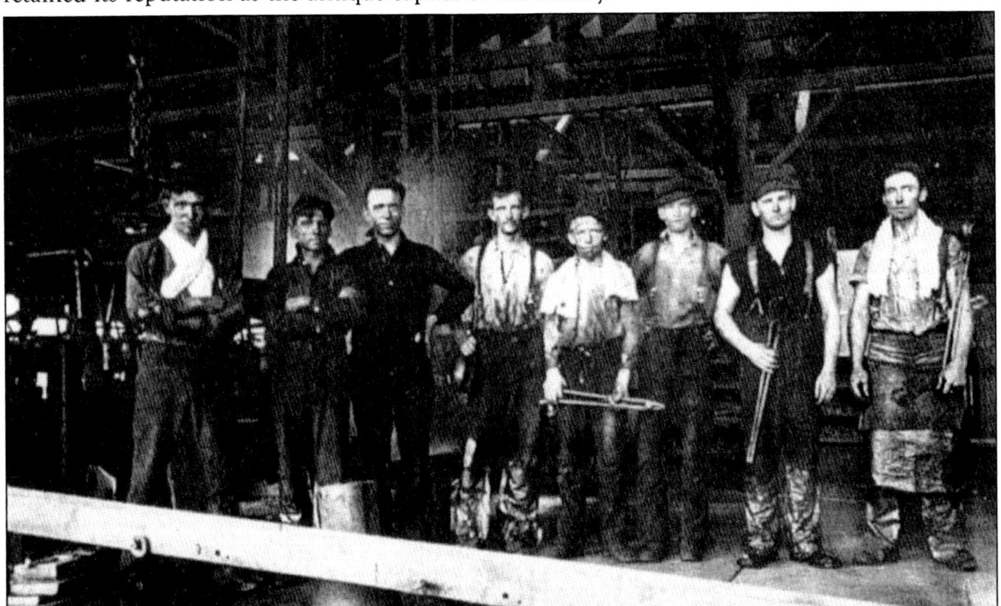

The little hamlet of Duncansville, nestled at the foothills of the Allegheny Mountains, measured only a mile long and a half mile wide. It buzzed, hummed, and resounded with activity throughout the 19th century. Machinery rumbled from foundries, factories, and forges. It became a stop for many famous turnpike travelers making their way over the rugged mountains. The Pittsburgh–Philadelphia Turnpike cut through the hamlet.

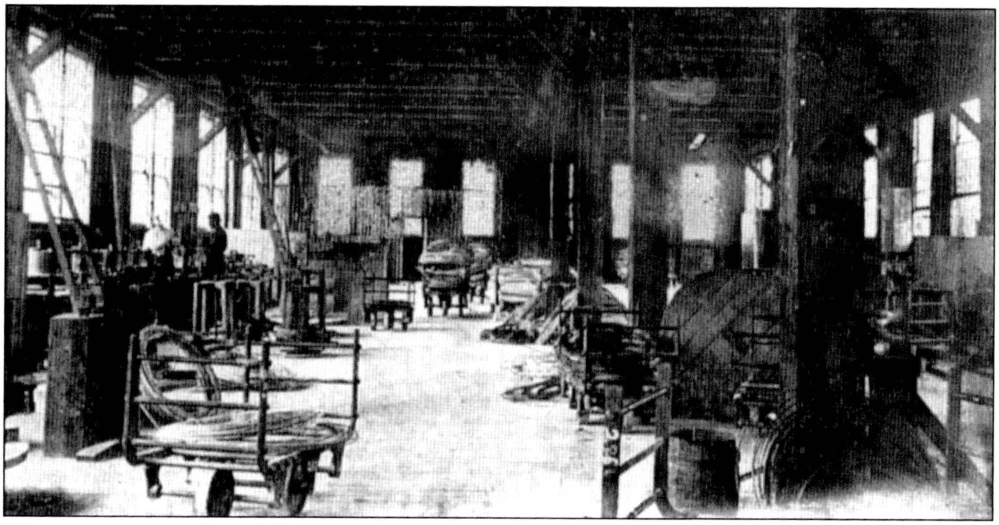

The construction of a nail factory adjacent to the ironworks in 1898 increased employment to 700 men. Some 400 kegs of nails were turned out daily, and business was a sensational success. A move to eradicate competition came first from the American Steel and Wire Company of Pittsburgh, which bought out the Duncansville plants. In 1904, the entire operation was sold, the equipment dismantled, and the buildings razed. Duncansville became a sleepy little picturesque hamlet along the main line of the Pennsylvania Railroad.

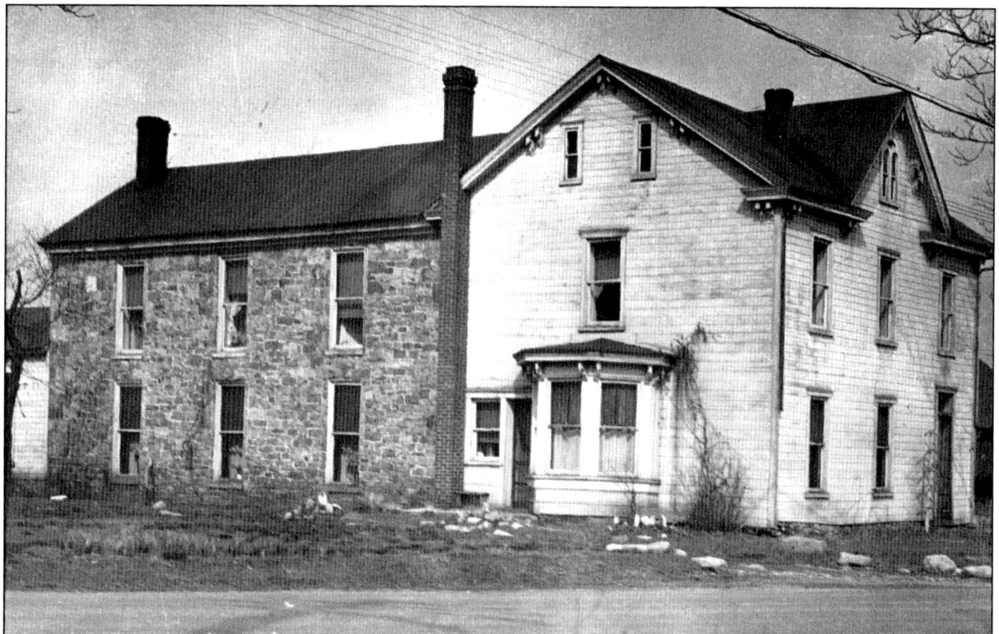

Pictured is the home of John Blair (1766–1832), for whom the county is named. Located west of Duncansville, the house was built in 1785. The stone section was added to the rear in 1827. Blair was a staunch advocate of establishing a county. He was a businessman who was active, progressive, and enterprising, with a keen interest in construction of roads, transportation, and commerce in western Pennsylvania. Blair County was carved from Huntingdon and Bedford Counties in 1846.

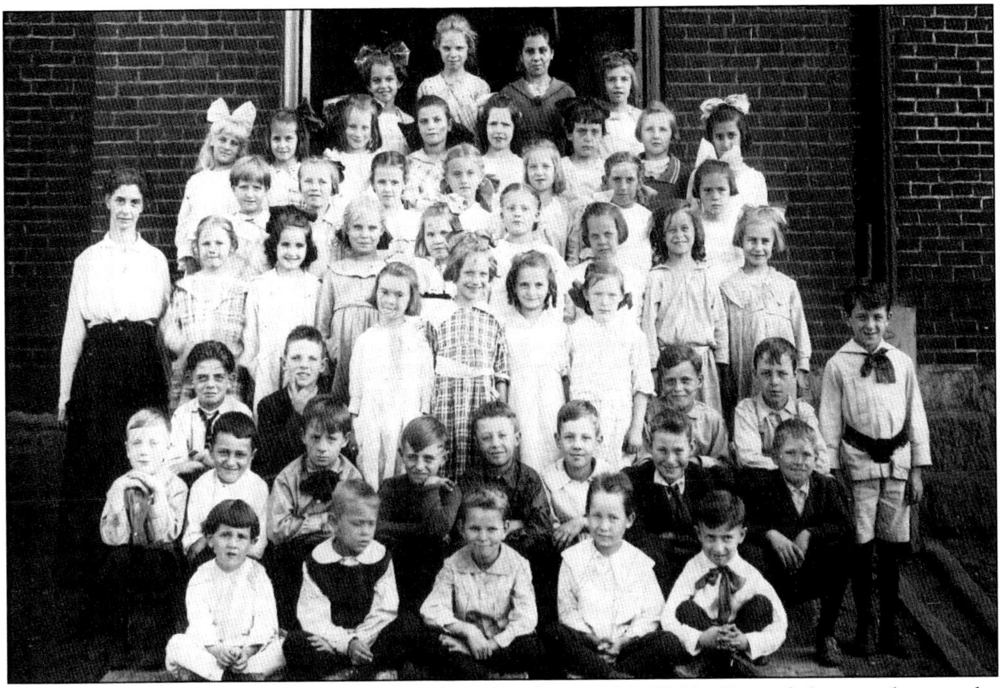

Pictured are the children of Duncansville School in 1920–1921. From left to right are the following: (first row) Paul Shaw, Erle Keller, Earl Johnston, Russel Buck, and George Ritchey; (second row) Clair Smith, Clair Henry, Harold Bouser, Charles Mobely, unidentified, Cloyd Neely, Paul Wilt, and Ellis Harris; (third row) Nelson Hicks, Ellis Plowman, Marie Deyarmine, unidentified, Marian Engle, Olive Kelly, Kirth Grove, Harry McCale, and Ralph Krider; (fourth row) teacher Myrtle Mountz, Christine Benton, Hilda Shaw, Dorothy Piper, Lois Treese, Madeline Neely, Lucille Neal, Wilma Grove, and Amy Burns; (fifth row) unidentified, Grace Leonard, Lilas Neely, Estelle Feathers, Lillian Brown, Mary Smith, and Catherine Yeckley; (sixth row) Elevyne Grove, Coletta Crawford, Martha McCready, Jane Decker, Hazle Shaw, Margaret Wilt, Effie Piper, and Ruth Young; (seventh row) Anna Marble, Violet Plowman, Martha Feathers, and unidentified.

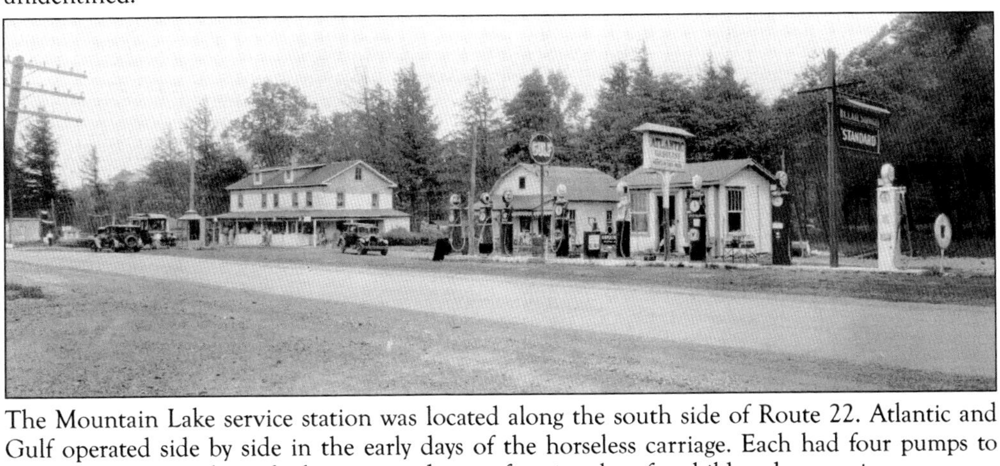

The Mountain Lake service station was located along the south side of Route 22. Atlantic and Gulf operated side by side in the early days of the horseless carriage. Each had four pumps to service the resort. This refreshment stand was a favorite place for children because ice cream was sold only in summer. Note the tiny stand that housed bus riders in inclement weather. It was also known as a guardhouse.

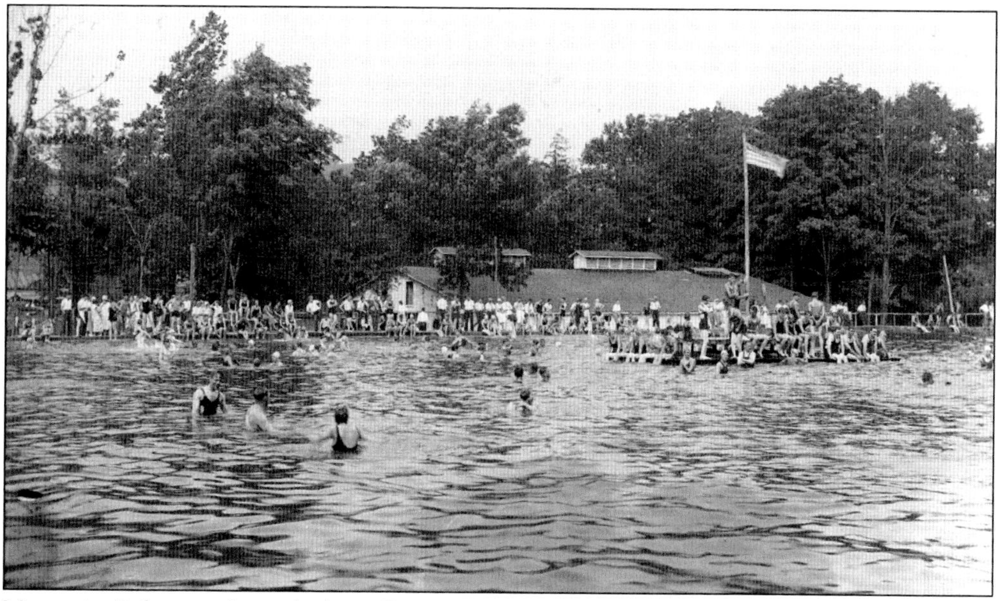

Mountain Lake was located along Route 22 on what was the old Philadelphia–Pittsburgh Turnpike. It was and still is the main route through the one-mile settlement. The freshwater lake was attractive as a summer resort. It provided recreation for townspeople and neighbors alike. The little island in the center of Mountain Lake became a sunbather's paradise. The huge bathhouse accommodated the large volume of swimmers each season.

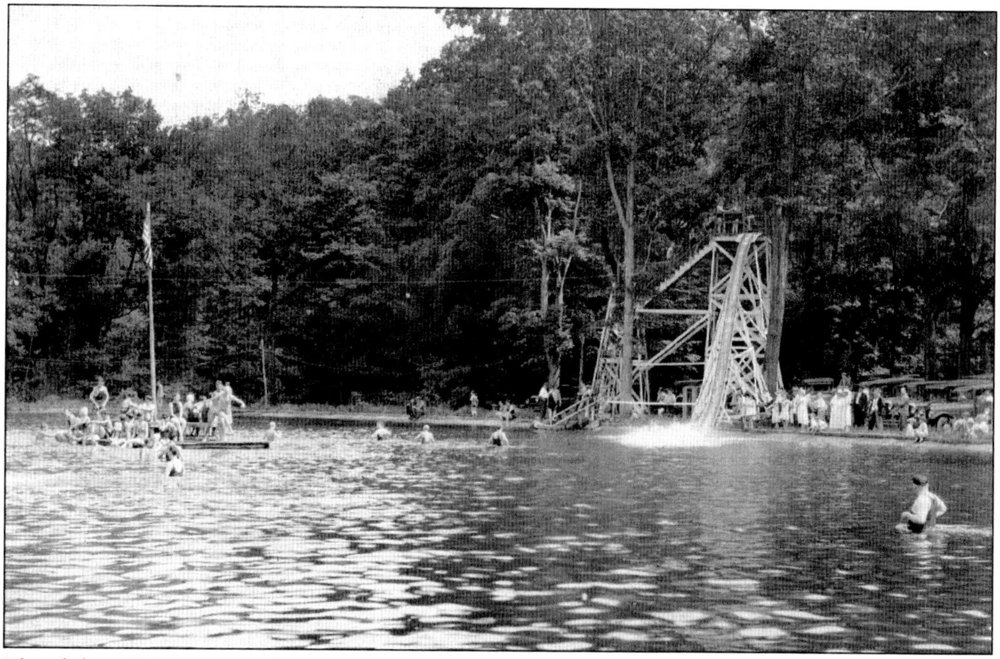

The slide at Mountain Lake was a huge wooden structure. Red Well was the original name of Mountain Lake. It was the largest rustic swimming pool in the state. Built by Kough in the 1920s, it was fed from mountain streams. In this photograph, boys at the top prepare for the big splash into the spring water. It was a long hike up the steps. Note the early-century Model T Fords on the right.

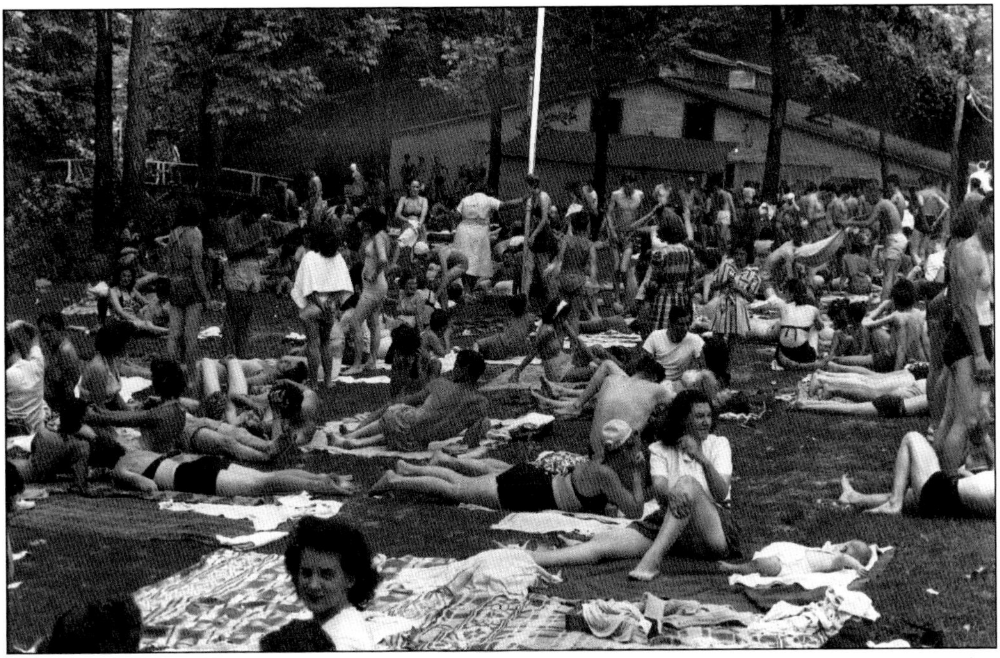

Hot summer days brought crowds from nearby communities to Mountain Lake in Duncansville. Sunbathers found a spot on the grassy area beside the huge bathhouse. In the background, note the rustic bridge that took one into the nearby forest. This photograph was taken on July 5, 1948. The rustic lake was used for many years. When the state wanted to put in a purification system, the recreational aspect ceased, the pool closed, and the numerous summer cottages became year-round dwellings.

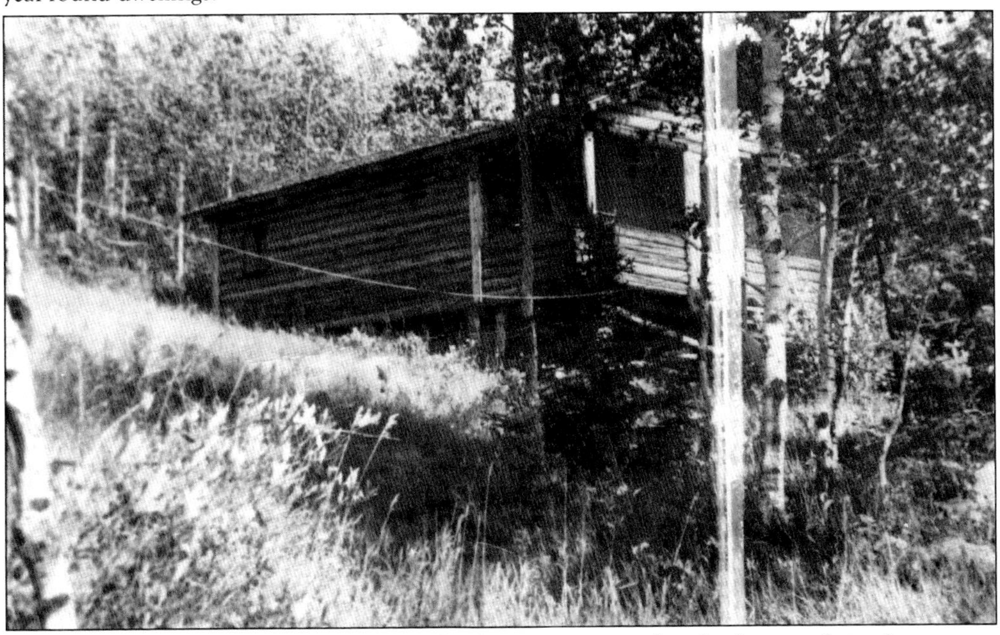

Summer homes surrounded Mountain Lake. Some were owned and others, early in the century, were rented. The notion of vacationing at the seaside was just beginning to take root when Mountain Lake was established in the 1920s.

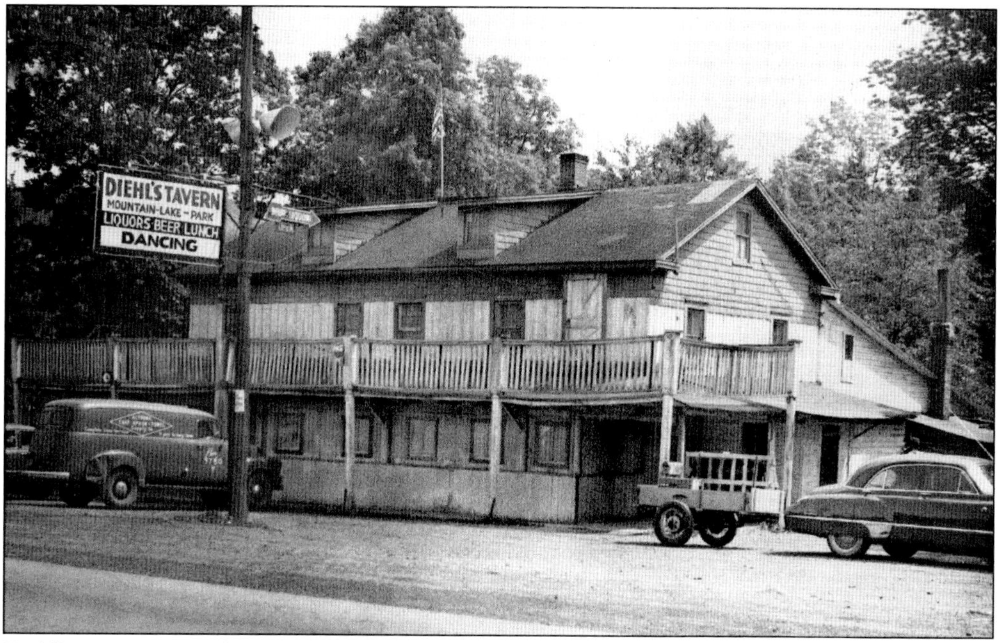

Diehl's Tavern opened at Mountain Lake to serve the patrons of the park. It came alive at night, when the jukebox of a bygone era supplied the music and the dancers swung into action. By day, Diehl's served lunches and dinners. It was located along the south side of Route 22. Across the street, Iconette's Pizza Shop was quite popular. It was one of the first fast-food establishments in the town.

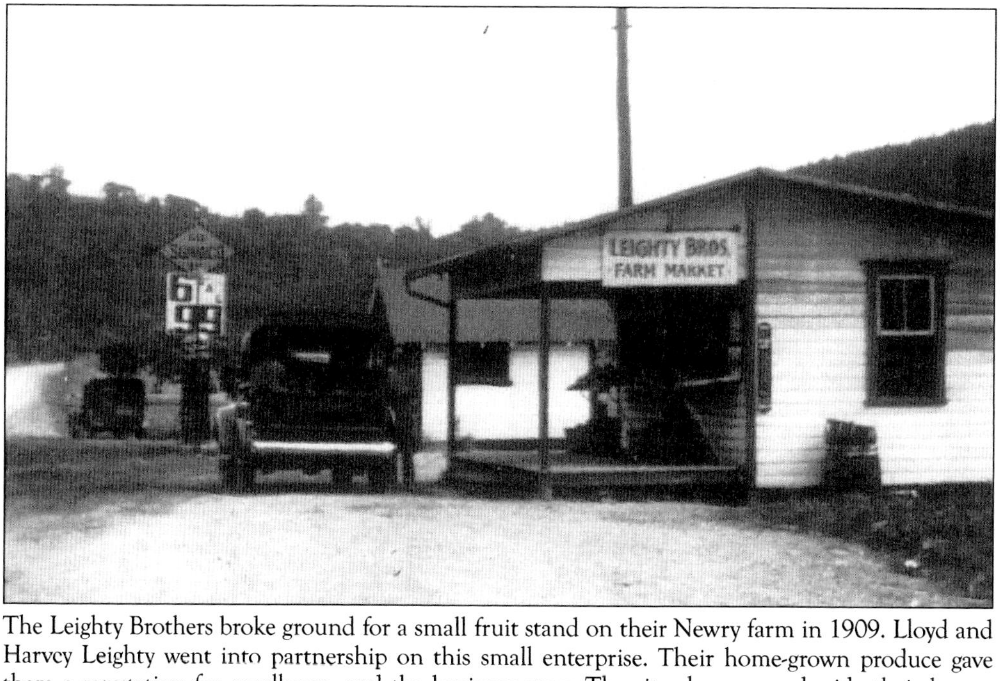

The Leighty Brothers broke ground for a small fruit stand on their Newry farm in 1909. Lloyd and Harvey Leighty went into partnership on this small enterprise. Their home-grown produce gave them a reputation for excellence, and the business grew. The site chosen was beside their home. The road on the left links Hollidaysburg and Altoona with Bedford. The business would always be transient. Note the Sunoco sign. Does anyone recall when six gallons of gasoline was 99¢?

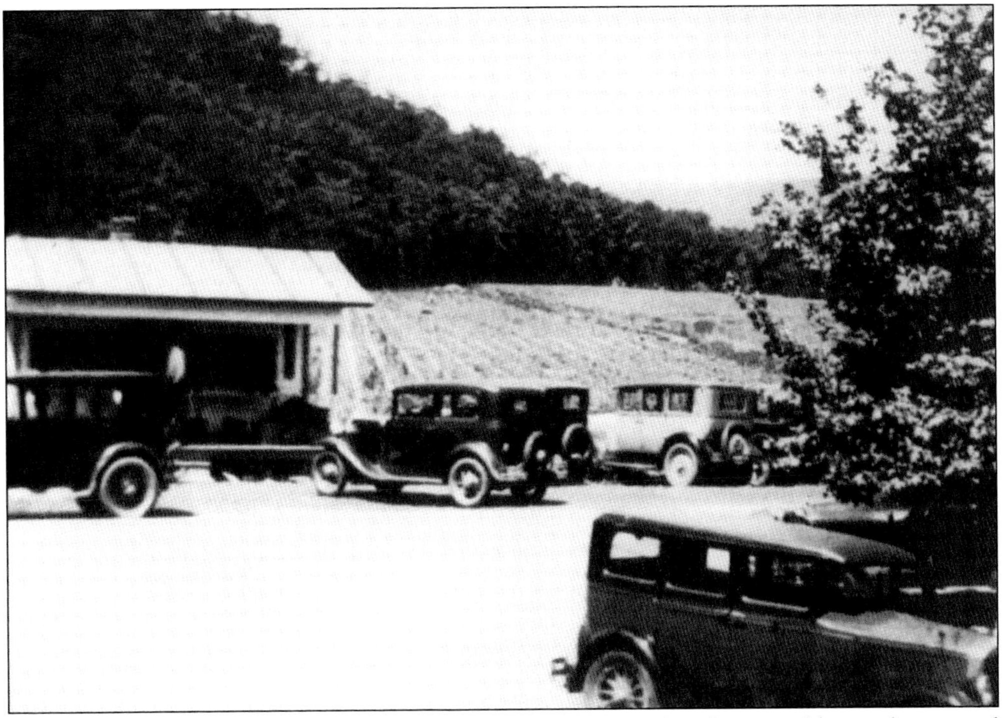

Don Leighty, son of Lloyd Leighty, took over the business in 1957. The vegetable stand measured just 20 by 22 feet. Don had been a buyer, a truck driver, and the delivery boy who often had to leave at 6:00 a.m. in his 1937 Chevy flatbed for produce markets. He procured peaches from Chambersburg and other items that were not grown on the Leighty farm.

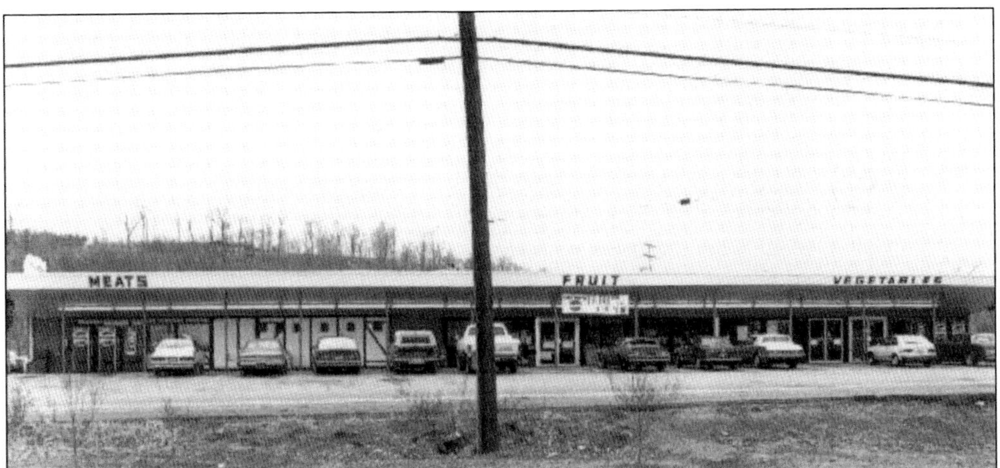

The little stall continued to grow. It now measures 40,000 square feet. Don Leighty, the entrepreneur of today, has cultivated his business into one of the largest establishments of its kind in Pennsylvania. What he does not grow is bought from local farmers or at least grown in Pennsylvania. The original farm still produces fresh cabbage, lettuce, strawberries, cucumbers, and corn. The market enjoys a wide reputation for its complete selection of incomparable produce. Now departmentalized, the market features centralized shopping services.

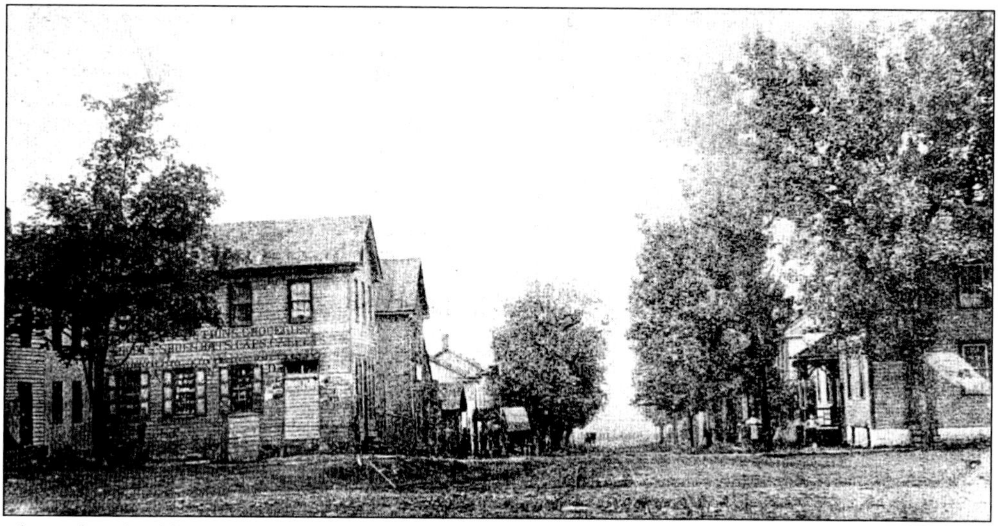

The earliest buildings in Newry were wooden. This scene on the lower Diamond dates from 1876. The horse and carriage has paused so its riders can procure water at the village pump. Founder Patrick Cassidy, a native of County Newry, Ireland, came to the United States at an early age while employed in the service of a British military officer. After the Revolutionary War, Cassidy, a professional surveyor, purchased 300 acres of land and then laid out the settlement.

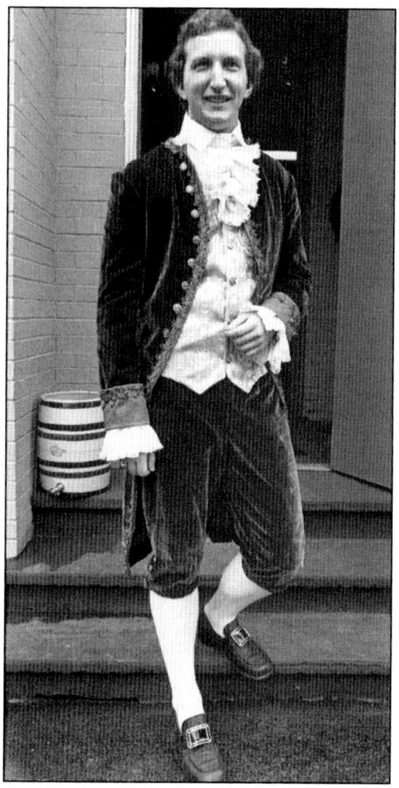

Michael Cassidy is the great-great-great-great-grandson of the founding father, Patrick Cassidy. In patriot attire, Michael Cassidy served as master of ceremonies for the bicentennial celebrations in June 1976. In 1977, he was elected to the Assembly of Pennsylvania. He opened his office on Bedford Street with a ribbon-cutting ceremony in February 1977. Establishing an office in Newry was a campaign promise that he made while seeking election.

The St. Patrick's parish enjoys a unique history. It is the oldest Catholic parish in Blair County. The parish was established by the prince priest, Fr. Demetrius Gallitzin, in 1816 on land donated by Patrick Cassidy. A little stone church was erected, and Gallitzin dedicated it to St. Patrick. He continued to care for the mission until his protege, Rev. Thomas Heyden took it over in 1821.

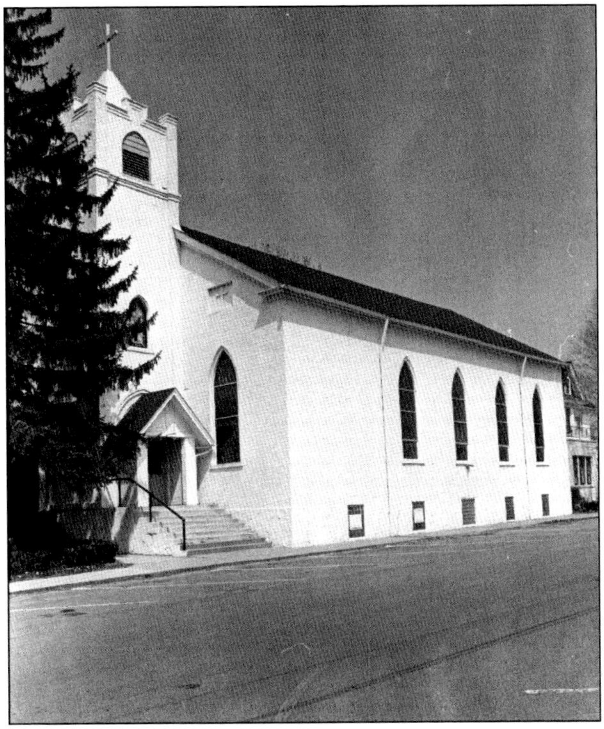

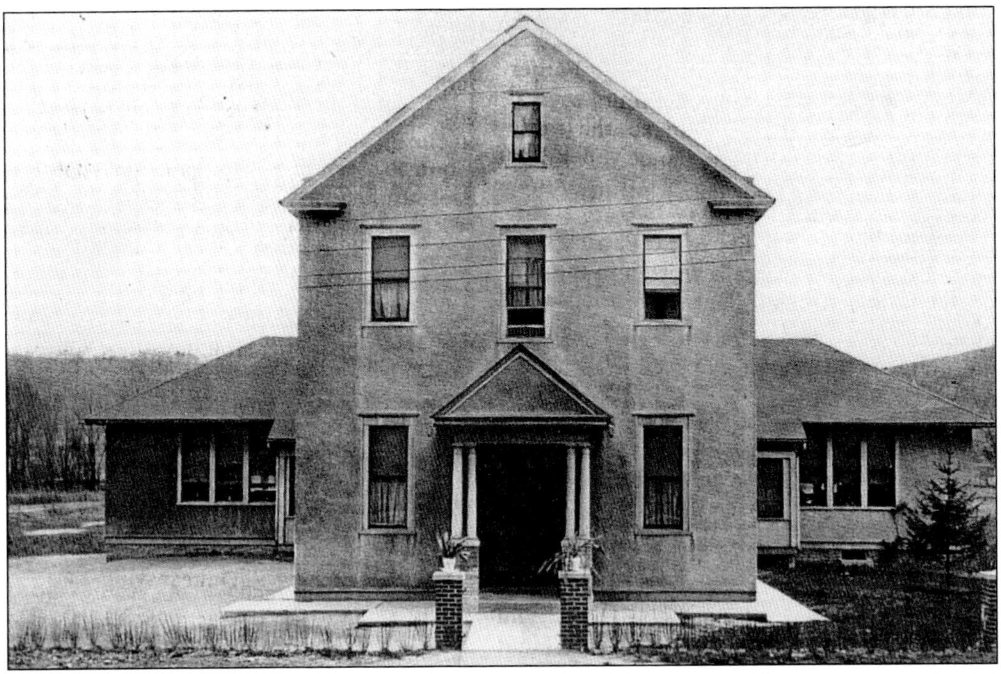

St. Patrick's School was opened by in 1921 in a former hall. Wings were added to accommodate 87 children. Four Sisters of Mercy from Cresson made up the first faculty and took up residence in the convent above the school. In March 1944, the entire complex burned to the ground. Despite wartime restrictions, a new school and convent were completed the following year. Rev. Jeremiah P. Flynn was pastor during this time.

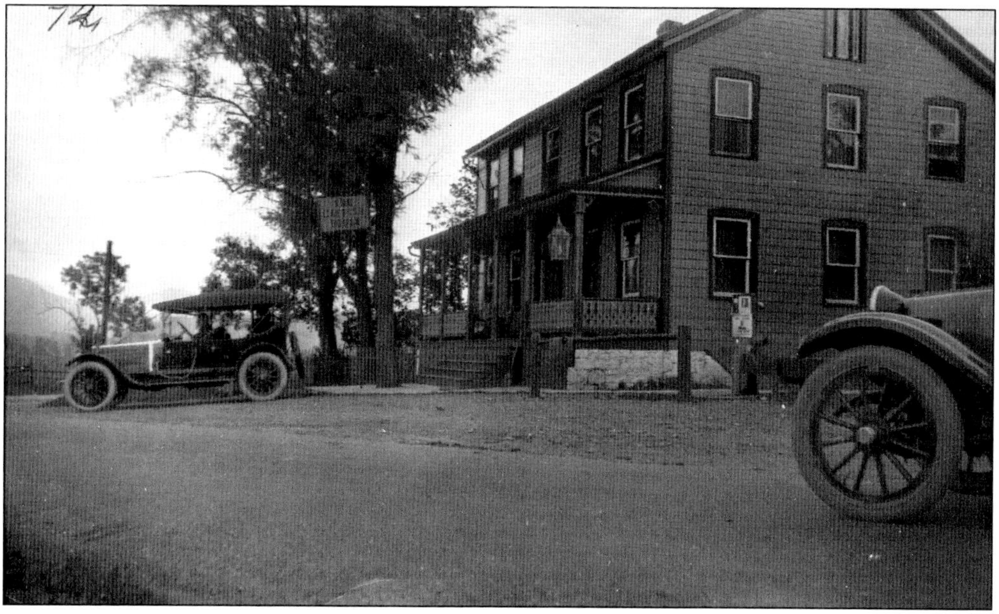

Catfish House was established prior to 1846 on an exclusive site near Kladder Station in Blair Township. It faced a picturesque reservoir that had been operational since 1839. The reservoir was stocked with a variety of food fish. The favorite fish among all patrons was called "catties." The second floor was a ballroom. When there were no social events, it became a dormitory. Beds were carried in, and travelers were accommodated at Catfish House.

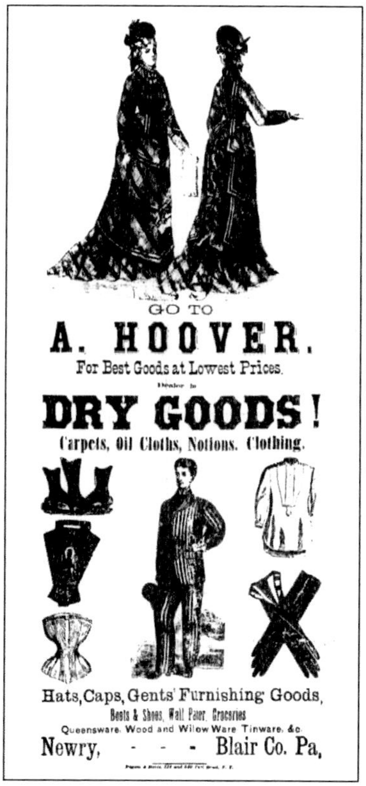

Newry had many businesses in its early days. Hoover General Store opened in 1832. Another was McIntosh Merchandising, which later became Smith Hardware. A hat factory, furniture shop, shoemaking shop, tin shop, wagon-making shop, blacksmith, carpet-weaving establishment, and grocery store all graced the town. Newry was a thriving hamlet when the Pennsylvania Railroad operated a passenger and freight train connecting with the trains at Duncansville.

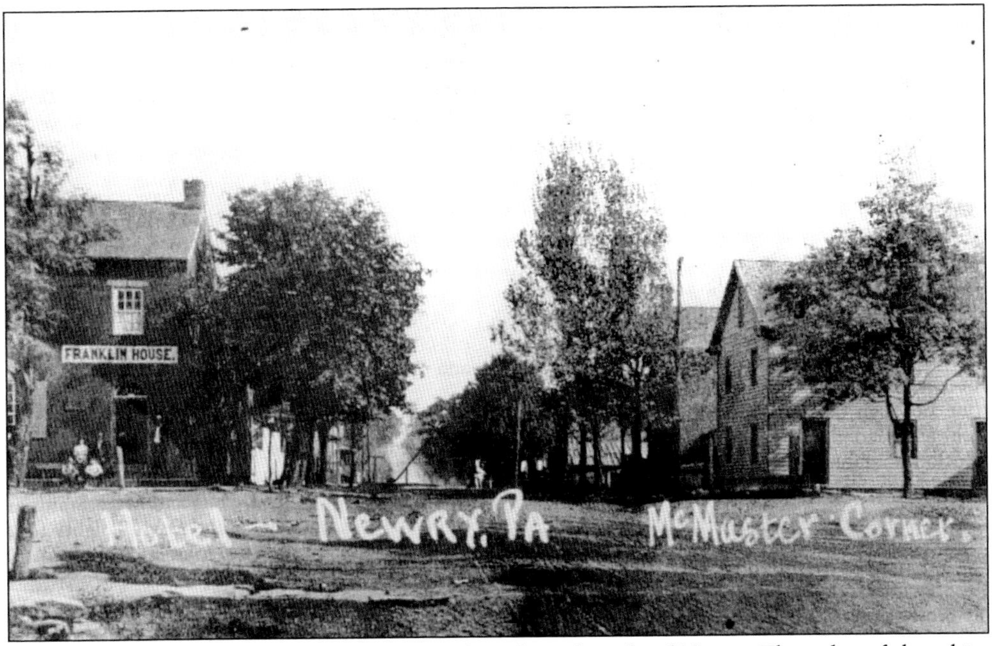

Toll gates were in operation at both the north and south ends of Newry. The rider of the white horse has just paid his nickel and will continue toward the crossroads, also known as McMaster's Corner. It was so named because a prominent citizen, James McMaster, had established a mercantile business on the Diamond. The Franklyn House was an early hostel and gathering place for townspeople. Joseph Diehl was the gatekeeper at the north end. The unpaved road was originally a trail and was later described as a turnpike.

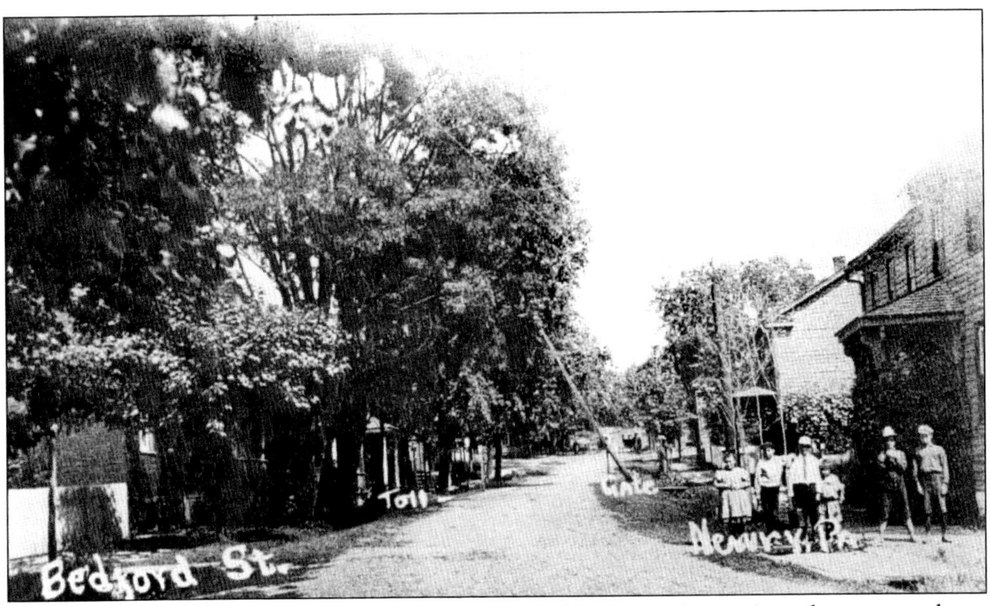

A toll gate was located at the south entrance on Bedford Street in Newry. A gatekeeper was always there to collect the nickel. This is approximately where Leighty's stands today. The unpaved road linked Bedford and Altoona.

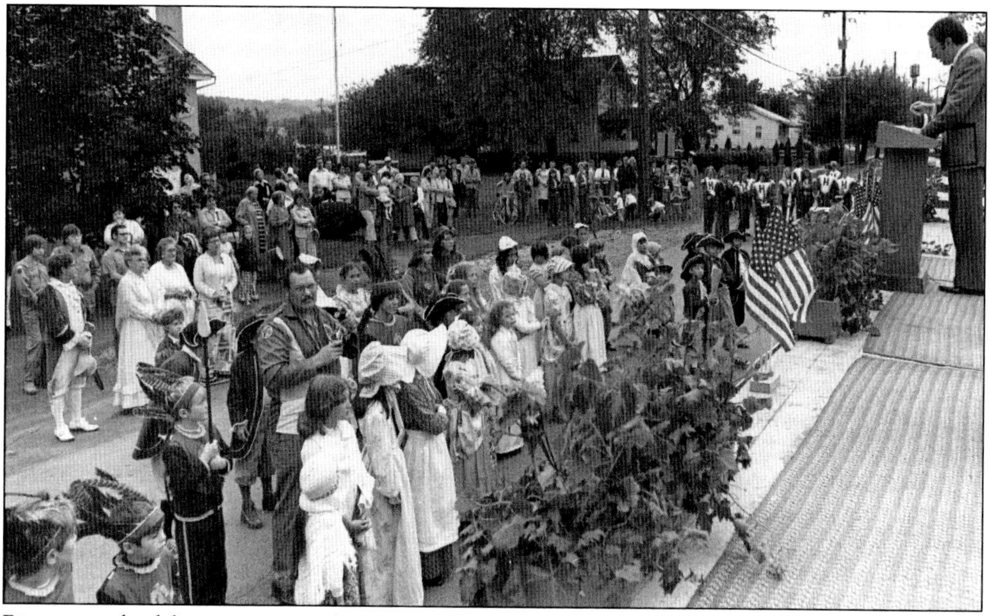

Bicentennial celebrations got under way in Newry with the reenactment of the Boston Tea Party. Children dressed as colonists and Native Americans dumped sacks of "tea" into "Newry Harbor" (better known as Poplar Run Creek). Many citizens appeared on the scene in the guise of colonists. Judge Paul S. Foreman delivered an address to the assemblage. Tea and cookies were served in the borough building following the reenactment. Note the protesters to the left.

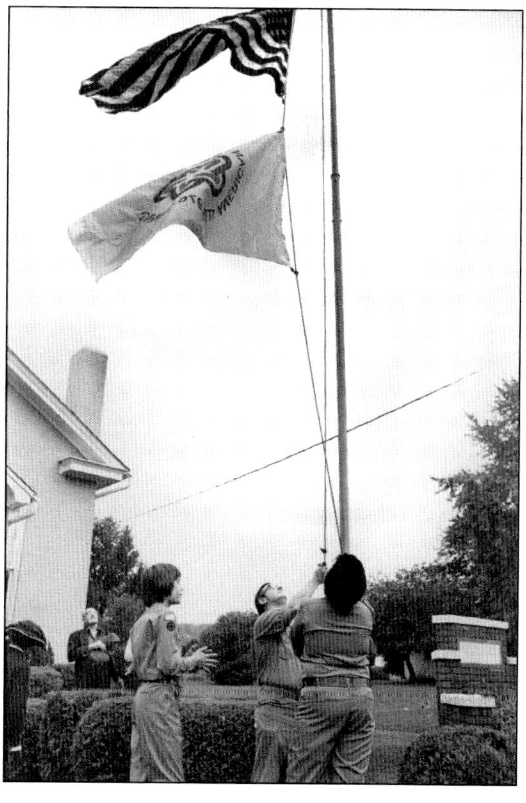

Old Glory rises above the bicentennial flag at the borough building in Newry during the bicentennial festivities. Edward Miller, chairman of the Newry Bicentennial Committee, received the flag from the county commissioner, Colin E. Jones. Both Jones and Miller were speakers. The Boy Scouts hoist the flags while patriots look on. Note the Revolutionary War uniform on the left.

Three

Nestled in the Valley

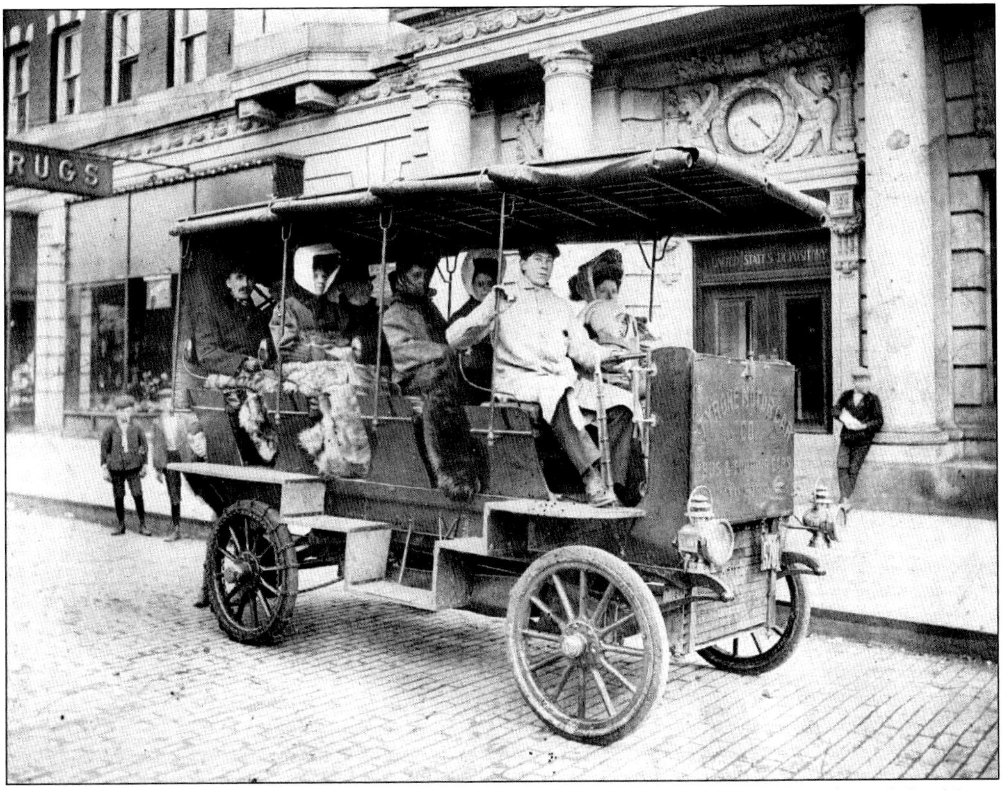

The Tyrone Motor Car Company parked its coach in front of the First National Bank building, which Ben Jones bought in later years, on Pennsylvania Avenue. This was a regular stop for the public-transportation coach. These open touring cars and early buses followed the horse-and-buggy era. Note the chains on the rear wheels to help prevent slipping on the ice. The sides were rolled down in inclement weather.

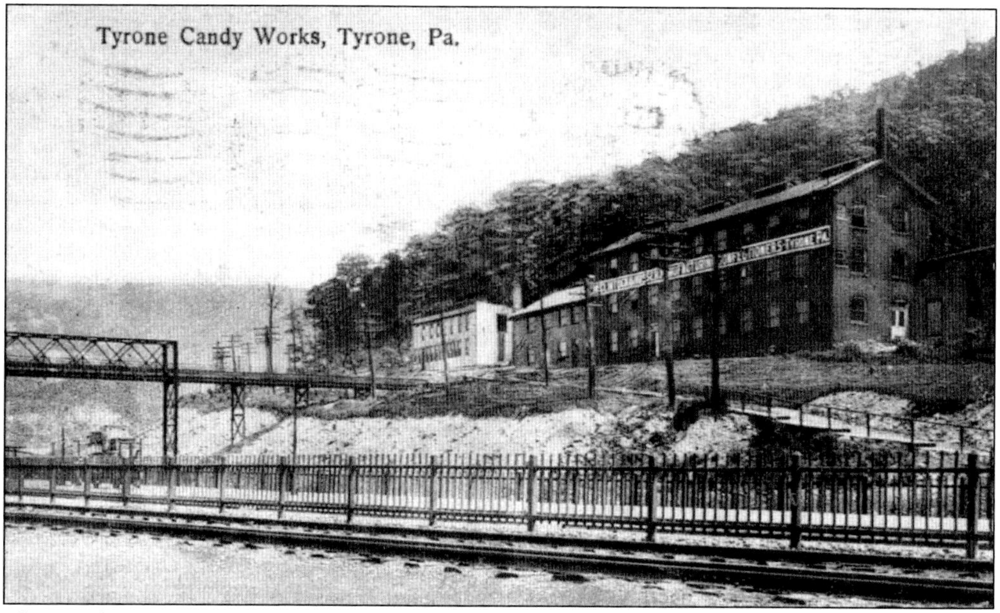

The McClintock and Musser Candy Company was located near the railroad. In 1908, McClintock solicited workers in County Cork, Ireland, for his candy manufacturing. John Seymour, an employee with Thompson's Bakery in Cork City, accepted the challenge, crossed the ocean, established himself in Tyrone, and sent for his family. When the parent company relocated to Florida, John Seymour established his own candy company in Tyrone.

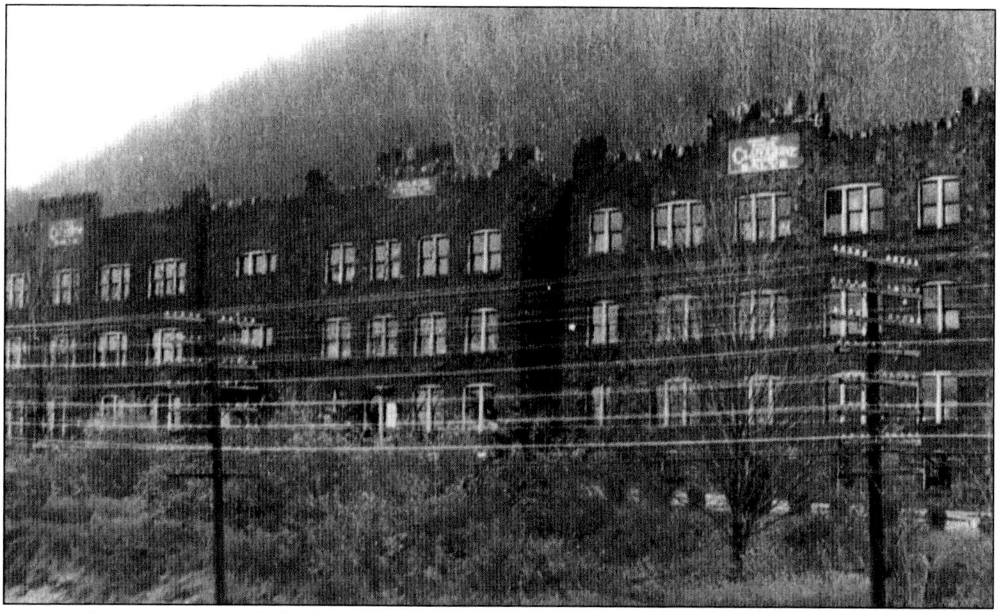

A shoe factory was established on this hillside in 1897. In 1903, the McClintock and Musser Candy Company came. Then, in 1904, George Wilson built a two-story wooden structure beside the candy factory to manufacture his famous Cloverline Salve. In 1915, he expanded to include the candy factory. A year later, fire destroyed the entire plant. A new building of natural stone from the nearby mountains was constructed within six months. In 1973, the plant was demolished to make way for the new Tyrone Bypass.

Burley Brothers Company Dry Goods, located on the corner of Pennsylvania Avenue and Tenth Street, was one of the first general stores in Tyrone. On the left, horses wait patiently to make deliveries throughout the area. The Burley, Study, and Jones building housed the First National Bank. A small Italian market was opened on Pennsylvania Avenue by Donato Idarola to service Italian immigrants.

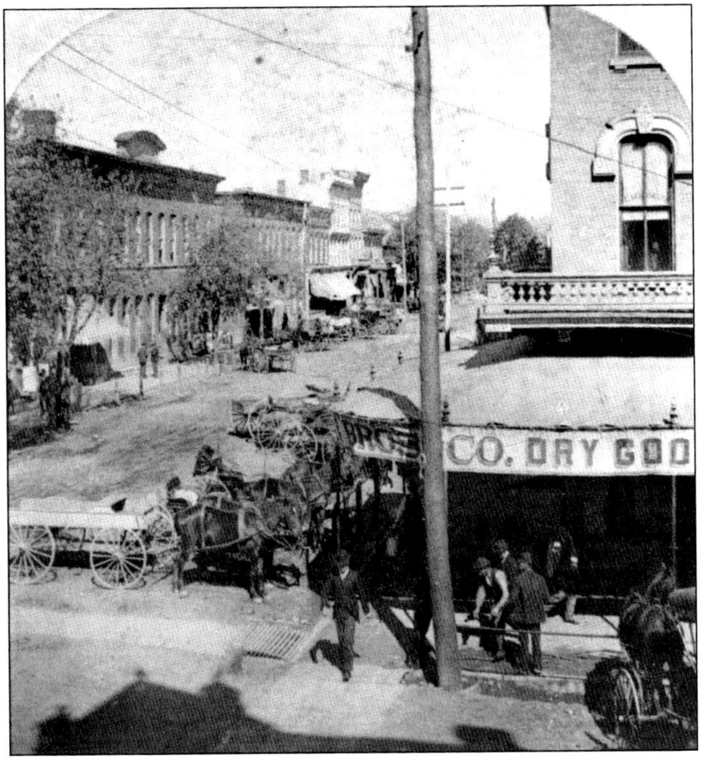

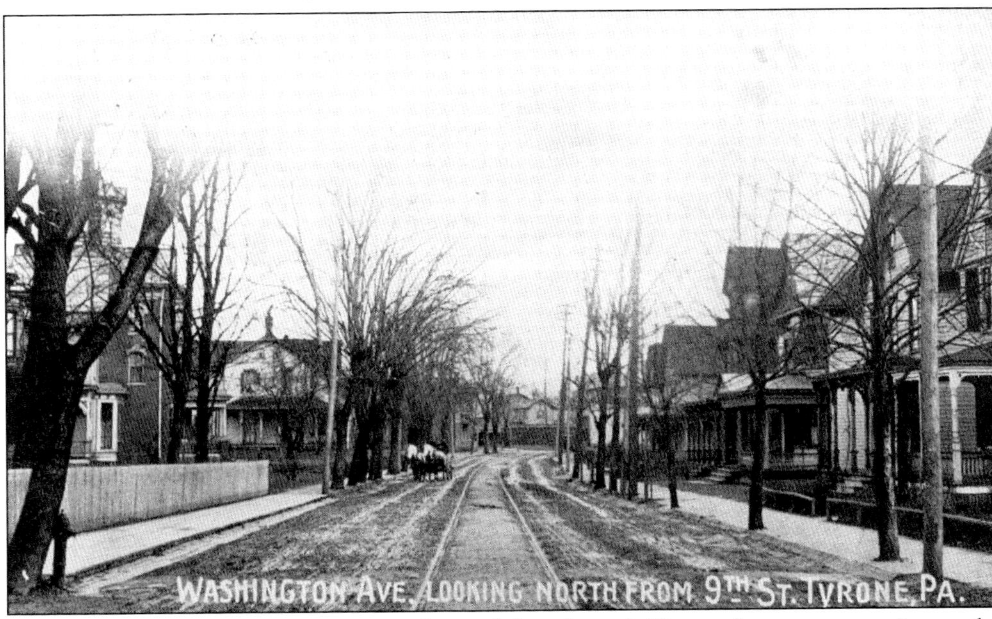

Washington Avenue was a prominent thoroughfare through Tyrone for many years. It was the celebrated highway to Altoona and points west. Its charm as a residential street gained popularity because of its location. In this early-20th-century scene, looking north from Ninth Street, the road is not yet paved, but the trolley tracks give the residents of Washington Avenue a source of transportation. Note the horses and wagon coming into town. It was on Washington Avenue that the Waring brothers first settled and established a nursery.

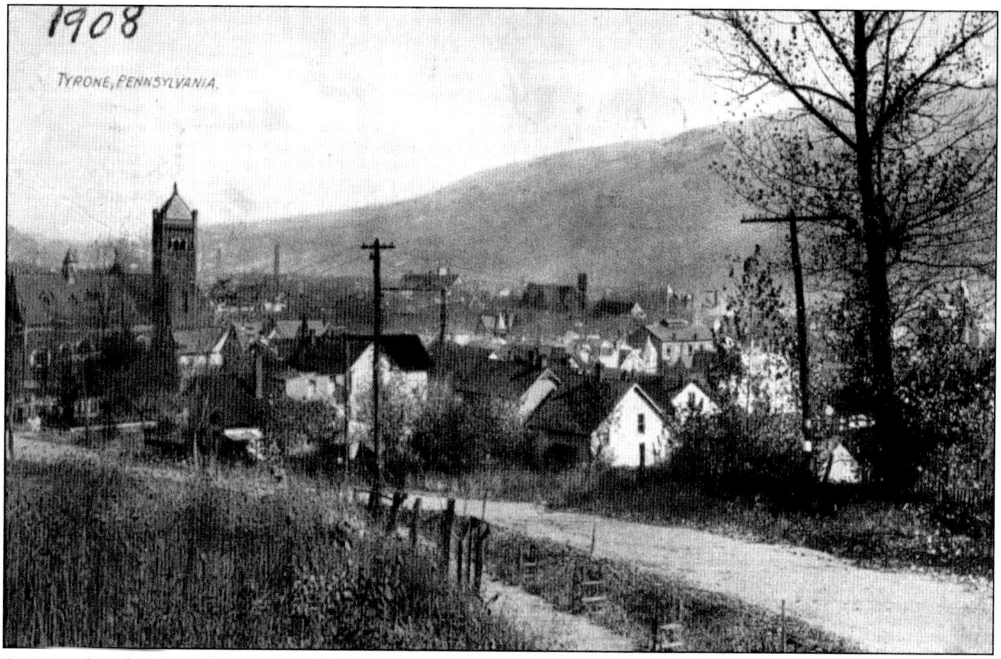

St. Matthew's Church is viewed from Henry Street in 1908. This early unpaved road was renamed Jefferson Street when a patriotic trend swept the country. Located at the junction of several branches of the Pennsylvania Railroad, Tyrone was an attractive hamlet of 7,000 inhabitants. It has always enjoyed excellent transportation facilities.

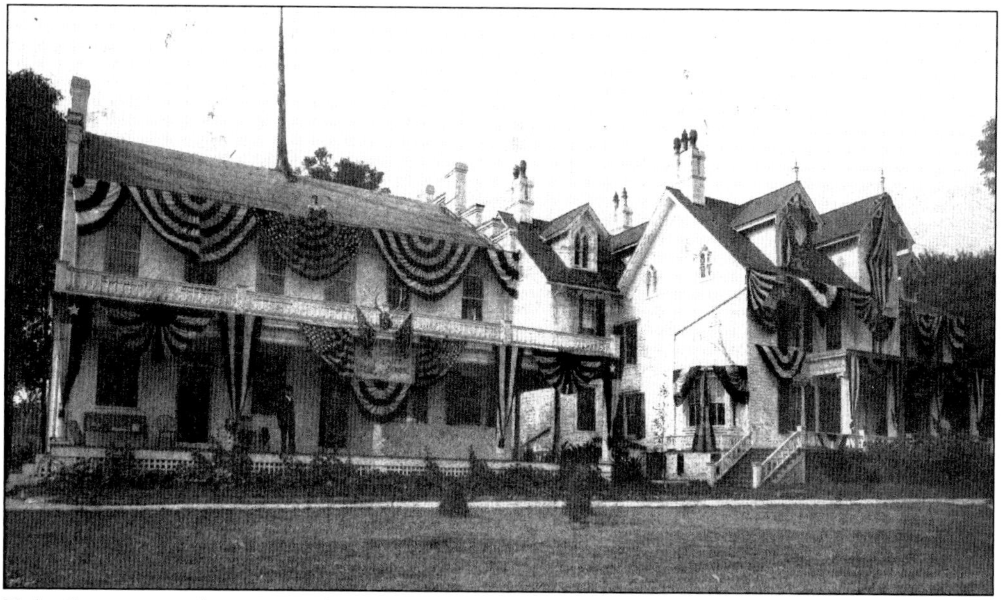

H.A. Gripp opened an art studio named Elkhurst in 1880. It was located at Villa Maria near Tyrone Forge on 165 acres of rustic woodland. Gripp was a German artist who made lifelike portraits from common photographs. His clientele included students from many foreign countries. Personal supervision was his hallmark. His complex of buildings faces the railroad and mountains that open into Warriors Mark Valley. Elkhurst was so named for the original inhabitants of Tyrone.

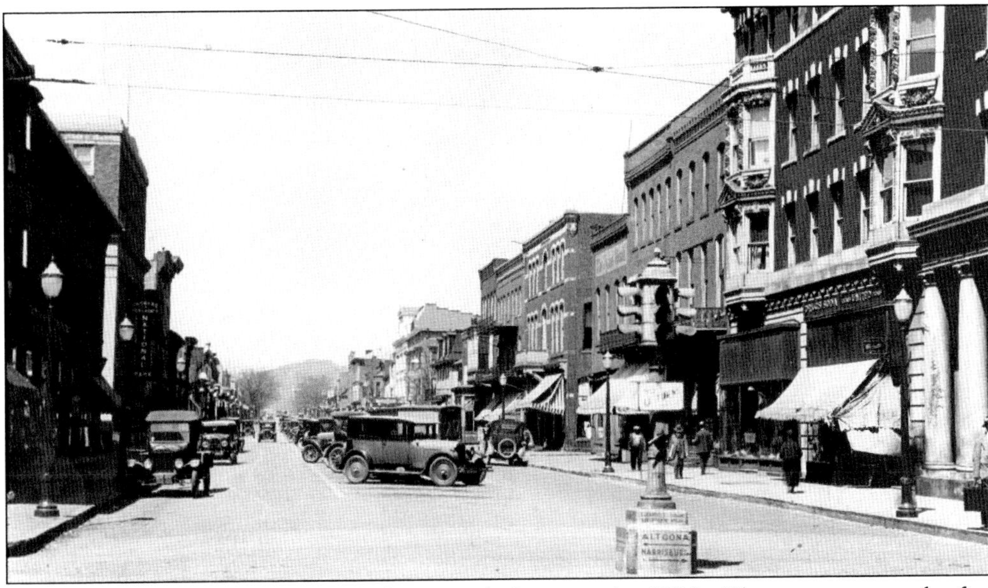

Streetlights were proudly displayed along Tenth Street in the 1920s. They were among the first traffic lights in town. Note the location in the center of the street with directional arrows for Altoona and Harrisburg. The Farmer's National Bank is on the left. The right side includes McClanhan Drugs, Dank's Clothing, the Herald office, Francisco's Hardware, and the Jones Building (which housed the First National Bank).

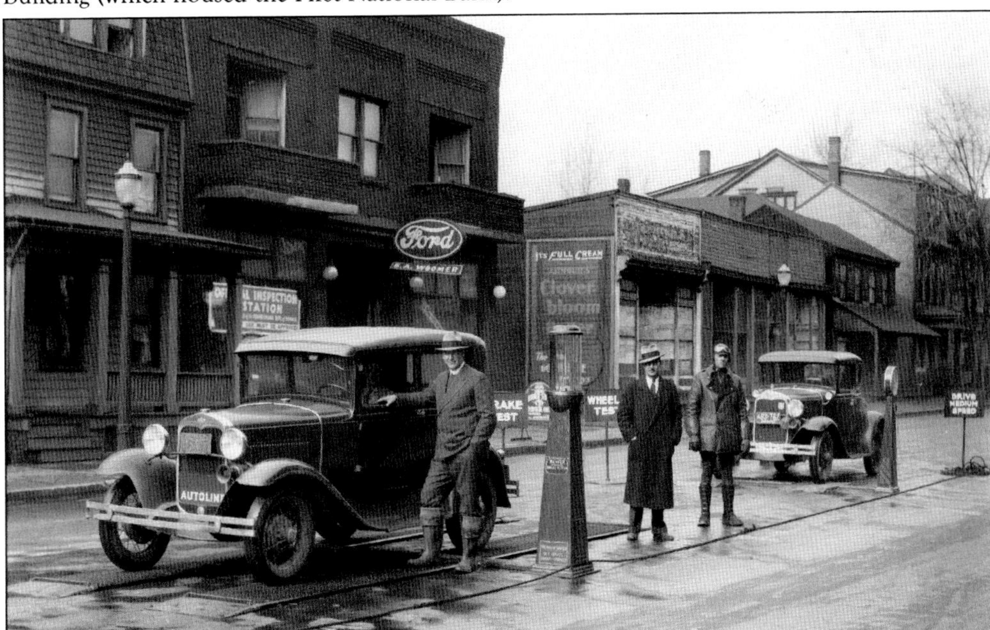

The first gas station in Tyrone was that of S.A. Woormer. It was a Ford dealership along Pennsylvania Avenue. The gentleman on the right in uniform is the chief of police, Dewey Menther. Note the tester that the sedan stands on. The device on the left is a Weaver brake tester. The wording indicates "medium speed, set brakes quickly and firmly." It was an official inspection station of the 1930s and advertised Quaker State motor oil. Armours Clover Bloom Butter is advertised next door.

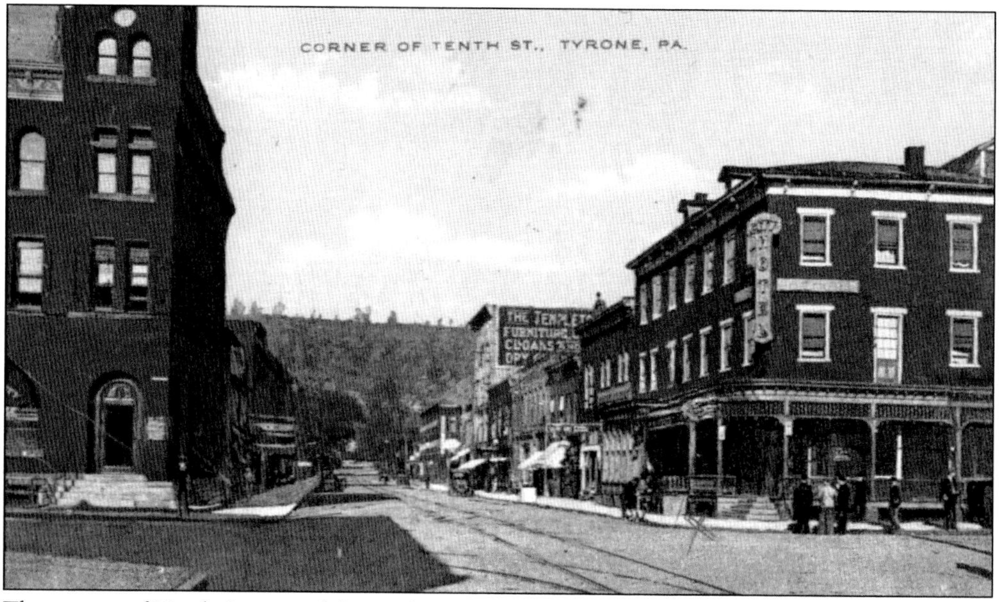

The corner of Tenth Street and Pennsylvania Avenue features the Blair County National Bank Building on the left. Established in 1874, it was chartered in 1902 and merged with First National Bank in 1932. It later became Mid State Bank. City Hotel (right) was built in 1881 and was opened by John D. Stewart and Jacob Burley. It was a favorite gathering place with its huge veranda. Frank Skelly operated a newsstand down the street on the right. His small establishment can be seen beneath the furniture store sign.

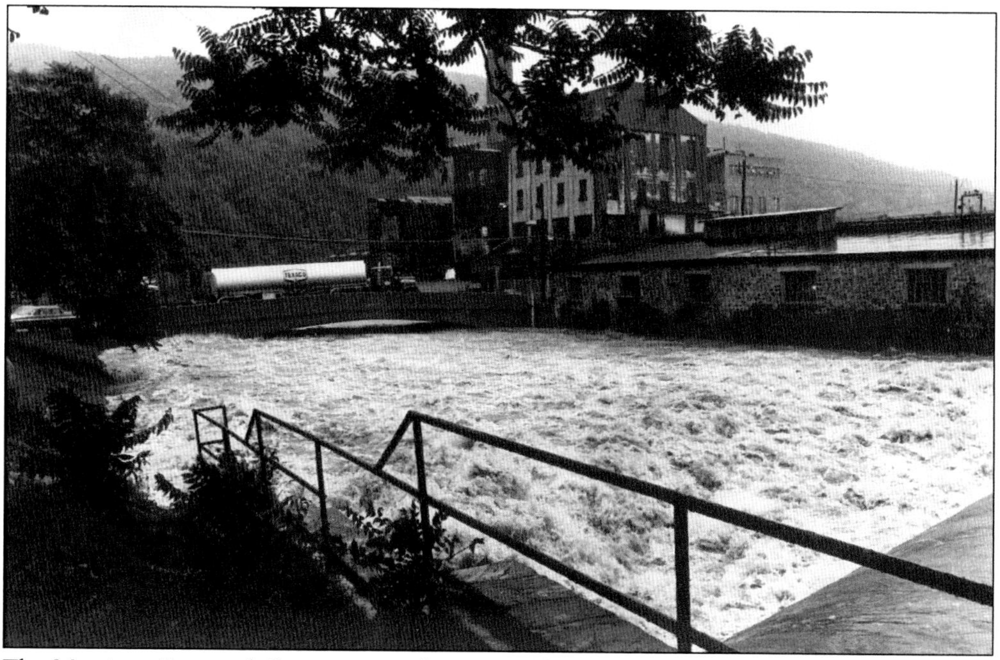

The Morrison Bare and Cass paper mill was established on the Juniata River in 1880. The buildings cover 825 feet of land (the length of a block), where various phases of the work were carried on. The paper mill, the largest industry in Tyrone, employed 225 people. It manufactured high-quality products that were in demand throughout the country and abroad.

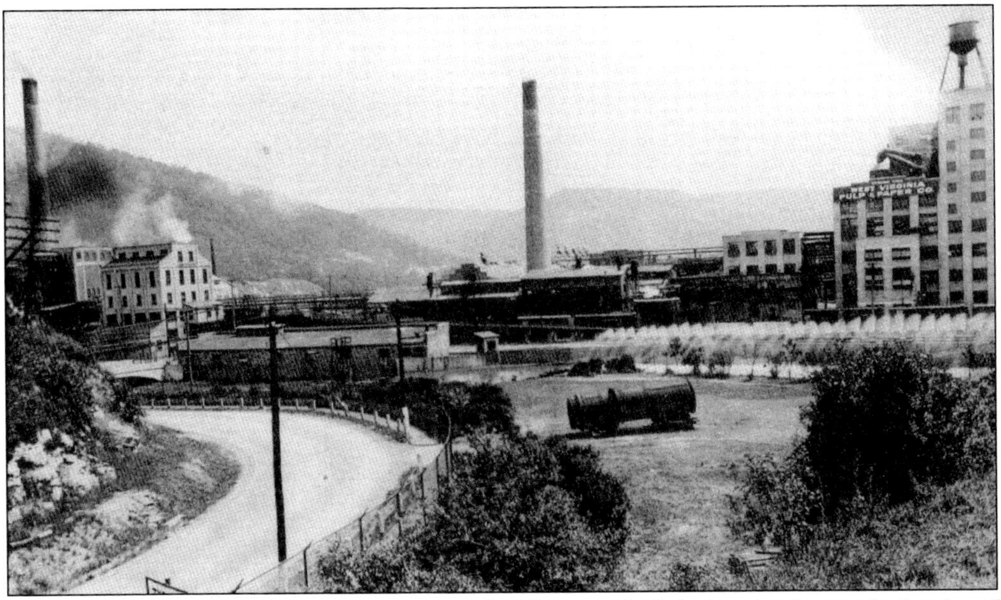

Tyrone will go down in history for the aroma that distinguished the hamlet during the heyday of its paper mill. To many natives, the very scent was "home sweet home." To others, it was a source of wonder. Two tall smokestacks characterized this little village in the valley. They gave off black vapor from the fires that operated its 24 steam boilers. These furnished power to its eight steam engines.

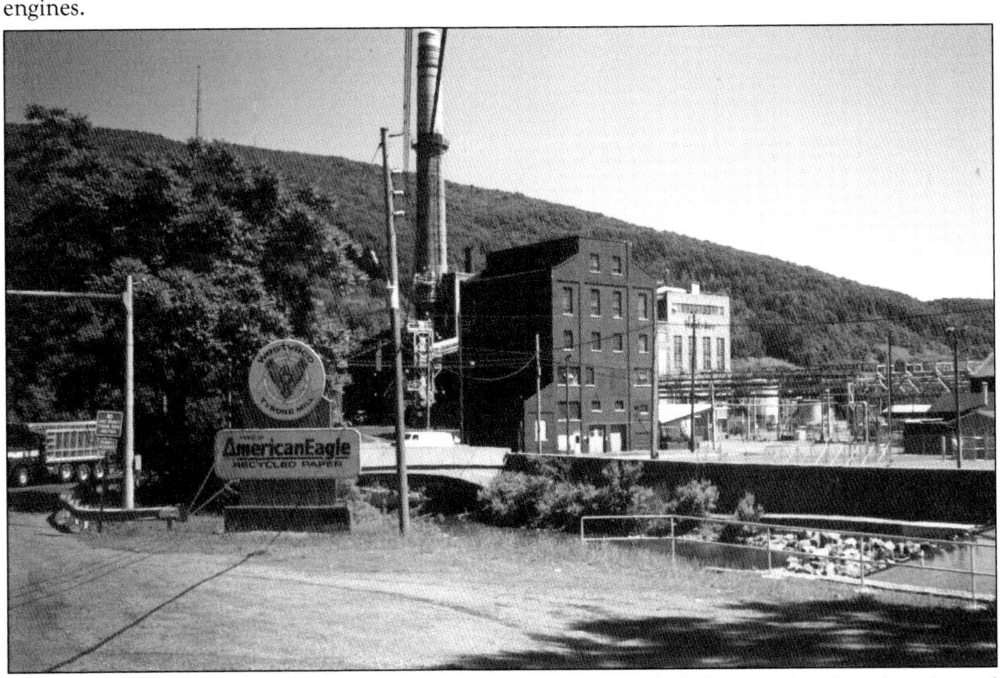

Thirty tons of paper were turned out in the Tyrone paper mill daily. Five-foot lengths of wood were thrown into the jaws of a giant steel chopper. This began the process of changing wood into paper. In 1899, the plant consolidated with the West Virginia Pulp and Paper Company. In 1970, a major part of the plant ceased operation. American Eagle recycled paper is produced here, as are covers for *National Geographic*.

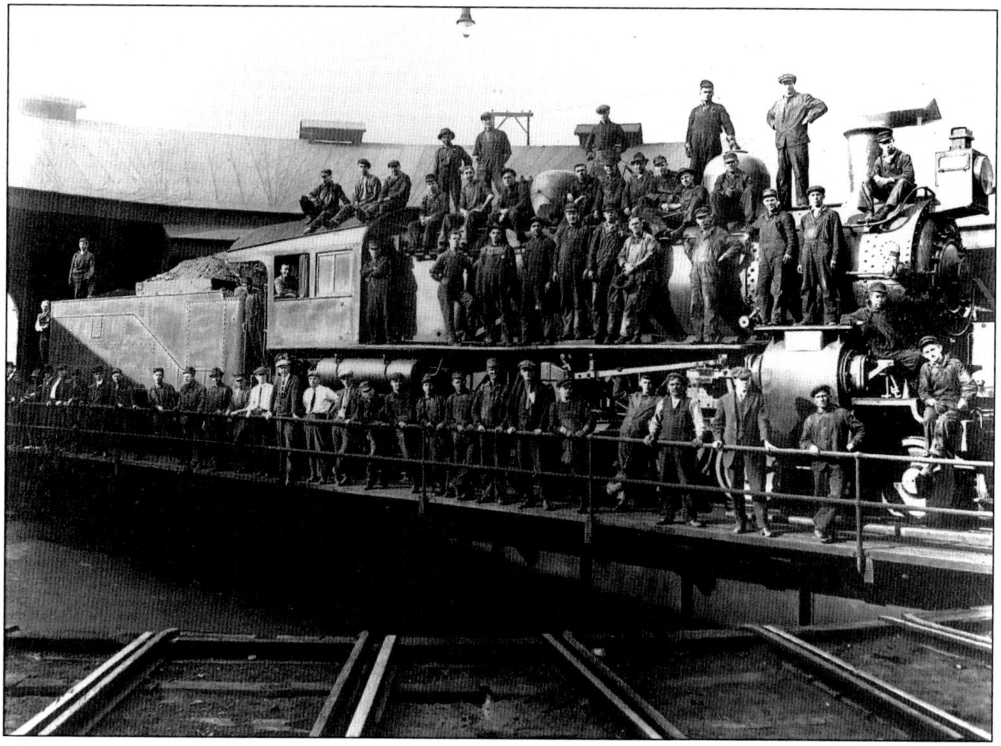

The roundhouse was located in east Tyrone at Eleventh Street and Lincoln Avenue. In this photograph, Tyrone railroad employees are gathered on the turntable for a ride as it makes a turn to travel in the opposite direction.

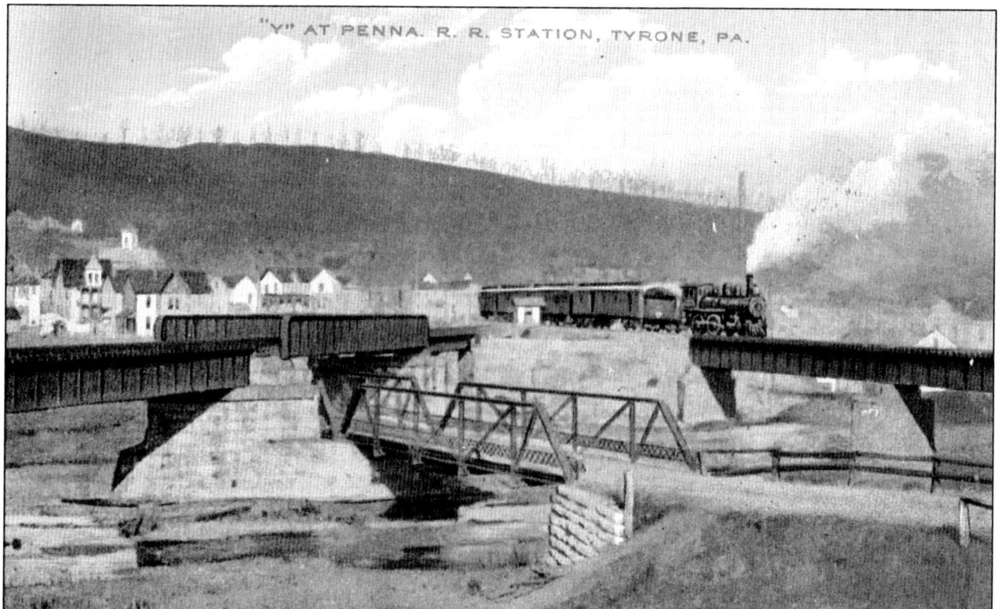

A wye was formed over the Juniata River at Ninth Street. The railroad bridge carried the train from Altoona to Bellefonte. This was part of the main line. St. Matthew's Church is on the left, and Bush Mountain rises in the background.

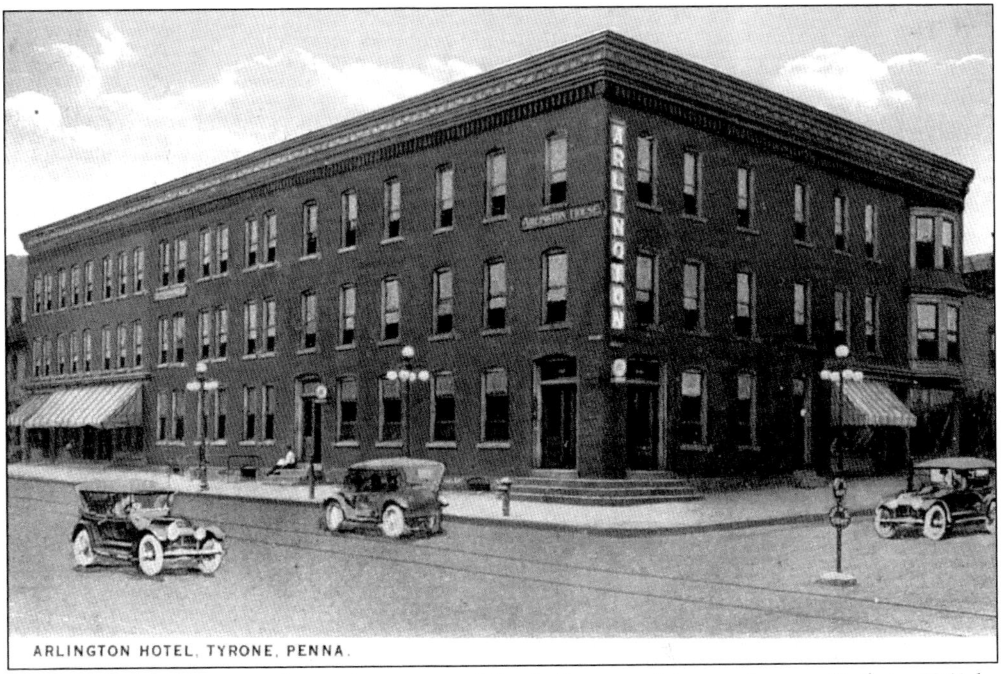

The Arlington House stands on the corner of Tenth Street and Logan Avenue. Built in 1853 by Joshua Burley and known as the Central for many years, the Arlington House maintains a popular homelike atmosphere. Hotels were a vital commodity in town when the railroad first came through. Men were needed and families resided in hotels while homes were under construction.

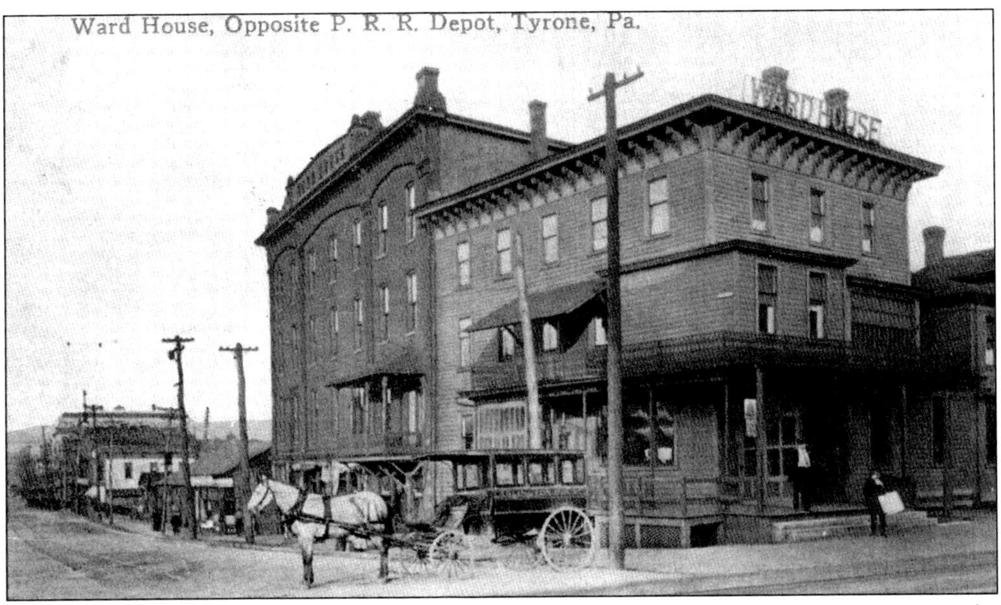

The Ward House was built in 1859 as a stopover for railroad travelers. Located opposite the railroad station, the hotel provided excellent hospitality and the most modern accommodations and conveniences. Initially, Mary Ward had a frame building constructed to house travelers. It was also an entertainment center that became increasingly popular. Expansion became necessary, and a brick extension was added.

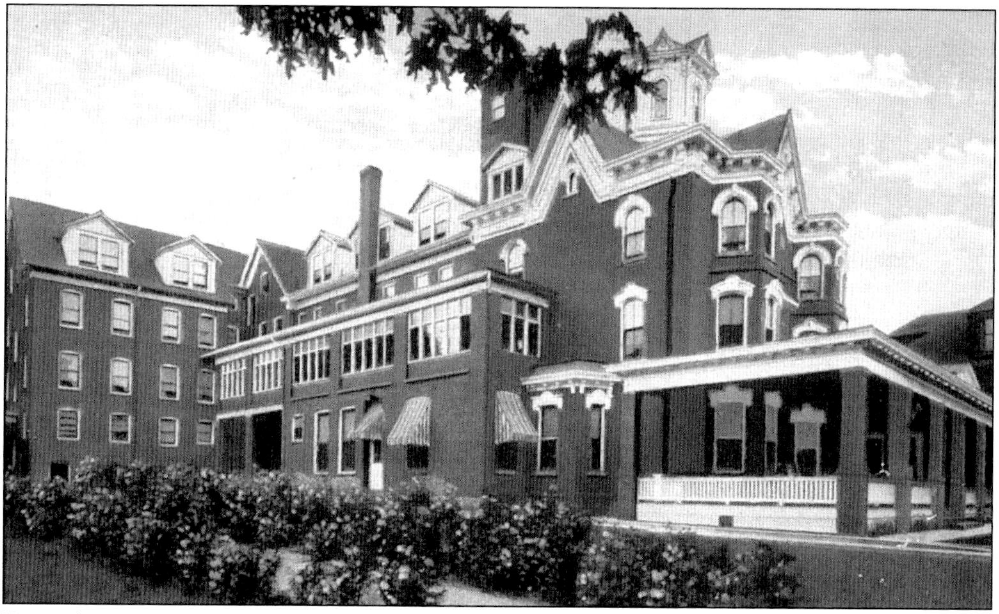

Epworth Manor is a Methodist home for the aged founded in 1919. The Central Pennsylvania Conference of the Methodist Church recognized the need for elderly housing and purchased the mansion of railroad superintendent S.S. Blair. Located on Washington Avenue, it was converted into a home that could accommodate 14 residents. Additions were built until 1974, when the mansion was demolished and a new four-story building was completed.

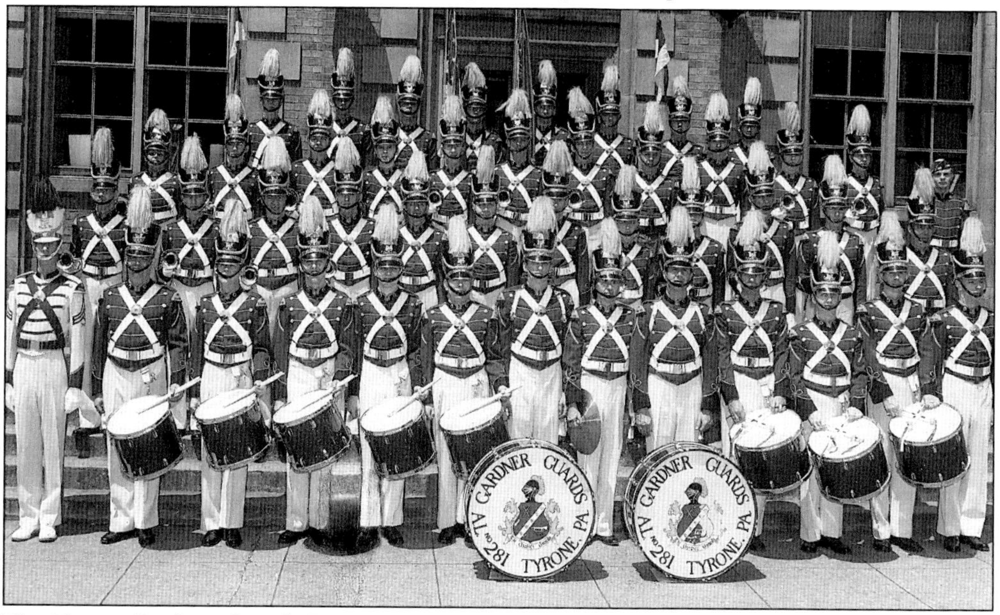

The Tyrone Gardner Guards Drum and Bugle Corps of Howard Gardner Post 281, American Legion, was organized in 1950. The unit appeared in many drill competitions and parades. They had acquired the services of Sgt. Truman Crawford, director of the U.S. Air Force Drum and Bugle Corps. They performed in the presidential inaugural parade in 1957. The group appeared on the Ed Sullivan Show and Fred Waring's Shawnee on the Delaware. They have won numerous drill championships.

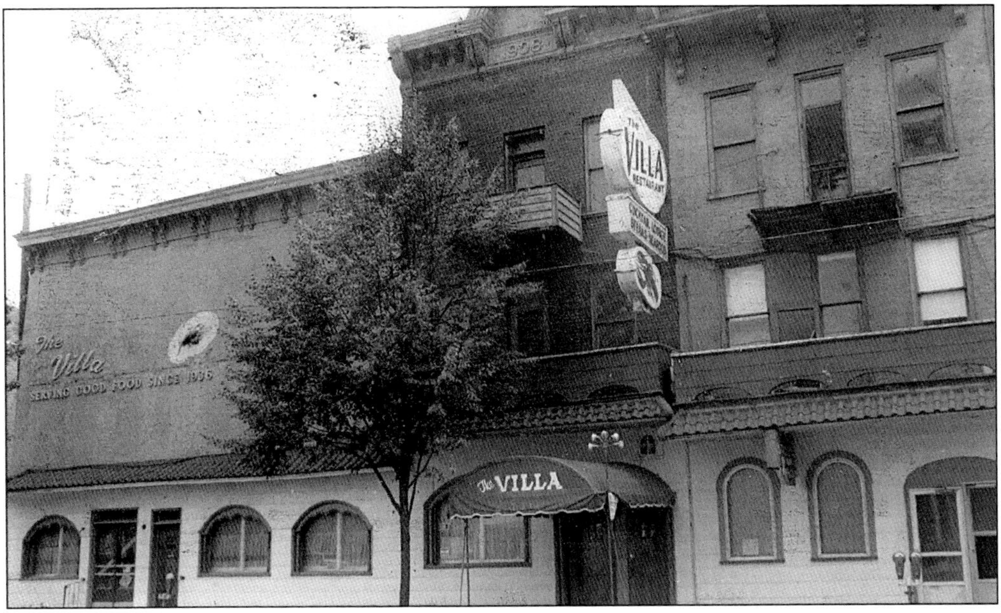

The Villa Restaurant was cited in *Good Housekeeping* in 1953 by columnist Dorothy Kilgallen as elaborate as any in New York City. Celebrities had to wait for tables. The Villa is a family-owned business. It was opened in 1936 by Santa Panasiti after the death of her husband, Dominic, and the disastrous flood of 1936. She originally specialized in her famous spaghetti sauce. She continued to improve, and eventually the third generation became proprietors. The Panasitis had been in Tyrone since 1920 and operated a small grocery store.

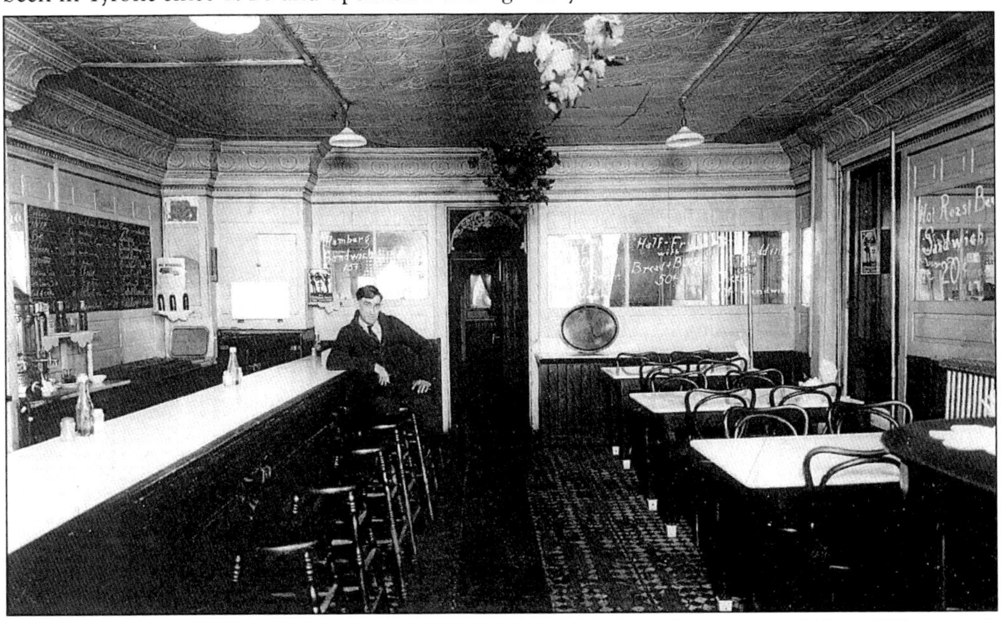

The Fifty Piper's Restaurant was located on Pennsylvania Avenue between Twelfth and Thirteenth Streets. Note the bus schedule posted in the left corner, the tin ceiling, and the furniture of another era. The unidentified gentleman is the waiting proprietor. The prices are those of a bygone era. A hamburger was 15¢; a half fry with bread and butter was 50¢; a hot roast beef sandwich was 20¢; and coffee, milk, and pop were 5¢.

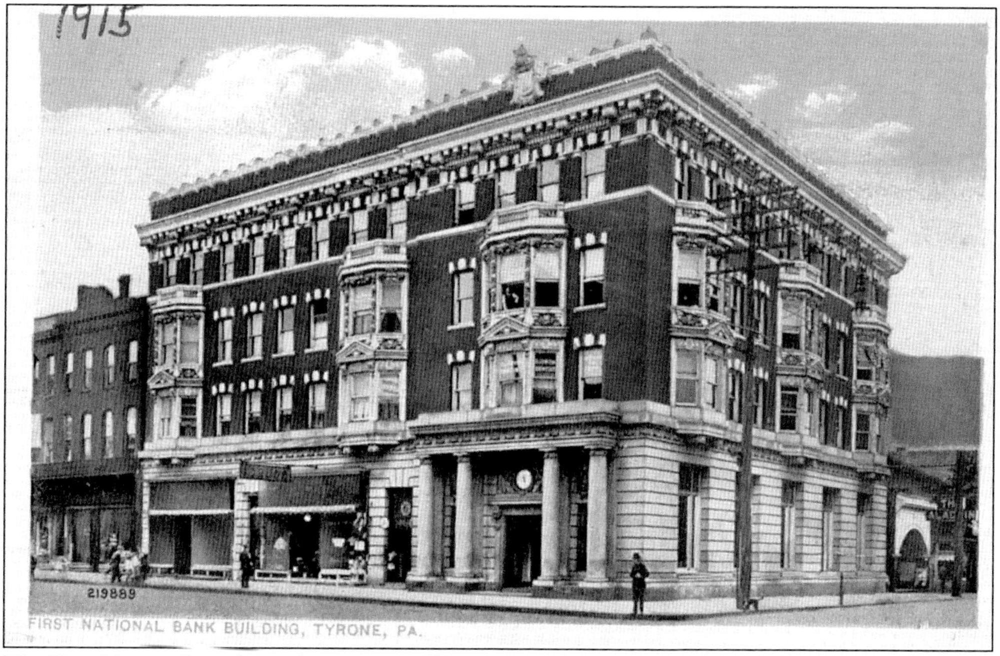

The First National Bank on the corner of Pennsylvania Avenue and Tenth Street was established in 1890. It gained a leading place among financial institutions. J.K. Cass, an honored businessman in the area, was president.

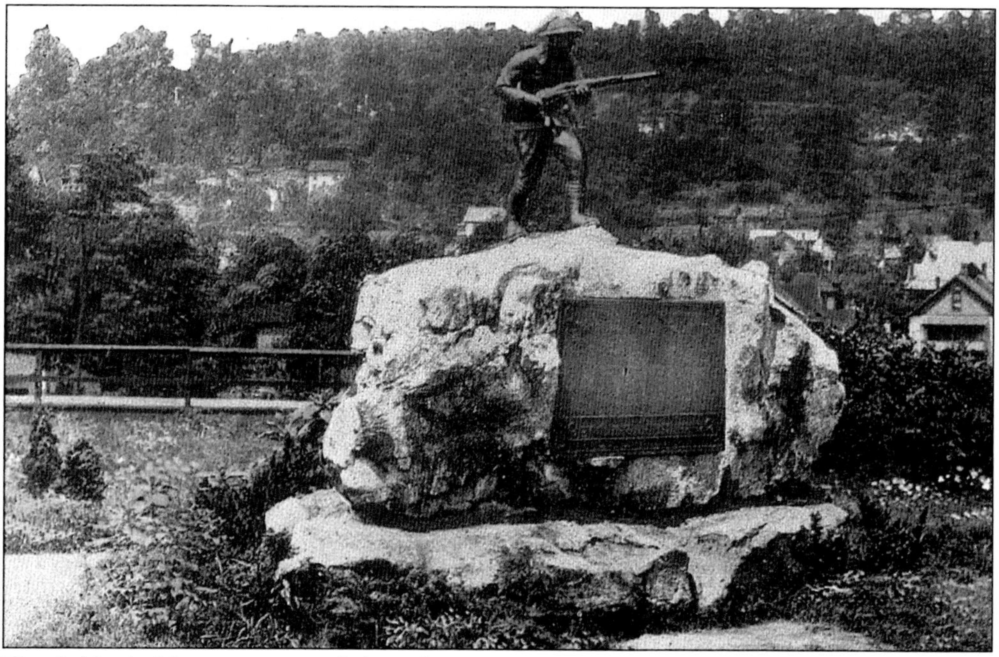

The Soldier's Monument was dedicated on May 30, 1921, by the Tyrone Division of the Pennsylvania Railroad. Located at the railroad depot on South Pennsylvania Avenue, it was dedicated to honor all those men who served in World War I. After World War II, the statue was moved to Soldier's Park on Fourteenth Street. The huge stone, too heavy to move over the Pennsylvania Avenue Bridge, had become part of the Tyrone Heritage Railroad Park.

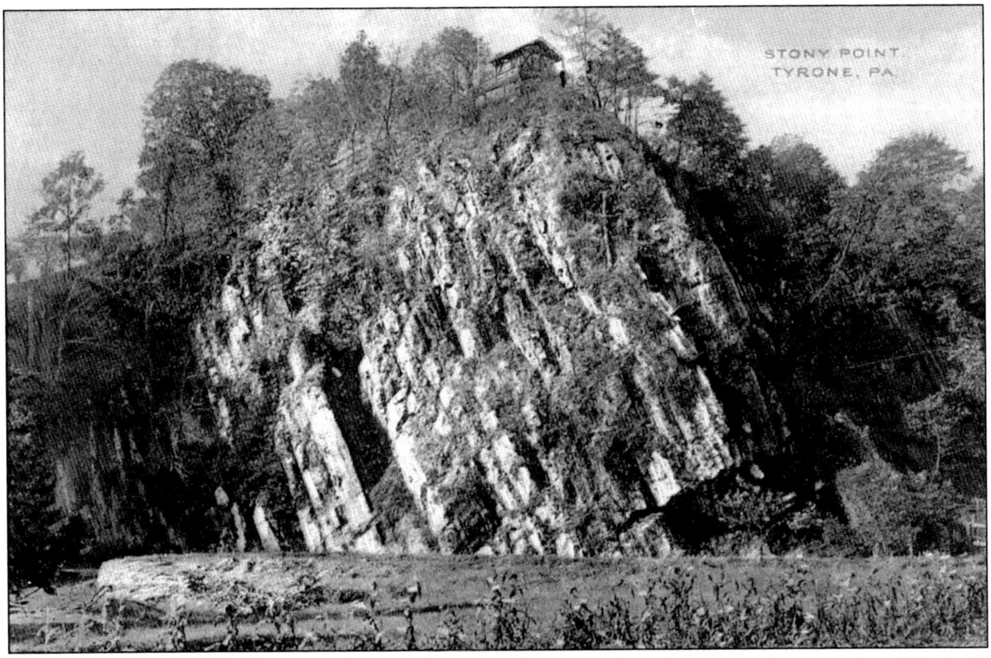

A.K. Johnston was the superintendent of the Pennsylvania Railroad and was also a gardner. He built a huge greenhouse in his backyard, where he grew vegetables and flowers. Located at the corner of Fifteenth and Lincoln Avenues, the American Legion now occupies this site. On the bluff behind his house, dubbed Stony Point, Johnston built a log cabin complete with hothouse.

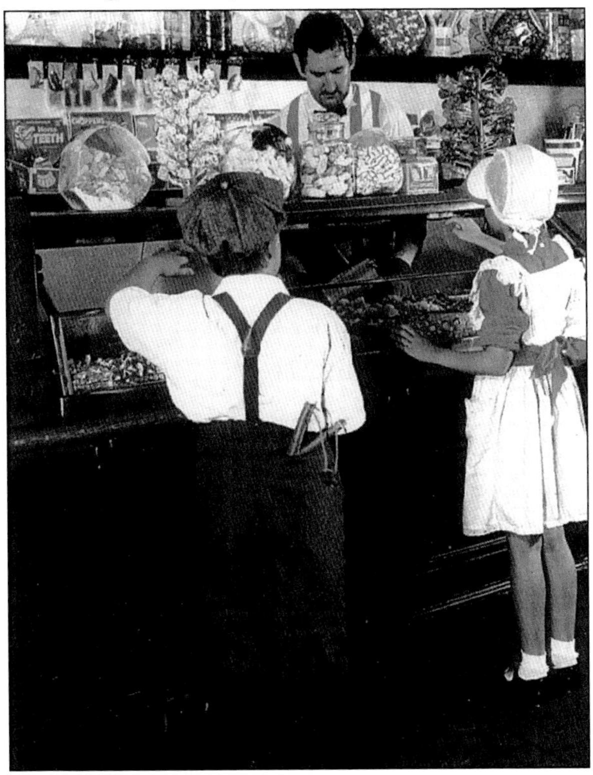

Gardner Candy has been a favorite for generations. Seventeen-year-old James A. "Pike" Gardner opened a candy shop on Pennsylvania Avenue in 1897. The business has moved several times. Many natives have memories of standing at the penny counter, making that big decision. In 1912, it was located in the Blair County Bank and featured a peanut wagon serving fresh-roasted peanuts, a novelty for Tyrone. Gardner initiated peanut butter meltaways and Valentine's Day heart-shaped boxes of chocolate.

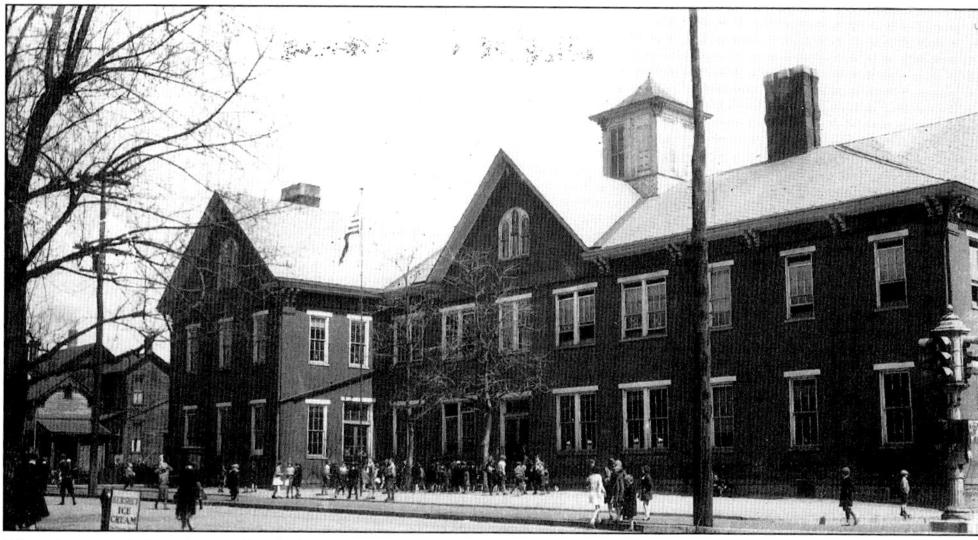

The Logan School was built by F.D. Beyer in 1866. Eleven years later, a high school was added. Adjoining properties were bought as the population grew. In 1911, a new high school was built. The Logan School location has become the site of Sheetz.

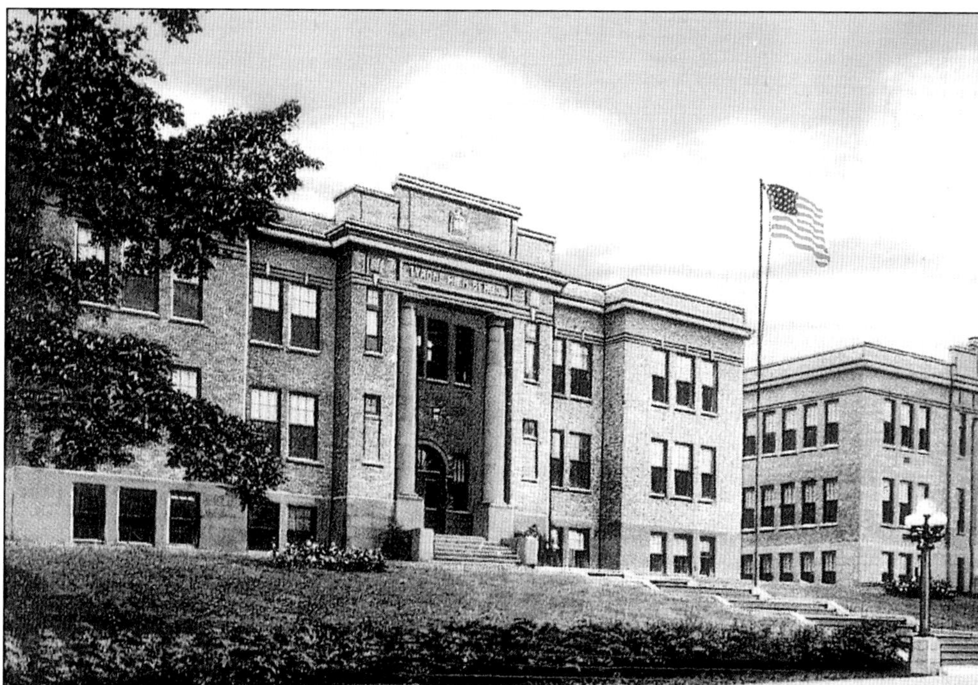

Education in Tyrone evolved into a modern complex of multilevel facilities. In 1895, an independent district was established. In 1939, Dr. Norman Miller, superintendent, undertook the construction of the new high school on Lincoln Avenue. School spirit is very strong among students. Tyrone considers itself a football town, but many other sports are part of the curriculum. High academic standards are achieved. The new senior high school was completed in 1962.

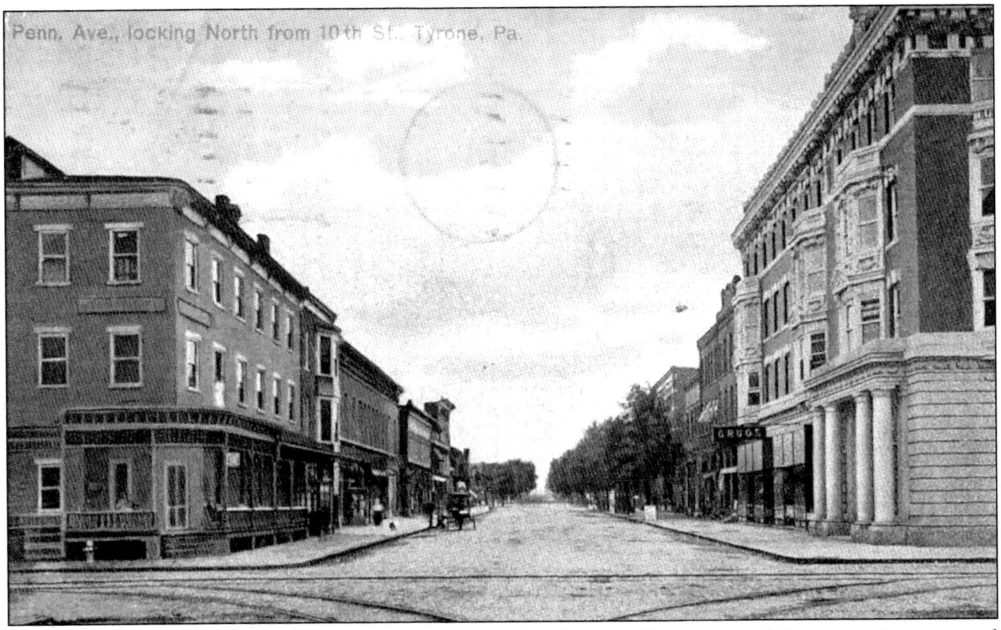

In 1902, a trolley line was installed in town. The first trolley operated between Tyrone and Altoona. Trolley tracks were laid along Pennsylvania Avenue and merged onto Tenth Street. Note the horse and buggy along Penn Avenue. The City Hotel is on the left, and the First National Bank is on the right. The trolley continued in use until March 1936, when the last trolley left for Altoona.

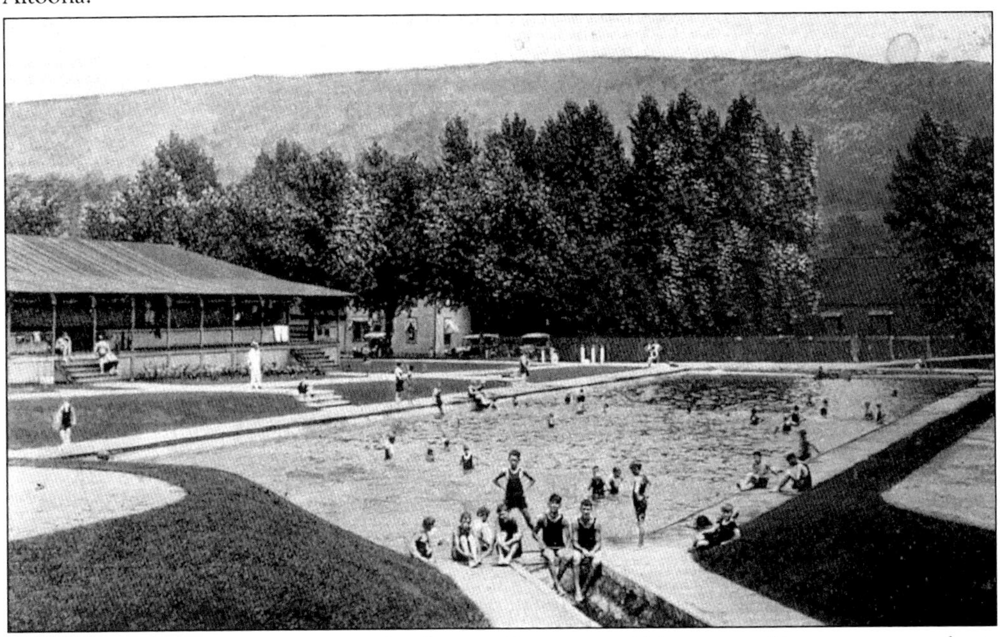

The Athletic Park was an attraction for those willing to pay 10¢ to enter. The water was only six feet deep and could not support a diving board. Patrons hiked a cinder path beside the railroad tracks to reach the park. The railroad owned the park until 1920s, when Tyrone Borough took it over. The large building on the left contained the bathhouses and refreshment stand. The park closed in 1948.

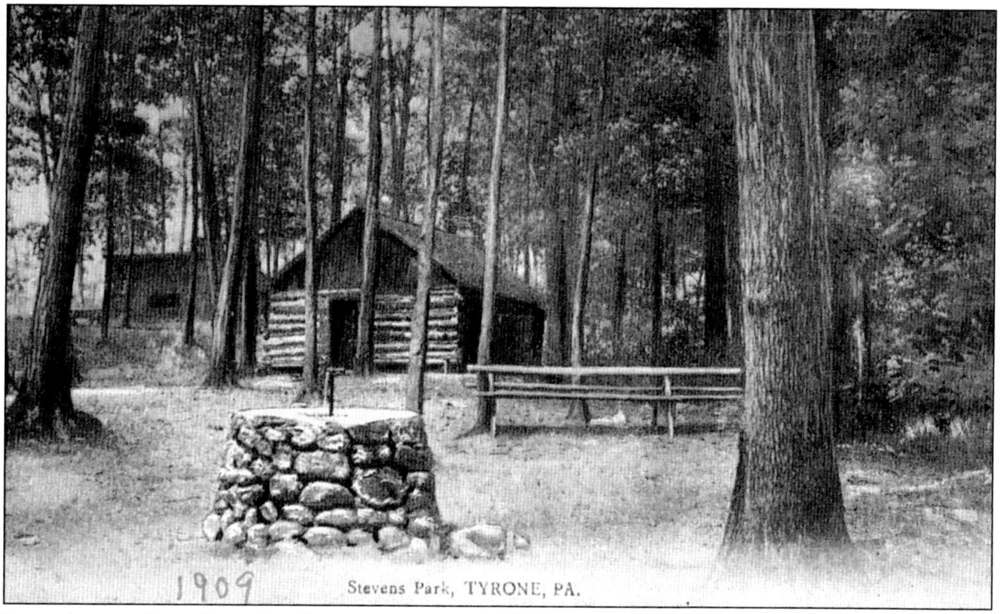

Log cabins and pavilions dot the picturesque woodlands of Stevens Park (now known as Reservoir Park). The park was established when A.A. Stevens donated 33 acres of land in Tyrone for this purpose. It was later owned by the water authority. Pavilions, complete with picnic tables and fireplaces, afford Tyroners and visitors alike opportunity for diversion. Rides for children are readily available, as is the unusually beautiful rustic scenery throughout the area.

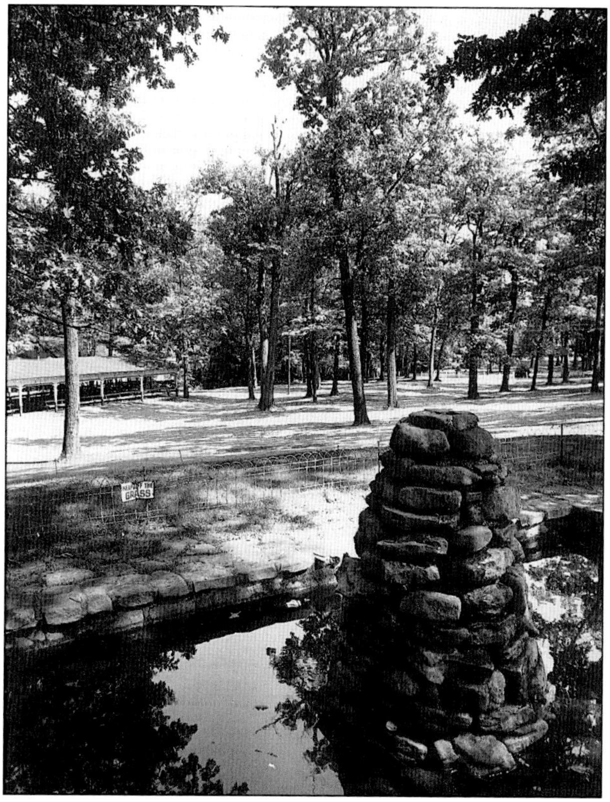

There was once a large wooden dance pavilion in Stevens Park that housed two dances a week in the mid-20th century. A cold, clear mountain stream flows through the park, where trout are often obtained. In winter, the stream becomes an ice-skating rink to the enjoyment of all.

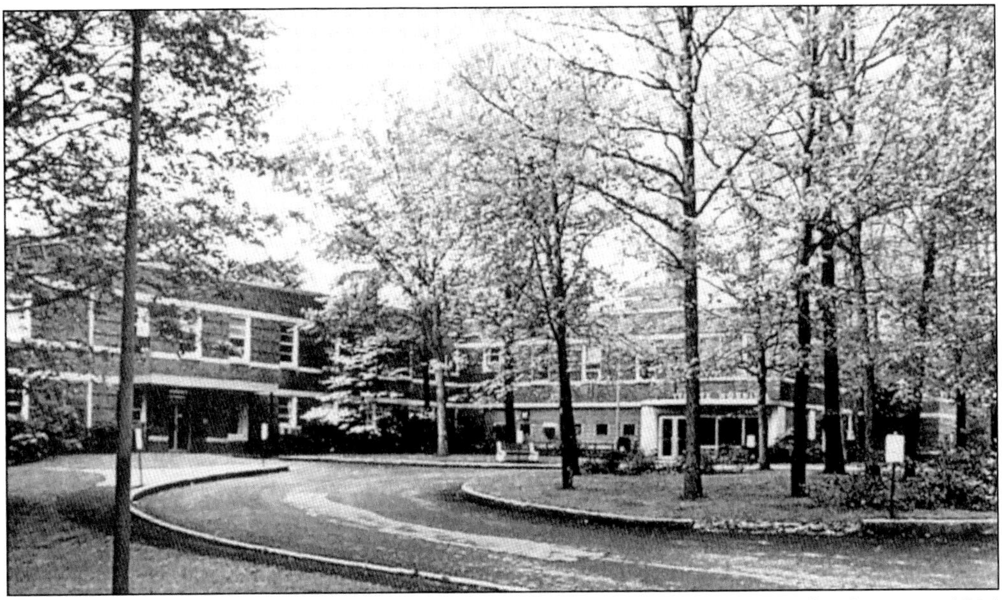

Tyrone Hospital came into existence in 1954. It was a long needed project that began in 1931 with a $150,000 bequest from Harvey and Addie Grey. The Great Depression and World War II intervened, during which time the project was on hold. Seventeen acres of high wooded land had been donated by the borough water department just west of Laurel Ridge. Many Tyroners assisted in bringing the hospital to reality.

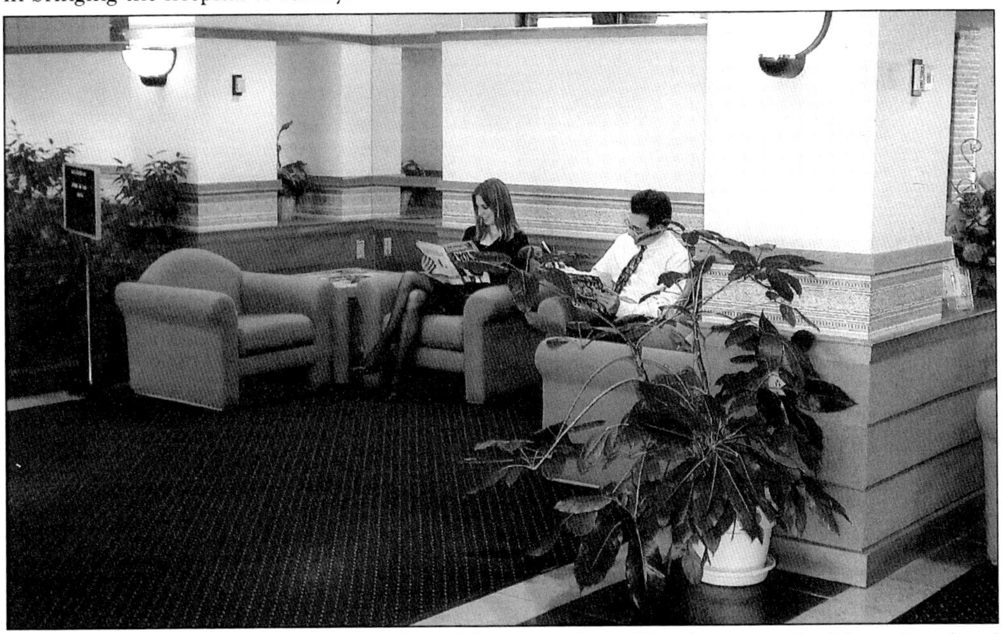

The lobby of Tyrone Hospital creates a homelike atmosphere. The three-story building of steel and red brick stands on a picturesque hillside. The dedication ceremony extended over two days and included many tours. The 50-bed institution was officially opened on September 20, 1954, when the first patient, Victor Getz, was admitted. The facility has kept pace with scientific advances in the medical field. An intensive-care unit, pediatric unit, outpatient clinic, and a new medical office building were added within the first decade.

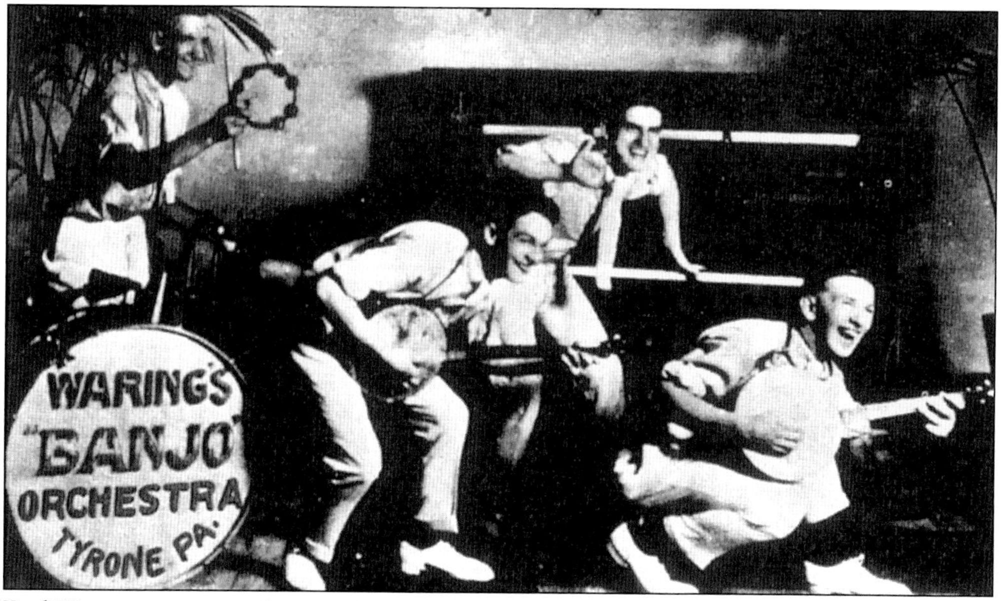

Fred Waring was a musical genius. Born in Tyrone in 1900, he formed the internationally famous Pennsylvanians. The quartet played at local parties and was popular at Penn State University and on Broadway. Waring's brother Thomas was the singer for the Pennsylvanians. Fred Waring never forgot his roots. In 1952, Tyrone Hospital was just a dream. Waring brought his orchestra home and gave the Concert beneath the Stars at Grey Memorial Field to benefit the hospital.

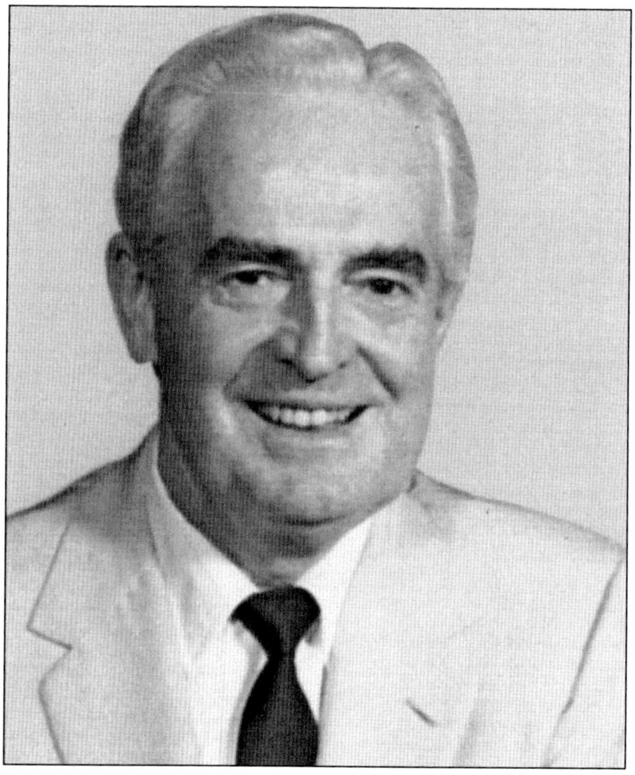

Fred Waring initiated a radio career in 1933 along with his wedding to Evelyn Nair. The couple settled at Shawnee-on-the-Delaware in the Pocono Mountains. His brother Thomas was the family pianist and composer. Fred Waring is world famous for his musical genius, glee clubs, and orchestra. However, he also invented a blender that became popular following World War II. A Waring blender made its way into nearly every kitchen in the country because it saved time and energy.

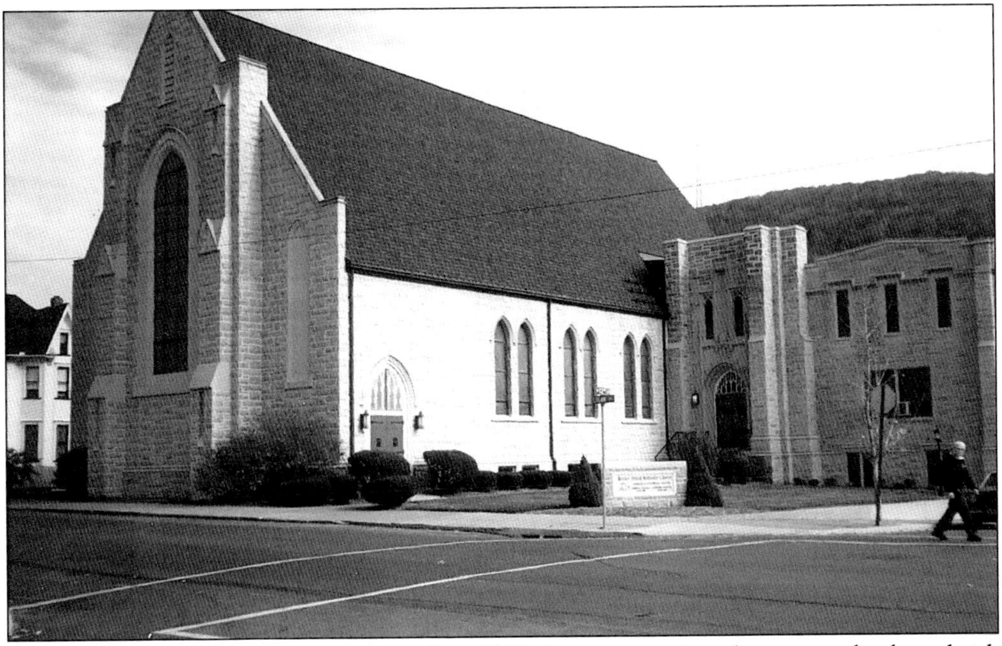

The Methodist congregation was formed in 1852. It met in private homes until a large brick building on the corner of Logan Avenue and Twelfth Street was procured. The congregation grew rapidly, and additions were made to the church building. In 1963, a new church was constructed to serve the growing congregation. In 1948, the nationally known Pennsylvanians sang at a church funeral for Fred Waring's mother, who had been an active member of the church choir for many years.

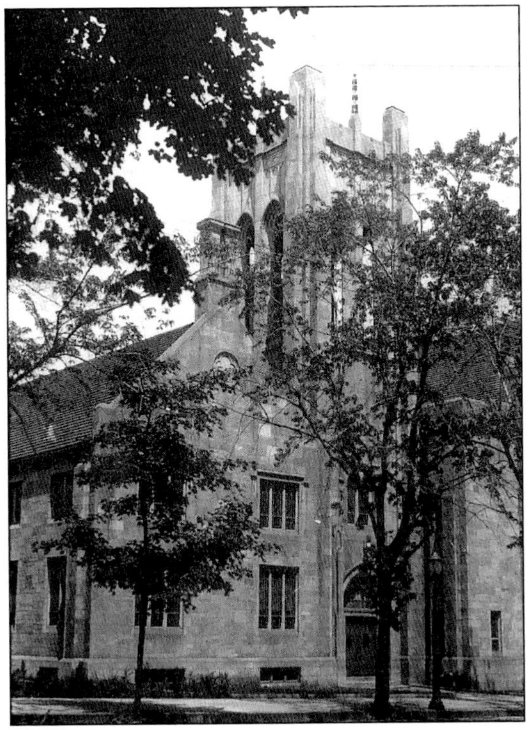

The Presbyterian congregation was formed in 1857, and its first church was the old United Brethren building. Services were previously held in an old schoolhouse on Spring Street. In 1867, the parish received its first resident pastor. Parishioners took turns as sexton. The present edifice on Logan Avenue and Thirteenth Street was built in 1882 and enlarged in 1891. In later years, during a renovation, carillon chimes were installed.

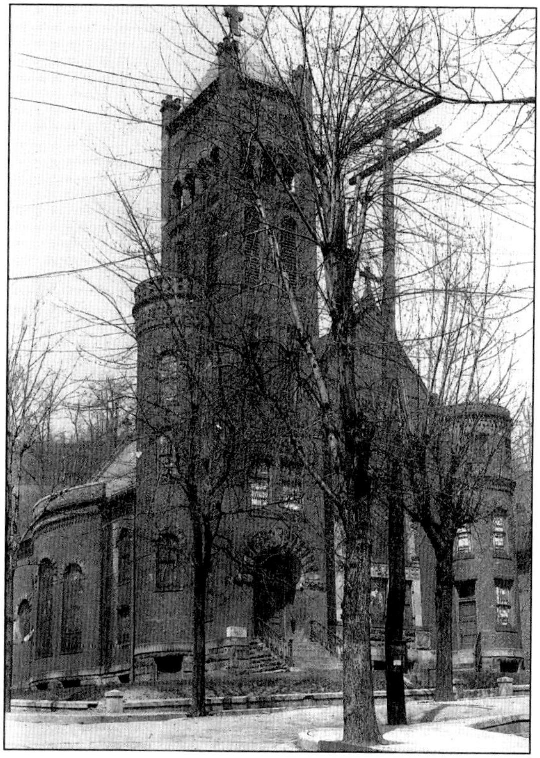

St. Matthew's Roman Catholic parish was established in 1851. Mass was celebrated in private homes, and plans were drawn up for a church building. Land was purchased along Cameron Street, and a small church was constructed. The parish grew rapidly and, in 1896, a larger church was dedicated. The architecture is a unique combination of Norman and Romanesque style, with a 25-foot tower. Farmers hauled in local stones that are visible in the base of the church today.

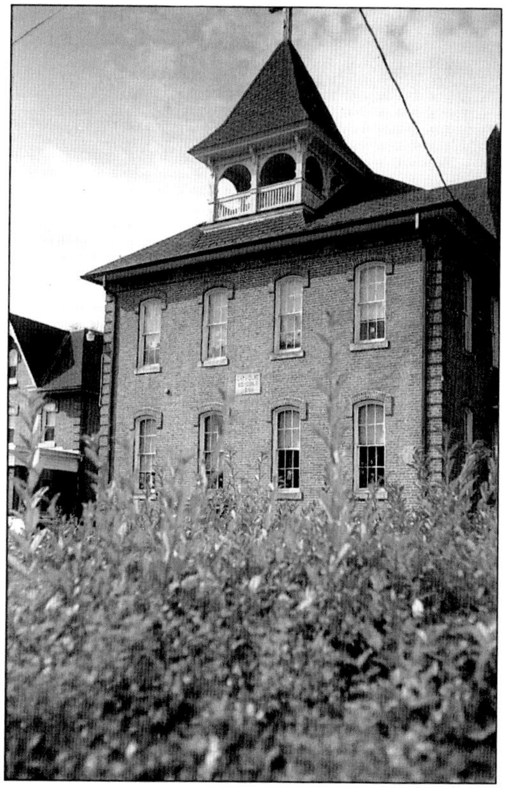

St. Matthew's School was a historical mission for the Sisters of Mercy. Rev. John C. Farran had begun construction on a school and invited the Sisters of Mercy to staff it. They arrived on April 16, 1885. It was their first mission from the newly established mother house in Loretto. Sr. Justina Daly was first principal, and 112 students were registered. The first convent was a converted house with adequate room for living quarters and classrooms.

Four

BIG ROCK MOUNTAIN

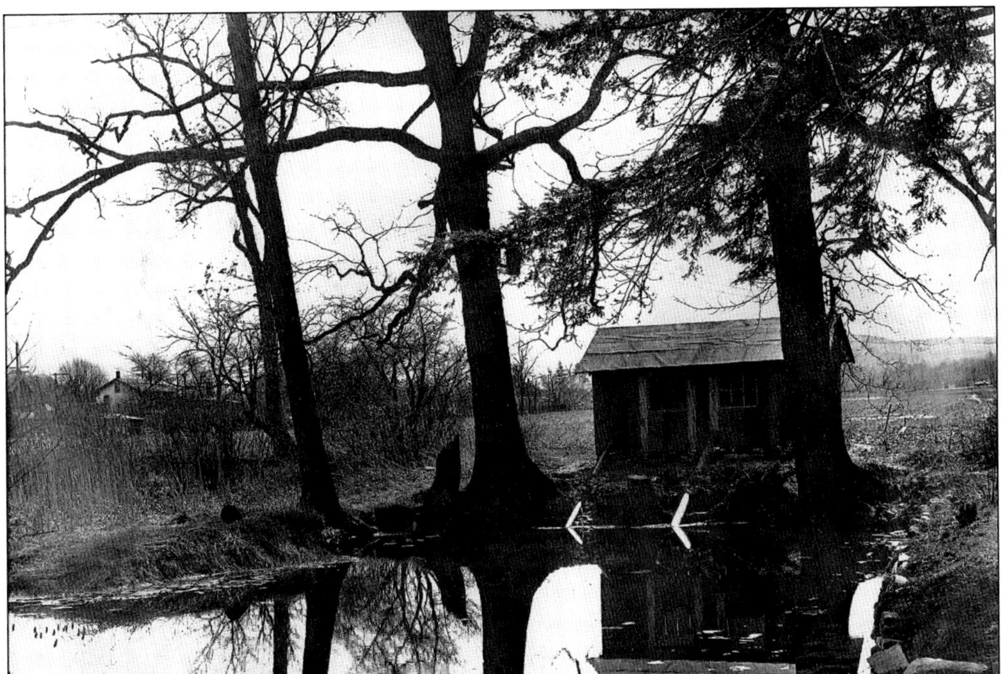

Logan Spring, located near Bellwood, was named for Chief John Logan. He was a prominent Native American Cayuga whose cheerful association and friendship with the whites earned him their esteem. He was educated by Moravian missionaries. In 1738, Logan married into the Shawnee tribe. The couple had six children. A plague took his wife and five of his six children. The remaining son was called Little Logan and lived to be 100 years old.

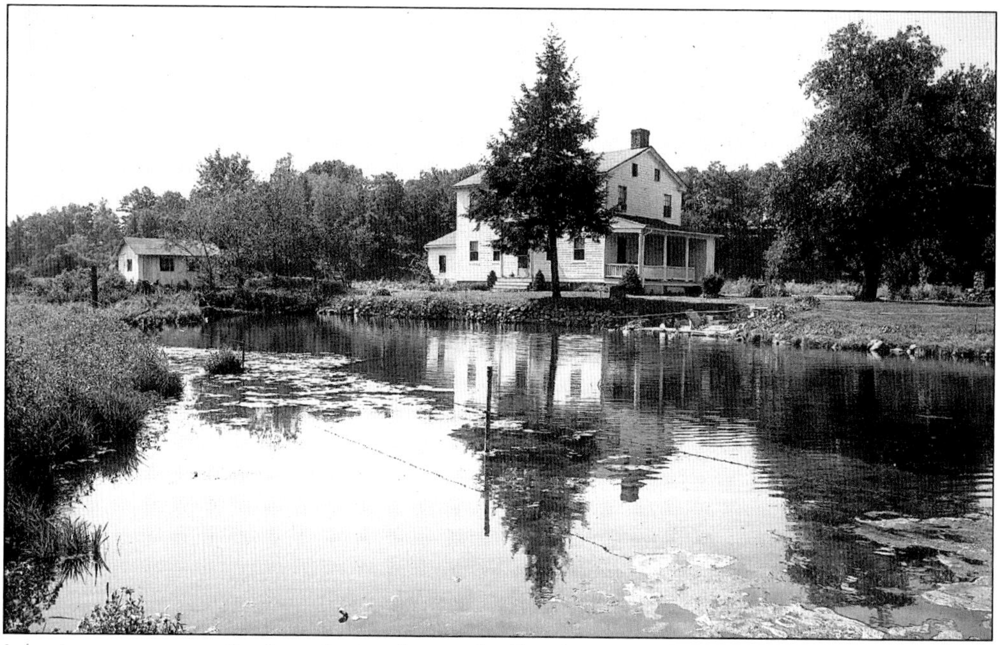

John Logan was a spy for the colonists during the Revolutionary War. Later, he lived at Tuckahoe near the Bell family. The renowned chieftain in the wilds of the Pennsylvania Mountains was held in deference by the whites when the largest and most prestigious establishment was named for him, Altoona's Logan House. In 1918, a historical marker was placed at the Big Spring in Bellwood in his memory by the Blair County Historical Society.

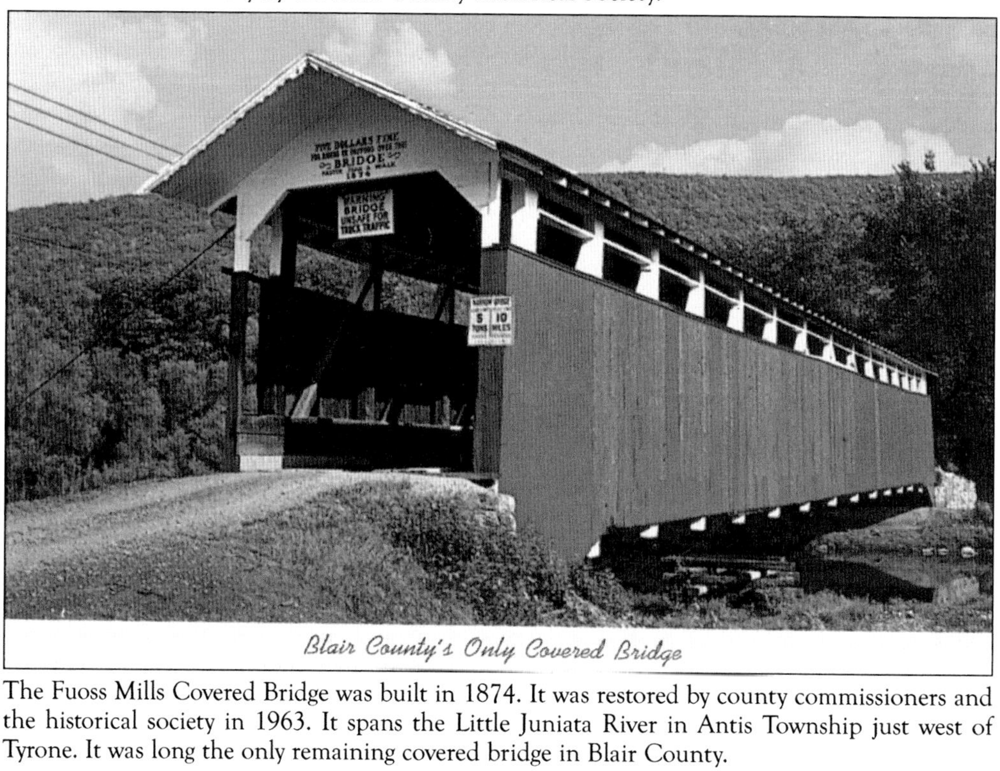

Blair County's Only Covered Bridge

The Fuoss Mills Covered Bridge was built in 1874. It was restored by county commissioners and the historical society in 1963. It spans the Little Juniata River in Antis Township just west of Tyrone. It was long the only remaining covered bridge in Blair County.

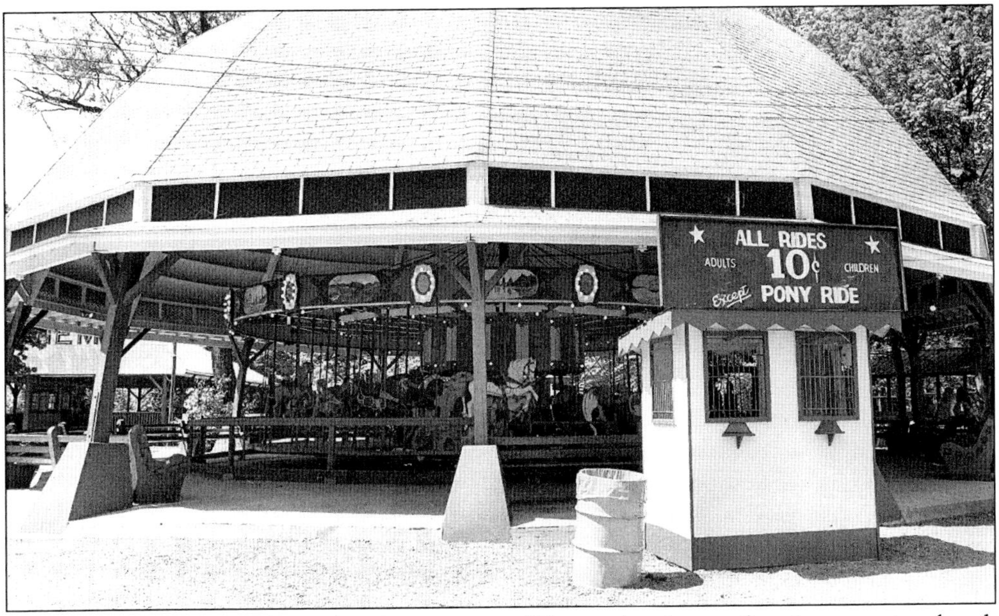

Bland Amusement Park, located in Tipton west of Tyrone, has been a favorite recreational park for generations. Many Tyroners met their mates at the skating rink, courted, married, and brought their children to enjoy the amusements. Established by the Bland family, it was sold to George Rinhard, who installed the merry-go-round. In 1946, Fred DelGrosso purchased the park. It is a modern family fun facility featuring an extensive water park, go-carts, miniature golf course, and more than 30 rides. DelGrosso also owns a packing company and a restaurant.

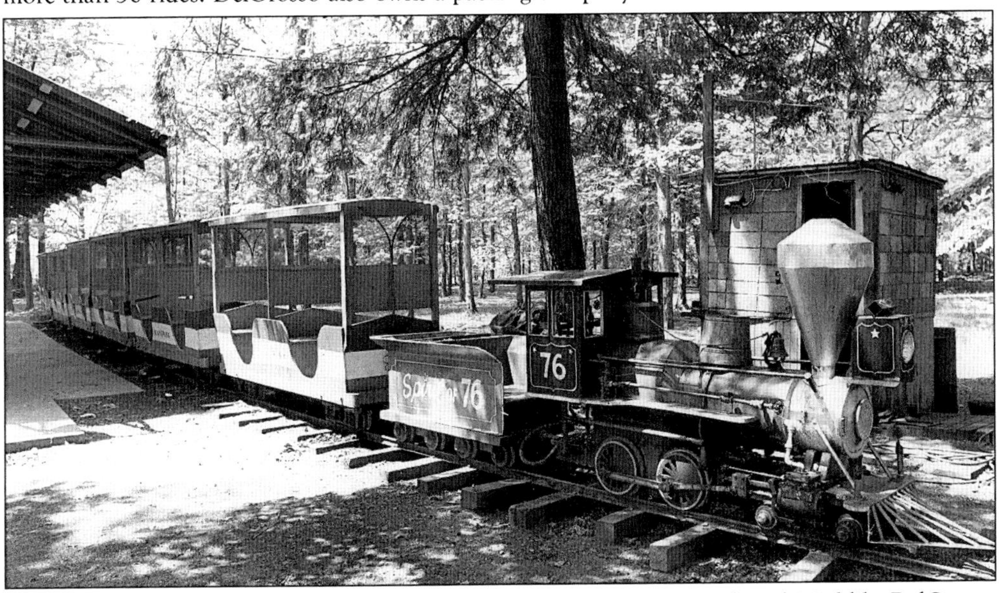

The train ride is one of many amusements in DelGrosso Park. Fred and Mafalda DelGrosso opened a small restaurant in Altoona in 1943. The homemade sauce they prepared for their pasta set the cafe apart from others. It was an original recipe brought from Italy. In 1946, DelGrosso sold the cafe and bought the Bland Amusement Park. There, he could experiment with the famous recipe in his restaurant. He used only the finest products. A small business took root, and DelGrosso Spaghetti Sauce branched into the commercial world.

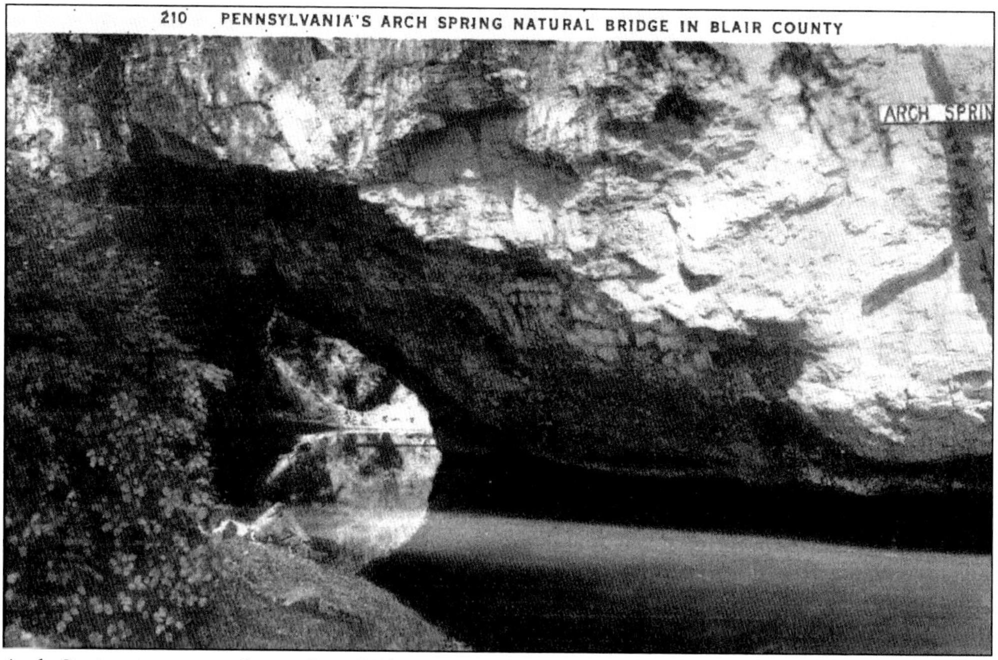

Arch Spring is a natural wonder of Blair County. Situated in Sinking Valley, it is a cave with a 15-foot opening in the middle of the valley. In springtime, a rapid stream of clear water fills the cave. In dry seasons, the cave can be explored 800 feet inside. The stream disappears into the cave and rises a mile east at Arch Spring. A perfect arch of rocks hangs over the entrance and is surrounded by stately pines.

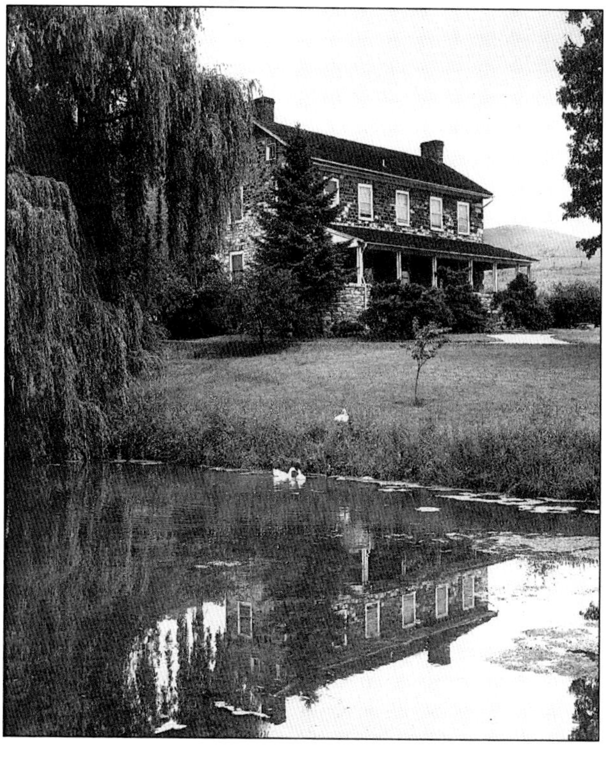

The original Lowry Homestead is located at the rear of Arch Spring in Sinking Valley. James Lowry was among the first settlers to acquire land from the Penn heirs. In 1755, he purchased from Frank Stephens about 300 acres on the spring branch of the old Native American trail called Frankstown. His house was built in 1778 and served as a fort or place of refuge during the Revolutionary War. Musket holes have been found in the building.

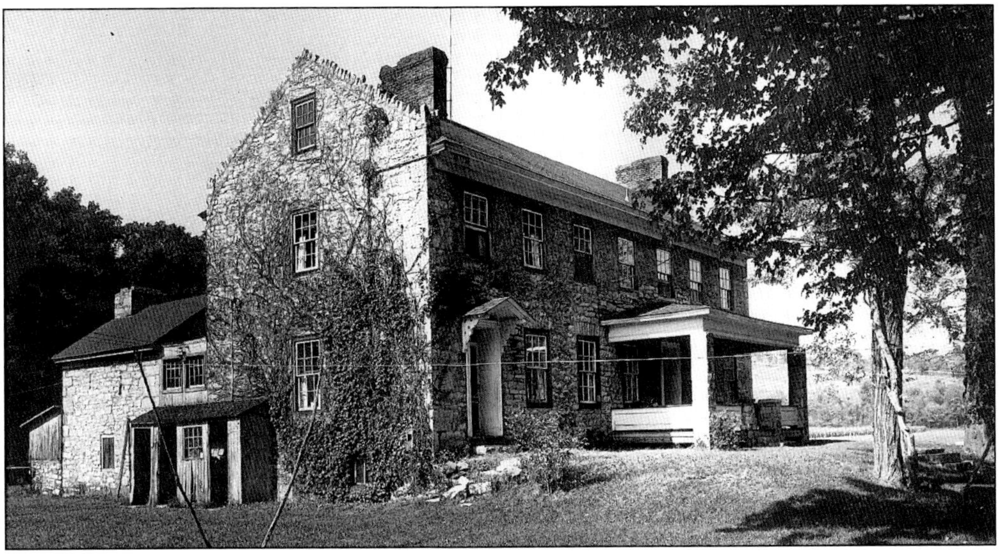

The Jacob Isett homestead stood in Sinking Valley. Isett built a gristmill just below Arch Spring in 1788. He was among the earliest settlers in the valley. Farming was the chief source of income until gristmills, tanning businesses, blacksmith shops, tin shops, and stores began to dot the valley.

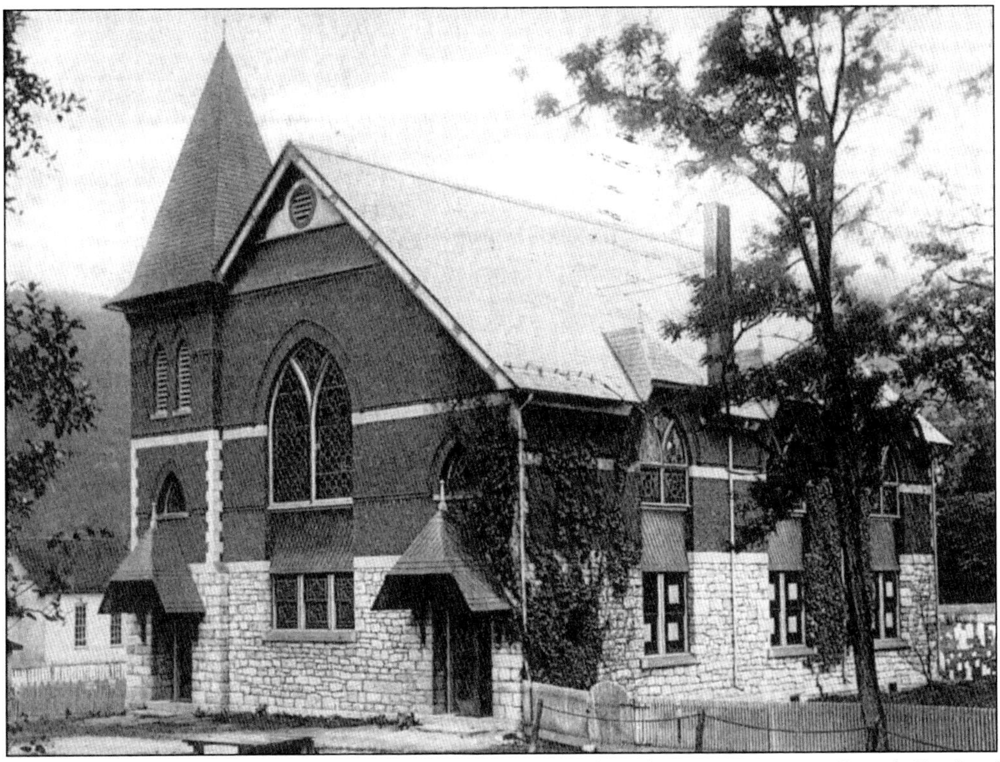

The Presbyterian parish of Sinking Valley was established in 1790. Rev. David Bard of Hollidaysburg, the supply pastor to the vicinity, was the first pastor conducting services in the area. Many members of the congregation were Scotch-Irish. Presbyterianism and Lutherism were the principal denominations in very early Blair County.

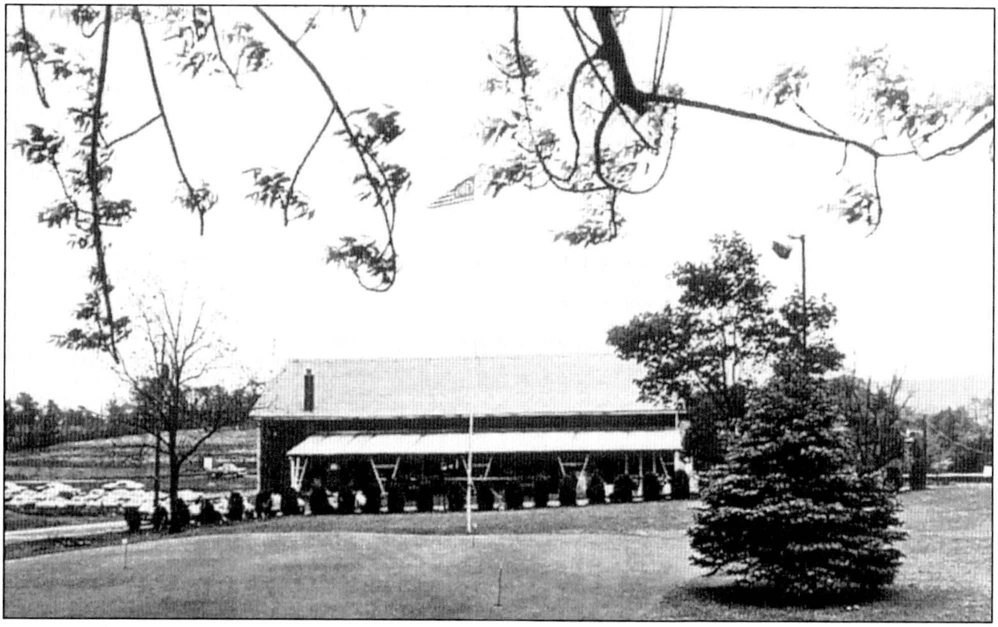

In 1961, the Jaycees of Tyrone conceived the idea of establishing a country club. A picturesque site was chosen, and a 216-acre farm in Sinking Valley was purchased in 1963. The farm contained a barn that had been constructed 150 years earlier. This was remodeled into the clubhouse and pro shop while retaining a rustic look with its hand-hewn beams. The lane was paved and the pond converted into a beautiful lake. The first nine holes were laid out in March 1962. Much of the work was done by volunteers and Boy Scouts.

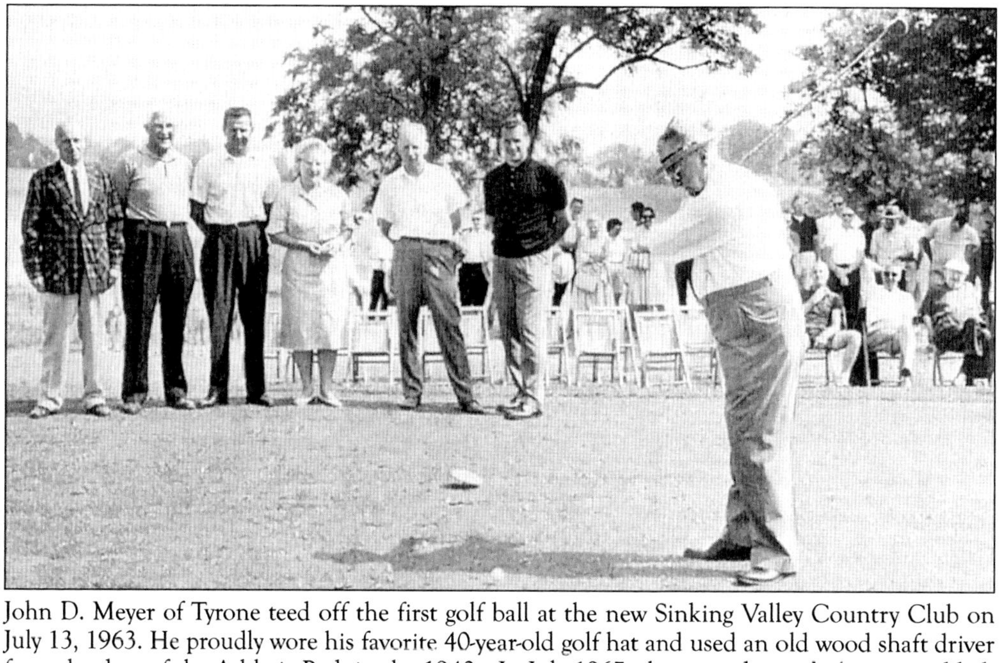

John D. Meyer of Tyrone teed off the first golf ball at the new Sinking Valley Country Club on July 13, 1963. He proudly wore his favorite 40-year-old golf hat and used an old wood shaft driver from the days of the Athletic Park in the 1940s. In July 1967, the second nine holes were added, making it a genuine championship course. In 1974, a tennis court and driving range were added through the generosity of Edward Sickler.

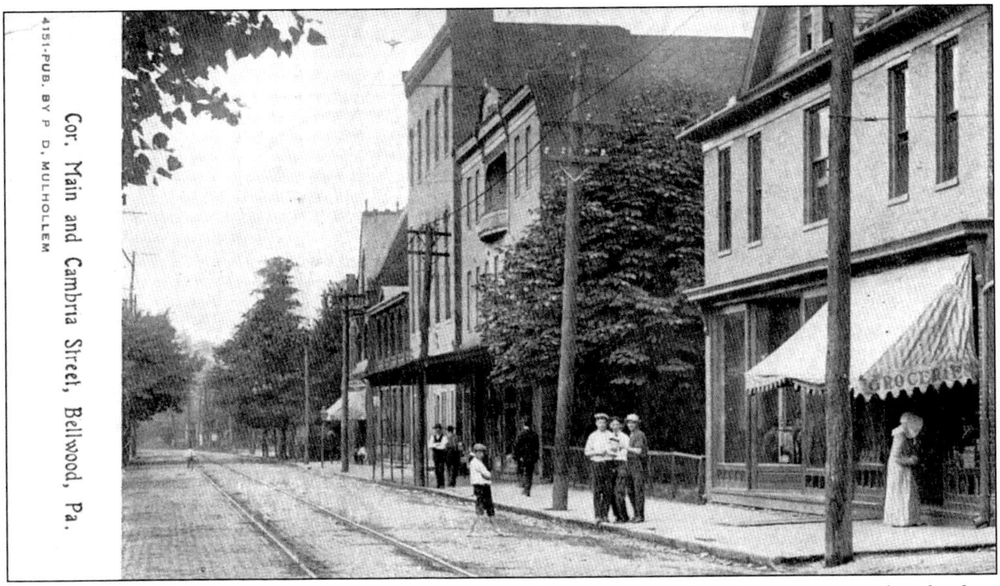

In 1914, Bellwood was a land of opportunity. Bells Mills, its original name, was ahead of its counterparts. The corner of Main and Cambria Streets featured a grocery store (right foreground). An opera house and clothing stores dotted the landscape. Bellwood was incorporated in 1887. The main roots of economic life had been iron, lumber, coal, mill, and grain products. Streetlights illuminated the roadways in 1892 and, a year later, the first telephone was installed. The year 1894 brought the first trolley.

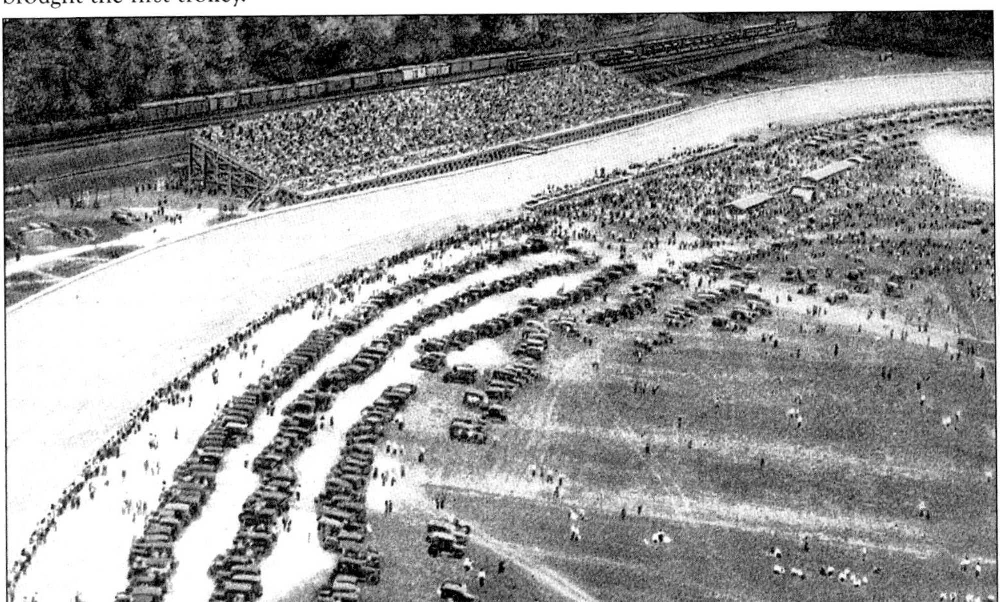

A speedway opened in Tipton and brought great prominence to the area. The wooden track, 60 feet wide and 1.5 miles long, featured its first race on Labor Day, September 3, 1923. Car races were held each Flag Day and Labor Day. Racing fans left home at daybreak lest a flat tire or overheated engine delay them. Others used the train or trolley. Ladies and gentlemen arrived in their finery. Hotels were filled, and many a Tyrone housewife rented a spare room to the stranded visitor. The track closed in 1929.

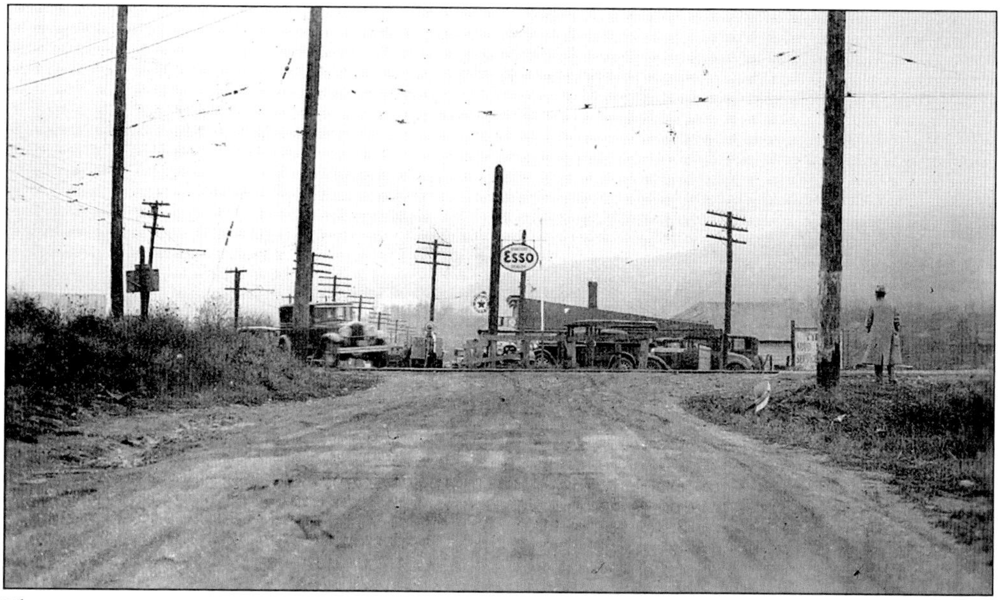

This is an intersection in Grazierville in 1935. Note the vintage Ford car and the Esso sign. A gentleman seems to be awaiting a ride. The view is from the railroad tracks, facing east along the turnpike. It is the north approach to the overhead bridge. Cold Spring Forge was located in Grazierville. It was built 1835 by John Kratzer and produced 175 tons of iron with 25 men daily.

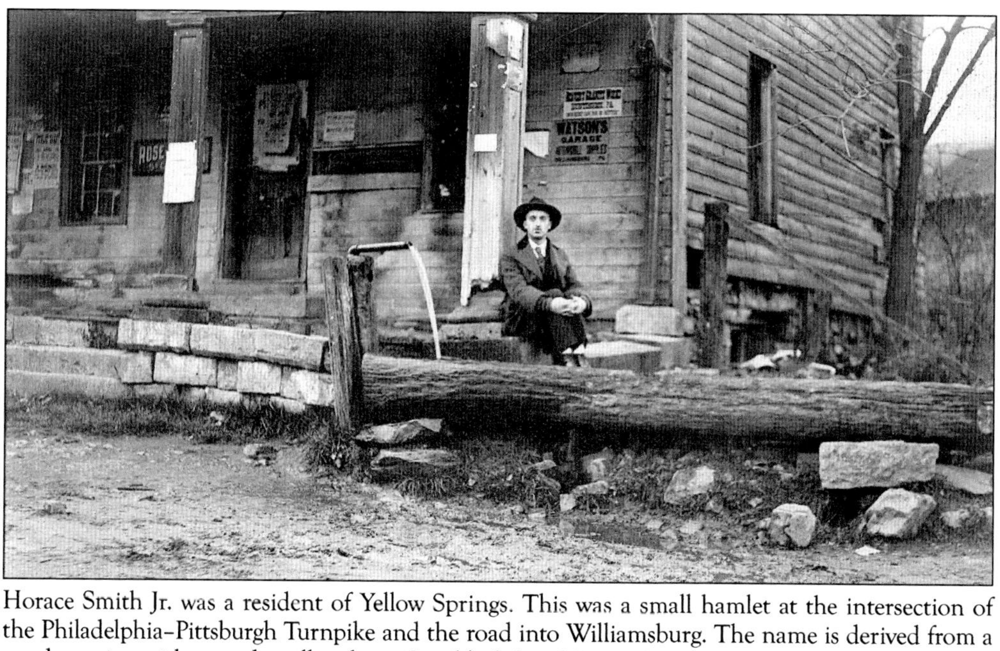

Horace Smith Jr. was a resident of Yellow Springs. This was a small hamlet at the intersection of the Philadelphia–Pittsburgh Turnpike and the road into Williamsburg. The name is derived from a nearby spring with a sandy, yellow base. Smith's father, Horace Smith Sr., wrote the first paper on x-ray machines in 1904. He lost his life as a result of experimentation with x-ray equipment.

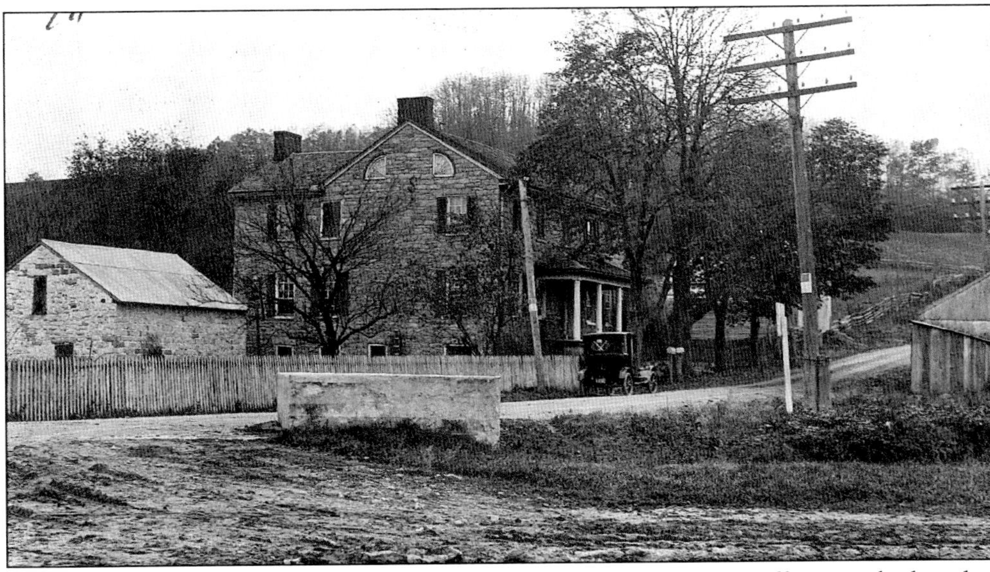

The home of Irvan Isenberg was located in Yellow Springs. He was an officer on the board of trustees of Mercy Hospital after 1935, when the Sisters of Nazareth came to staff the institution. Irvan was the secretary and treasurer of the board. Note the car of a bygone period parked in front of his house.

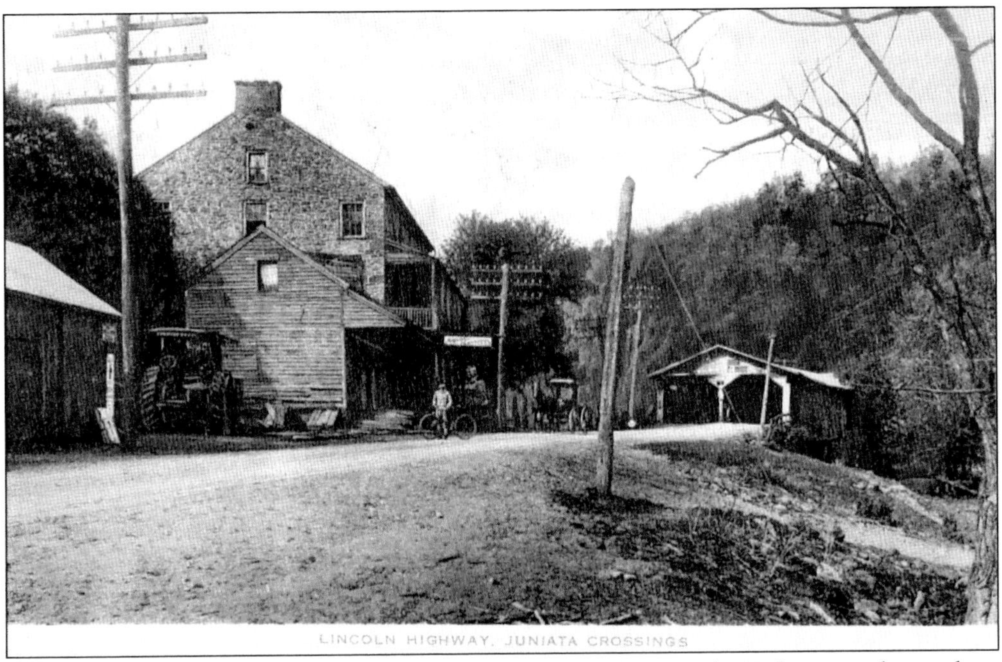

The Juniata Crossing Hotel was established in 1818 along the Lincoln Highway on the outskirts of Blair County. The bridge was one of many that crossed the Juniata River. Formed during the prehistoric era, the multiple springs in the ridges of the mountains united to form the Juniata River. It shaped the terrain of the region and features in much of its history. Claysburg is located where Poplar Run and Beaver Dam Creek unite to form the north branch of the Juniata River.

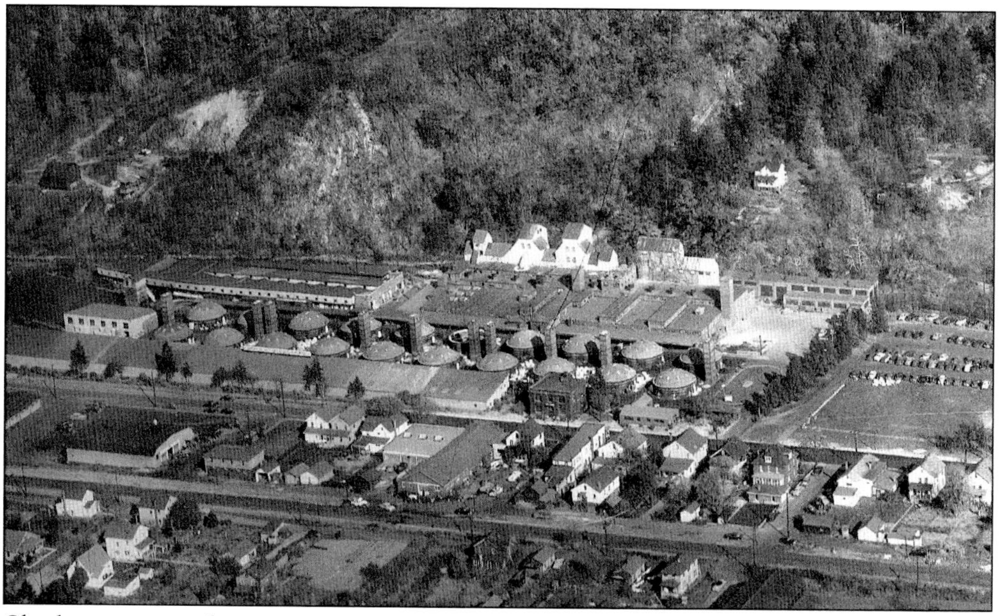

Claysburg owes its fame to ganister, a quartz rock composed almost entirely of silica. A tram road, called a dinky track, is visible along the right side of the mountain. The raw material had to be blasted. Anthony Berrich was among the chief blasters. It was brought down from the Dunning Mountain to the refractory plant on a tram. Employees lived in row houses in the right foreground. The clay works were built in 1913 by the Standard Refractories Company. In 1922, they were acquired by General Refractories.

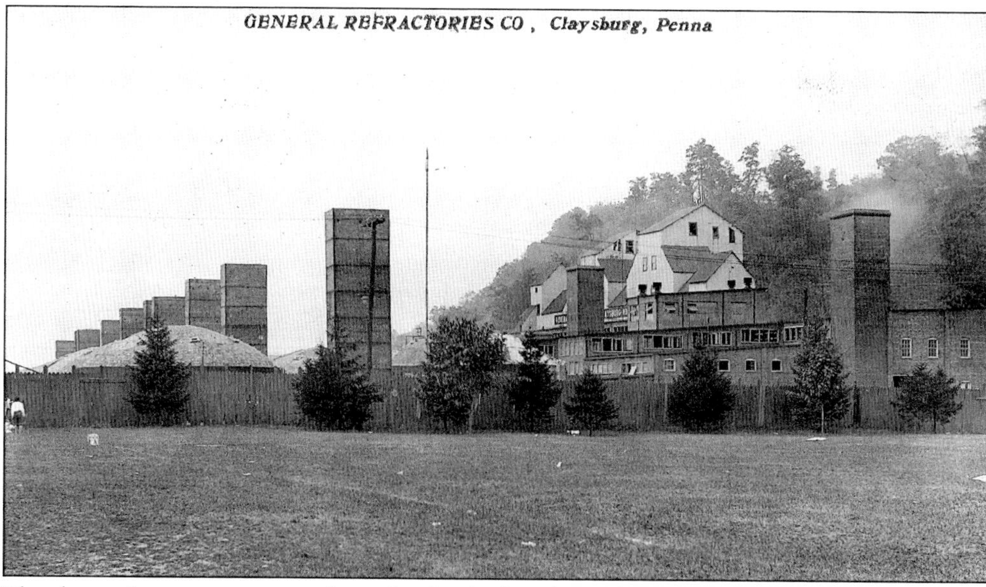

The clay works were an outstanding silica brick plant located at the foot of Dunnings Mountain. The plant was capable of producing 100,000 handmade bricks per day. Twenty 35-foot periodic downdraft kilns made up part of the facility. These are identified by the domes. The Eastern Silica District Laboratory, located here, handled all analytical work for the various plants. Refractory brick is used as lining for furnaces and makes possible the manufacture of steel, coke copper, and glass.

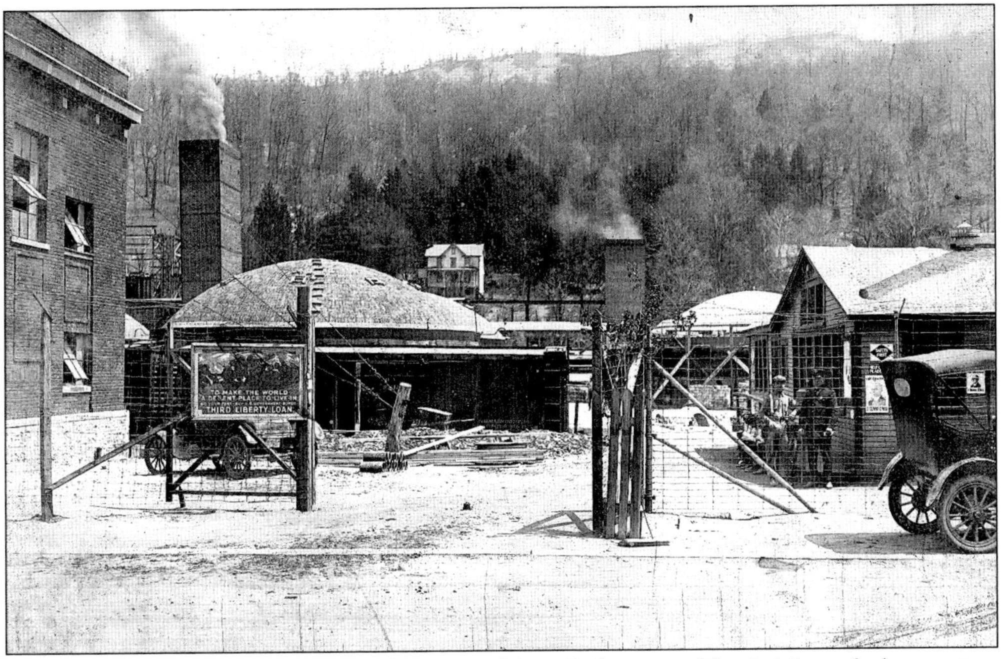

A large machine shop manufactured parts and handled repairs. The brick made here enjoys worldwide distribution. The pioneer in the developing of domestic granite as a refractory product was Jesse L. Hartman of Blair County. He discovered that stratified layers of rock contained valuable silica. The mountains of Blair County contain a substantial portion of this precious material. The plant closed in 1987. McCabe Transport now occupies the site.

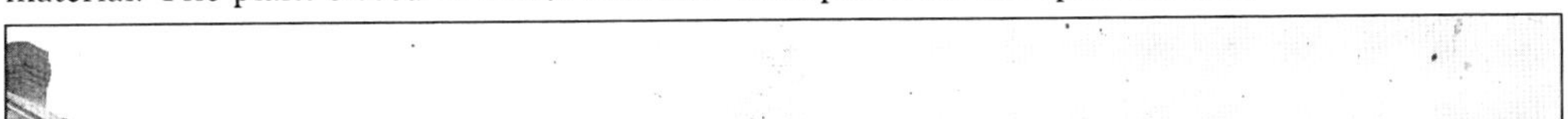

Row houses went up rapidly when the clay works came into town. The many employees availed themselves the opportunity to live close to their employment. Row houses were closely connected and were usually built by the company. Unlike many residents of company towns, employees and row house dwellers were not always required to purchase food and medicine from the company store.

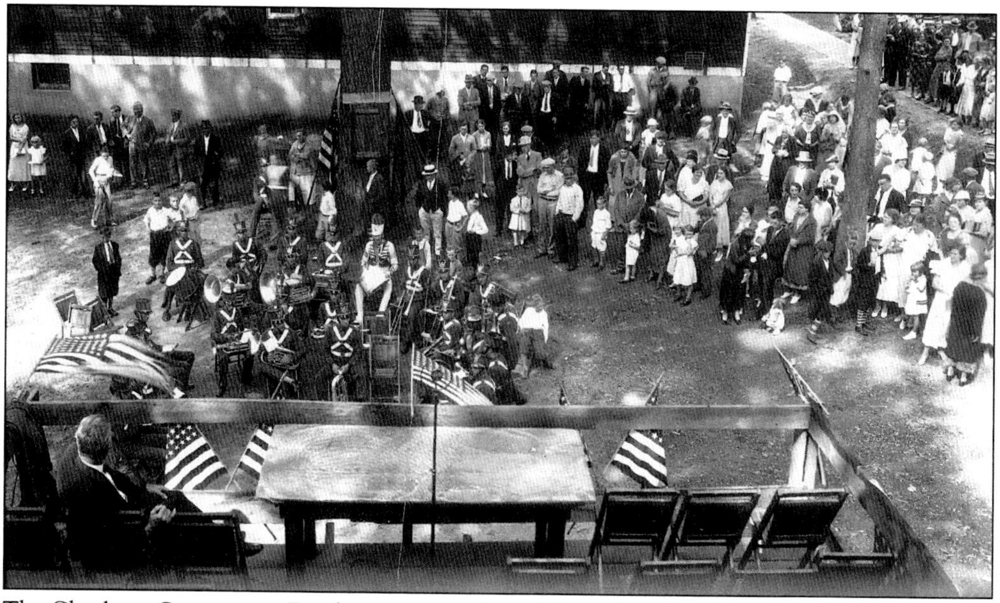

The Claysburg Community Band was organized in 1879 and retained its status until 1934, when the American Legion post became its sponsor. The band won the state championship in 1936 and again in 1953. Majorettes were added in 1941. The band appeared in many functions throughout Blair County and did many performances at the state legion convention.

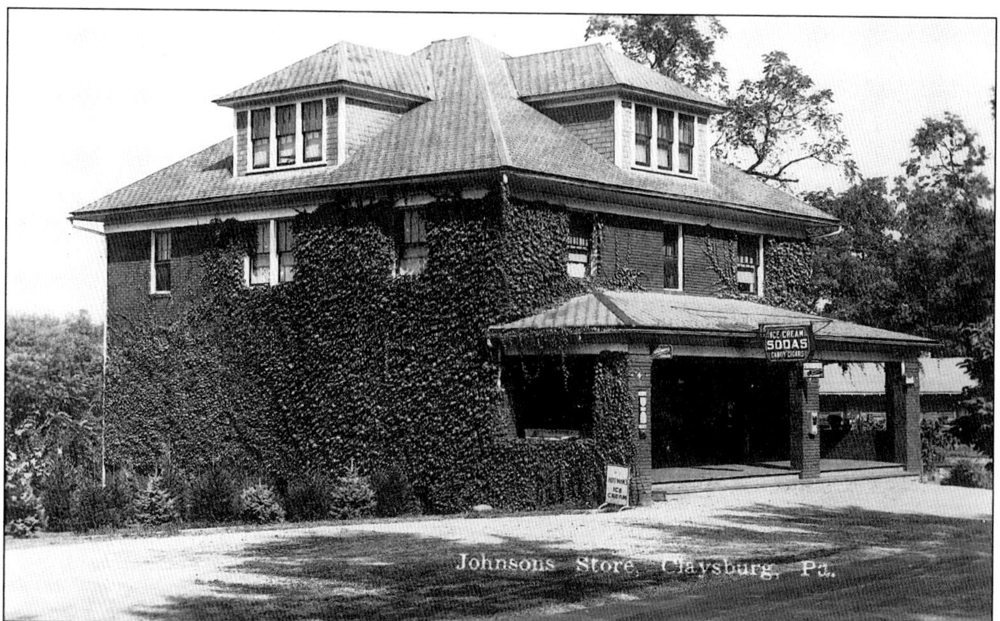

This ivy-covered building was Johnston Pharmacy. Ice-cream sodas, candy, and cigars were sold here early in the 20th century. It was bought by Zerelda Long in 1947. A complete renovation was done with new fixtures, fountain, and lunch service. Departments were added, specializing in such things as jewelry, flowers, and gift items. In 1953, a millenary department was added. The building later became Dick's Pharmacy and now houses the Cat's Meow.

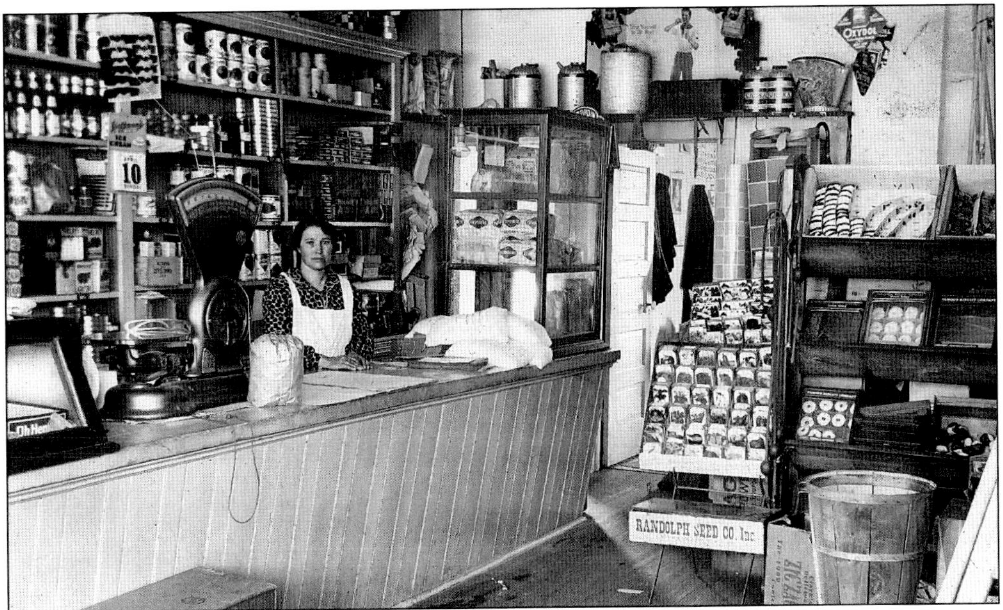

Joseph and Maria Gazzara were Italian immigrants in 1913. When the clay works were established, they relocated to Claysburg. Maria opened a grocery store on Bedford Street beside what is now the library. Note the cookie bins (right), Randolph's seeds, and the tall vegetable basket. Oxydol is advertised on the wall. Girls sat under the counter so as not to be seen by men. In 1926, the Gazzaras established a dance hall in Claysburg.

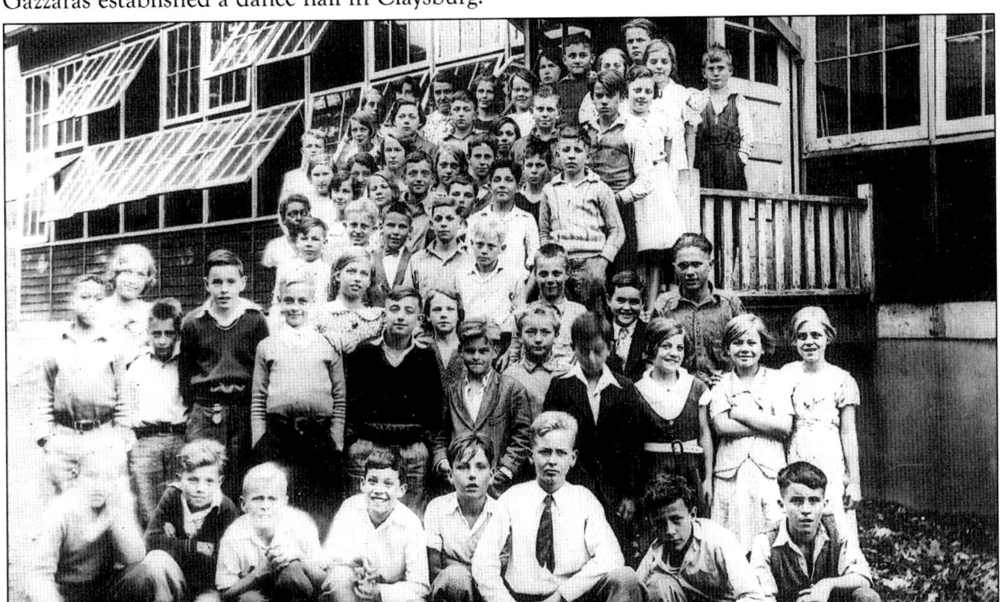

This is a chicken coop school. These were built in the 1920s to alleviate crowded conditions. Two portable buildings, near the brickyards, were so dubbed because of their construction. Among the identified are Bill and Arthur Dively; Earl, Reuben, and Bob Black; John, Ken, and Dorothy Burkett; Gary, Ray, and Ross McDonald; Fred Eicher; Bill Musselman; Charles Beegle; Cleve Winters; Ken Zeigler; Bob Brumbaugh; Regis Nale; Bruce Weyandt; Dean Lewis; Oliver Stein; James Scritchfield; Bill Water; and Morris McCollough.

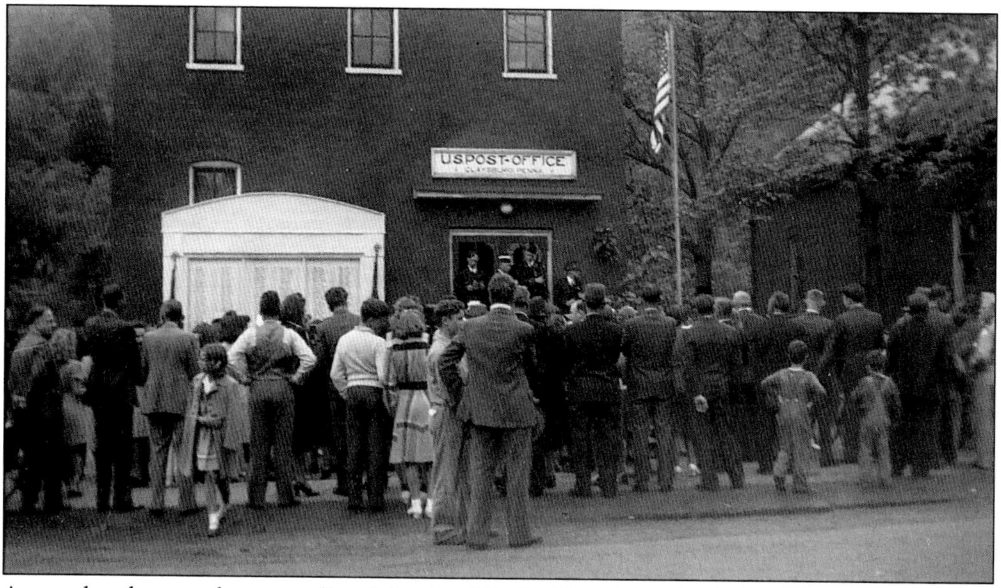

A crowd gathers at the post office following World War II for the dedication of a monument honoring local servicemen. Claysburg lost two native sons. The American Legion post was named in honor of John Earnest of World War I and Morgan Dively of World War II, both of whom gave their lives for their country. It is called the Earnest-Dively Post. Following World War II, it was a common practice to erect such memorials that would later become more permanent.

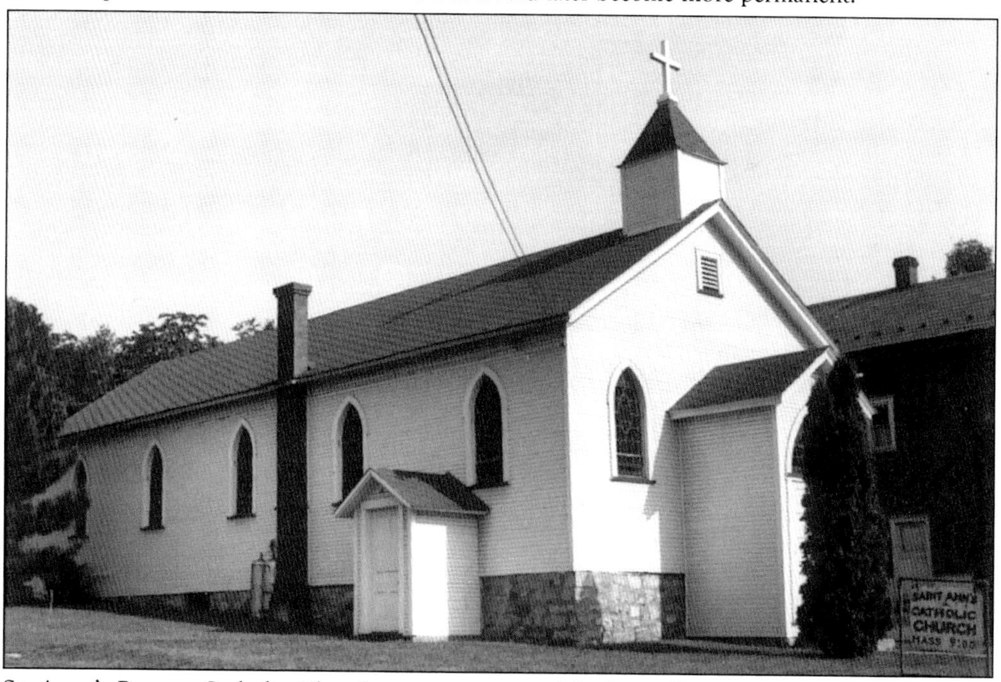

St. Anne's Roman Catholic Church was a mission of St. Patrick's in Newry. Distance posed a hardship for the early settlers. In 1913, land was purchased for the mission. It became a reality in 1914, when the church was dedicated by Bishop Eugene Garvey. The statues were hauled from the railroad station by horse and wagon. Ralph Hite of Newry drove the bishop to the dedication in his father's new Buick. The Diehl's of Puzzletown arrived by horse and buggy.

Five

Vibrant Mountain Streams

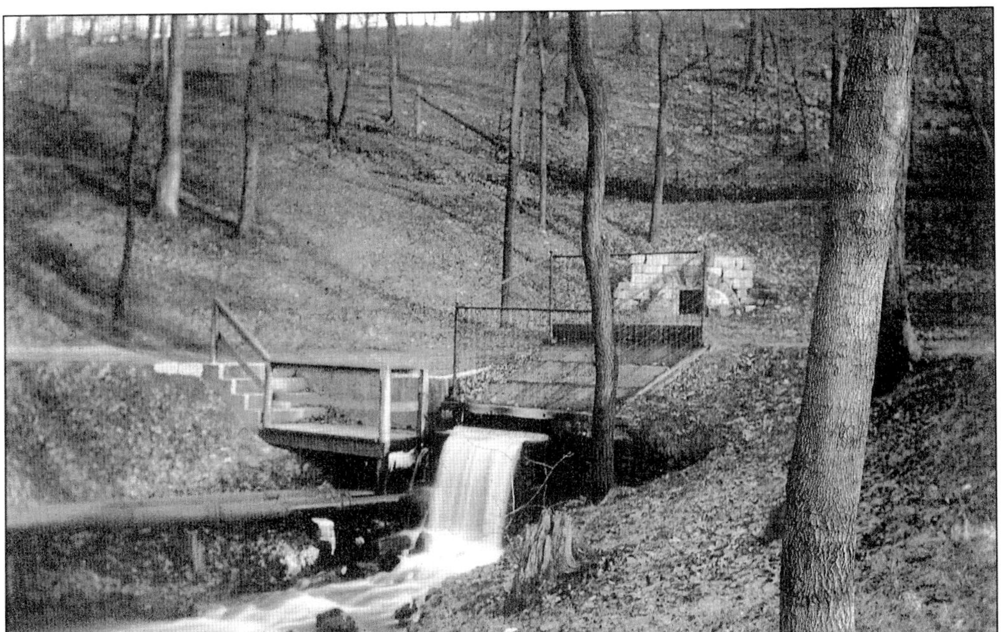

Roaring Spring derived its name from its most prominent natural resource, the Great Spring. The rapid cascade of falling water created a roaring noise. Early settlers controlled this sound by removing several huge stones from beneath the torrential water. The roaring ceased, but the name remained. The natural spring provided power facilities unparalleled in the area. The first white inhabitants in the cove found arrowheads and Native American mounds near the spring. The famous Blank Book Building is in the background.

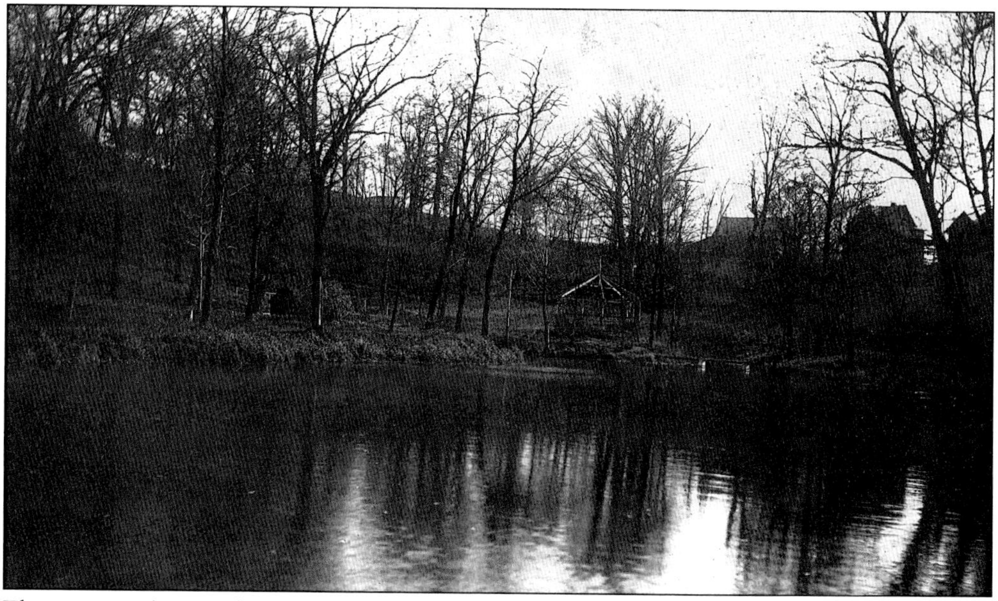

The spring is charmingly situated near the head of Morrison's Cove. The flow of 252,000 gallons of fresh, clear water per day supports the needs of the community with its varied businesses and industries. Authorities wanted to name Roaring Spring (once called Sprangs Mills) Baretown, but Daniel Bare declined the honor. When he became postmaster, the original name was reinstated. In 1854, Daniel Bare established a general store and post office.

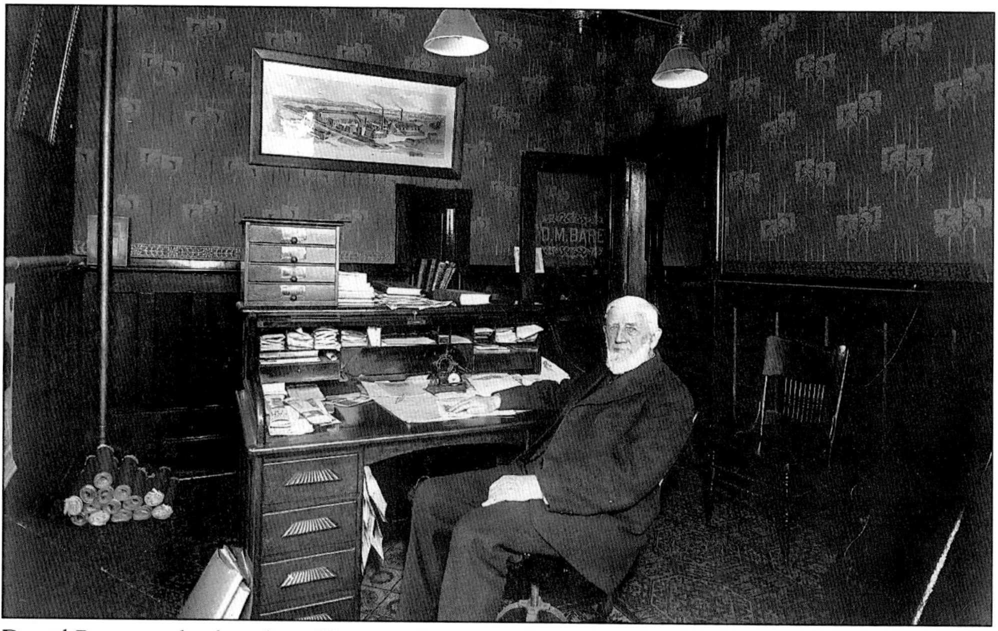

Daniel Bare was the founder of Roaring Spring. Born in 1834 in Sinking Valley, he grew up and devoted his life to family, church, business, and the community of Roaring Spring. Bare was instrumental in establishing the paper industry, the railroad, the blank book business, and the general store. In 1863, he bought 90 acres around the spring and began immediately to improve the industrial life of the hamlet. His many enterprises prospered. He addressed the religious, educational, and cultural needs of the townspeople.

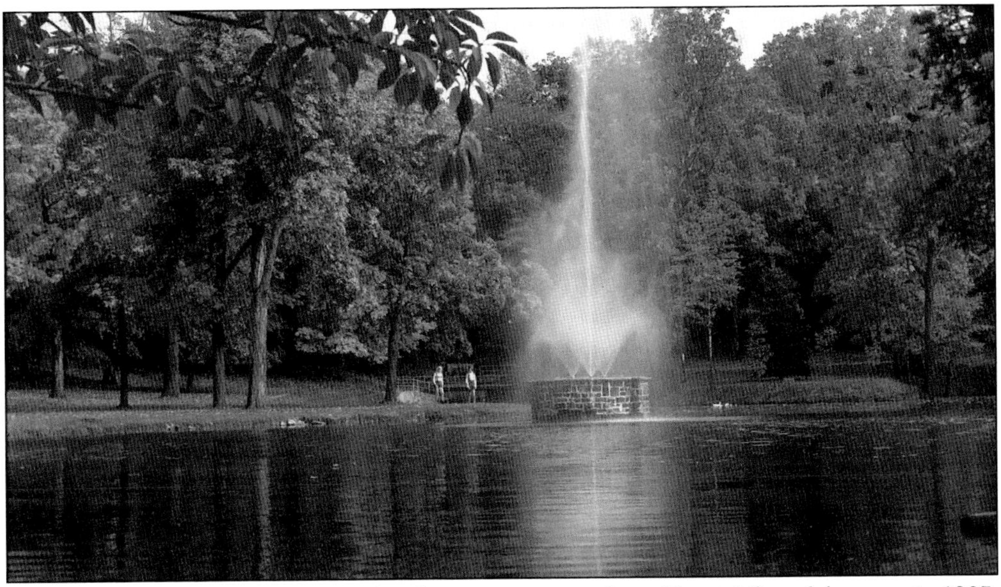

The Bare Memorial Fountain was placed in operation on the golden jubilee of the town in 1937. There were natural challenges encountered as the architects and engineers had to combat the water of the Big Pool in order to place the stone foundation for the fountain. Indiana limestone on the north side is engraved with the inscription "Erected 1837 in memory of D.M. Bare." It has long been in operation and is turned on for special occasions and during the Christmas season.

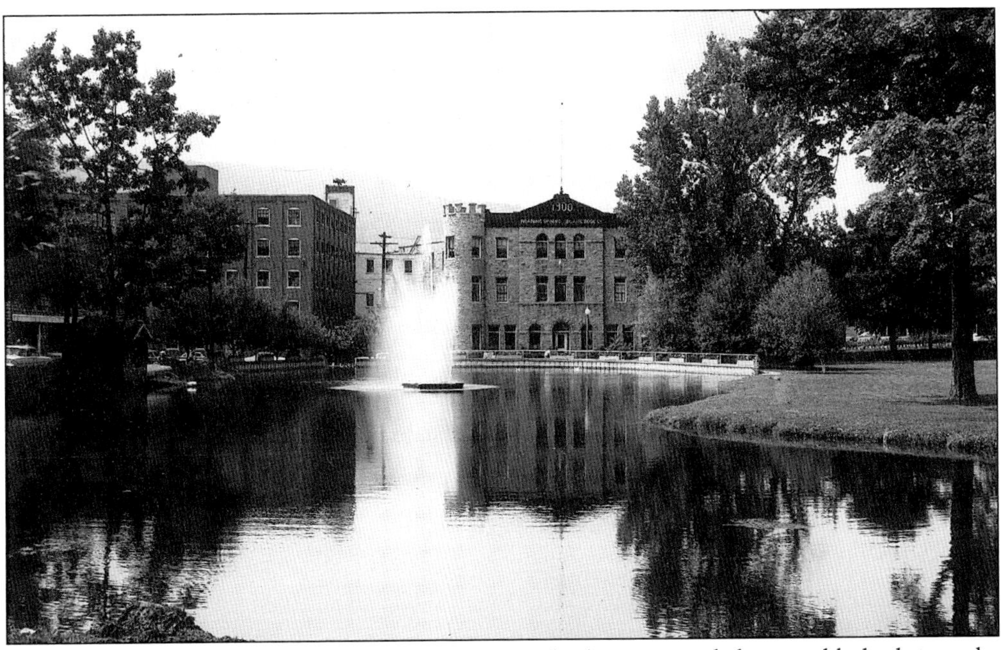

The fountain sends cascades of water soaring into the heavens, and they tumble back into the pool. The architect of the fountain was General Electric Supply of Pittsburgh. Three primary colors were used in the intricate lighting arrangement. They produce magnificent shades and hues of remarkable beauty. The fountain was dedicated to Daniel Bare, founder of the town and its industries. The Blank Book Building is in the background.

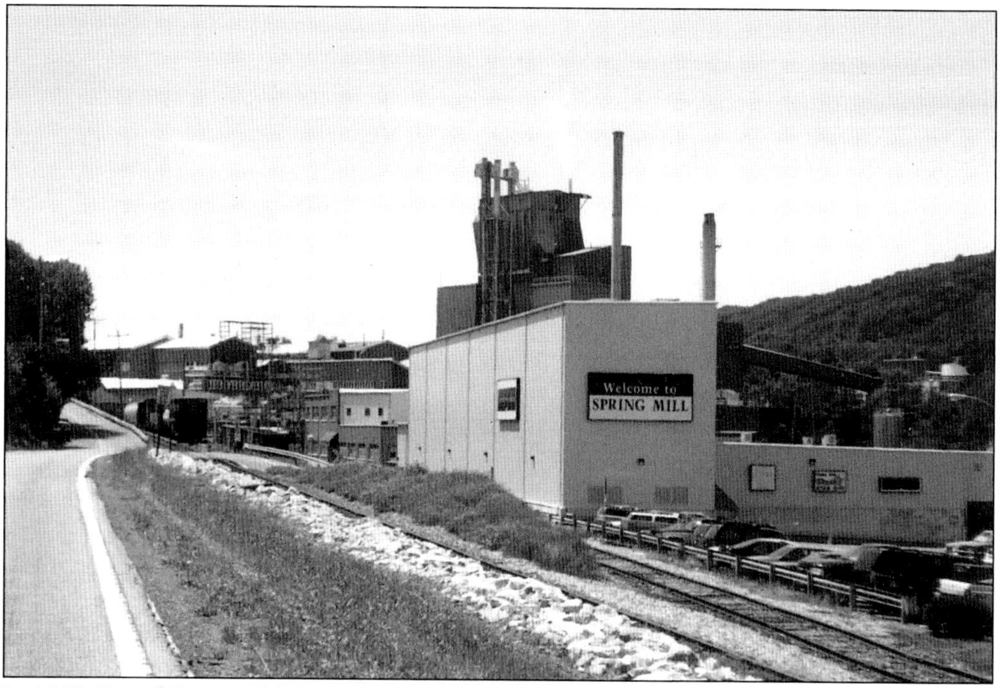

In 1865, Daniel Bare established a paper mill on the banks of the Juniata River. Early industrial life centered around the paper mill and the waterfall. The Bare family was a leader in the paper industry. The cove was blessed with rolling forests, an ample supply of coal, and sufficient water. The original paper was a manila sheet made of straw and gummy bagging. In 1870, rags replaced the bagging and, in 1875, the first wood pulp mill was built. It produced wood pulp from linden and poplar trees.

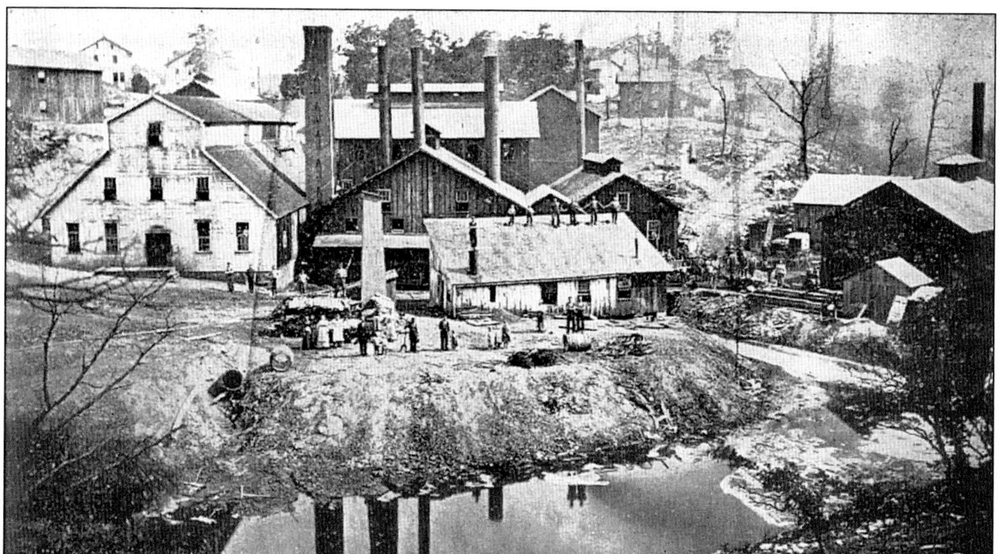

The paper mill underwent many changes and expansions over the 13 decades of its existence. Today, it is known as the Appleton Paper Company and dominates the landscape in the village. In 1972, the mill production was changed to concentrating on carbonless paper. This is paper that transmits an image from mechanical pressure without using carbon paper.

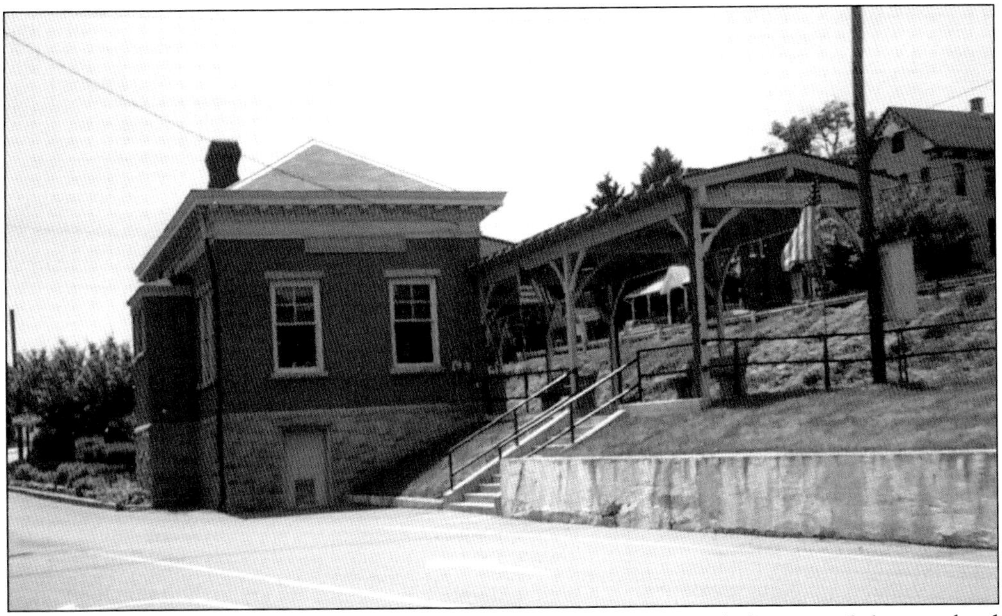

The railroad was extended into Morrison's Cove in 1871. Bare and the town fathers realized a need for more efficient shipping facilities for their products. They needed to connect with Altoona, 17 miles to the north. Bare was instrumental in bringing a branch of the Pennsylvania Railroad into Roaring Spring. The railroad brought a new era of prosperity to the already bustling town.

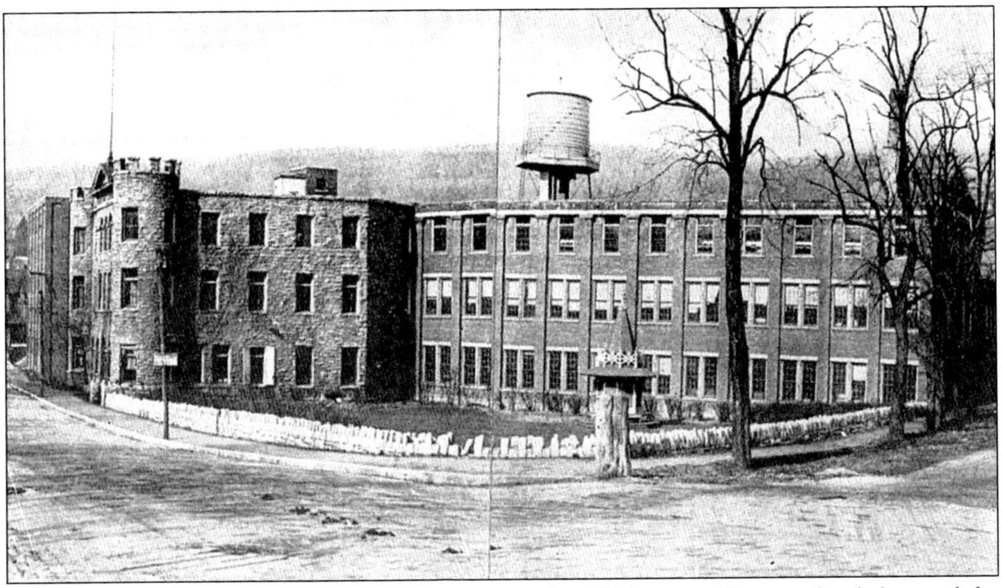

The Blank Book Company came into existence in the 1886. Daniel Bare realized the need for a plant that would convert paper into usable consumer goods. Ledgers were very popular. The business outgrew several sites until 1900, when a stately building of native blue limestone was constructed near the spring to house the expanding business. This would occupy three acres. Tablets, accounting books, passbooks, and composition books are just a few of its many products. This company is known around the globe.

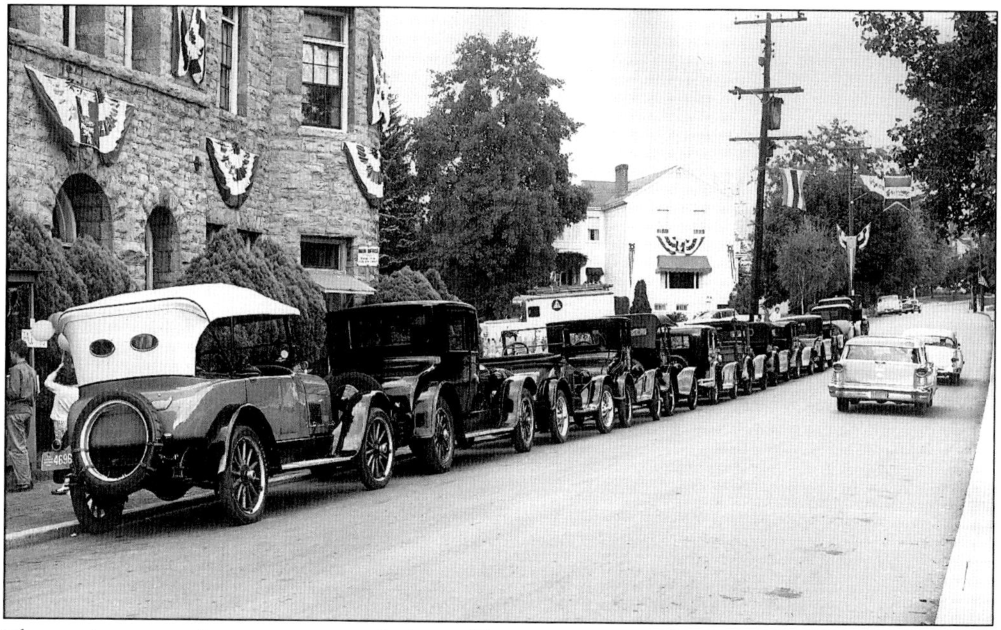

The antique car show was part of the golden anniversary festivities. Roaring Spring was incorporated on June 27, 1888. A prosperous industrial community had sprung up around the Great Spring. Main Street was once Woodbury Turnpike. The antique cars, parked in front of the Blank Book factory, represent all makes and various years. The Blank Book business was a vibrant industry. It was established by founding father, Daniel Bare.

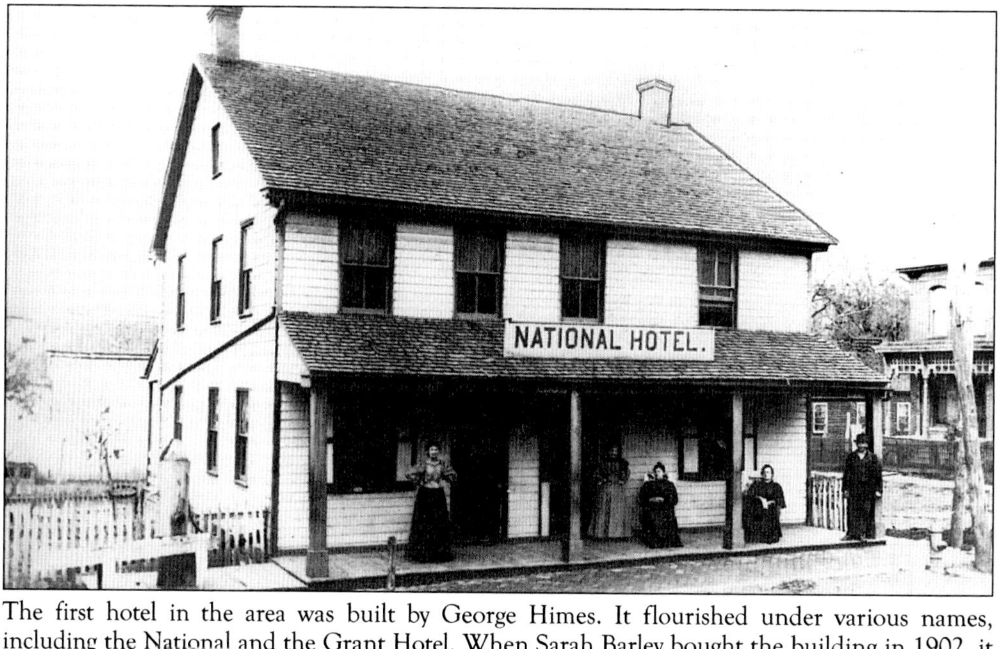

The first hotel in the area was built by George Himes. It flourished under various names, including the National and the Grant Hotel. When Sarah Barley bought the building in 1902, it became the Barley Hotel. This became a meeting place for peddlers who sold merchandise to the cove dwellers. It was located across from the railroad station. In the late 1800s, an attempt was made to establish a summer resort hotel near the famous spring.

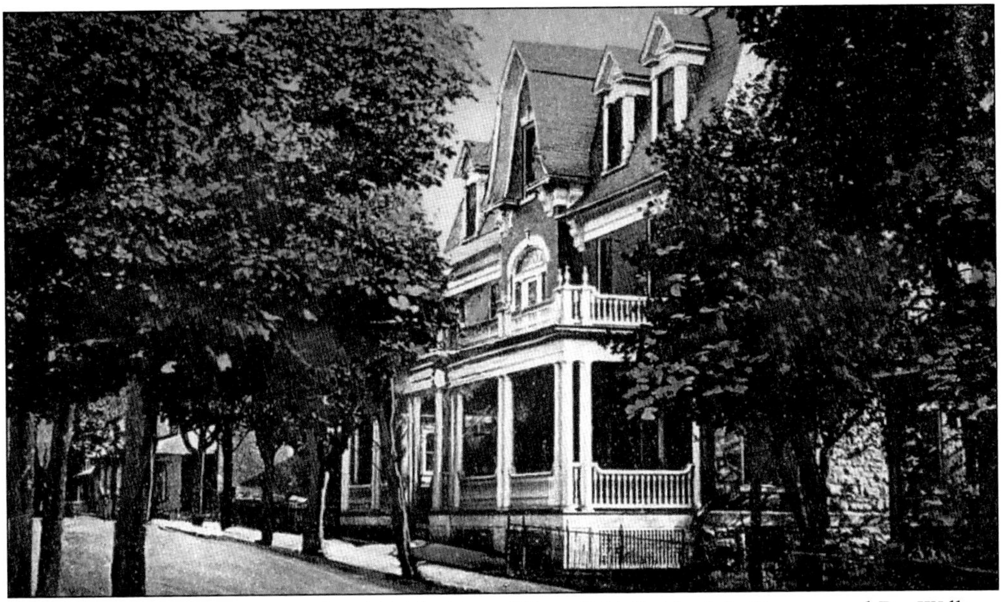

The Eldon Inn was constructed in 1908 by Daniel Bare, E.G. Bobb, A.L. Garver, and Dr. William Elton. It was designed as a first-class inn for the traveling public and was to function strictly without the sale of liquor. The spacious brick structure was fitted with all modern conveniences. It operated for many years as the only hotel in the community. Its earliest managers included Simon Kauffman and Jesse Replogle. A salesman from New York credited the hotel as the best he ever slept in.

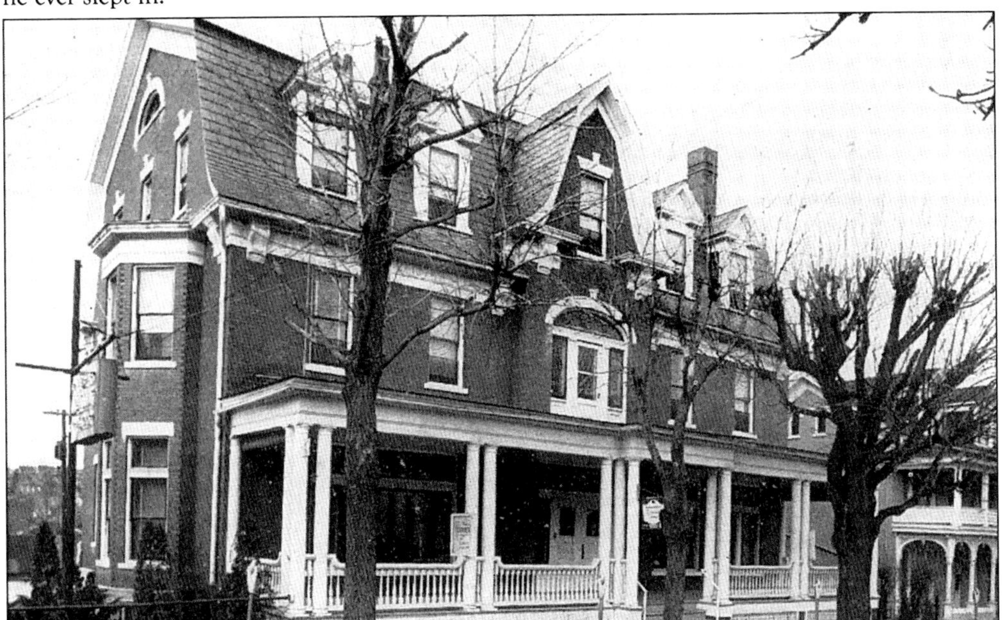

Eldon Inn became a library in January 1966. The library had been established in 1959 by George Kesinger and his wife. It was housed in various sites throughout the borough. Each time, a larger site was needed. The borough council purchased the Eldon Inn. The Blank Book Company contributed toward a new furnace. The charming library today contains all modern equipment in a delightful Victorian setting.

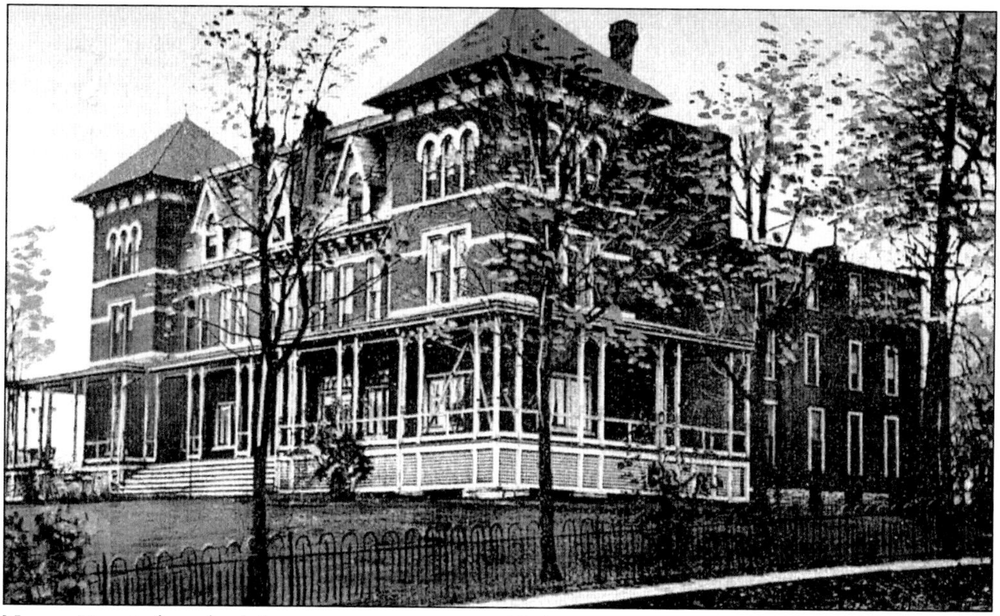

Nason Hospital evolved from an attempt to establish a summer resort at Roaring Spring. The spacious Park Hotel was built on the corner of Main and Grove Streets in 1880 to entice summer guests. The medicinal benefits of the limestone spring and pure mountain air were publicized, but the project never materialized. Dr. William A. Nason arrived in Roaring Spring in 1896 and, with six partners, bought the abandoned Park Hotel. He then established the Nason Sanitarium.

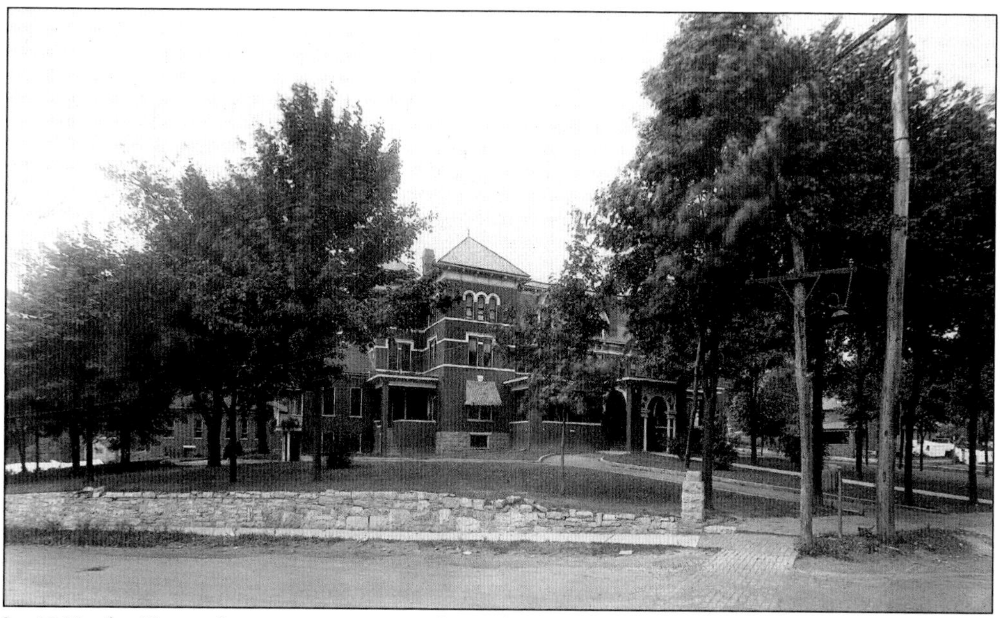

In 1900, the Nason Sanitarium was transformed to a charitable hospital. It was complete with the first nurses' training school in the county. The hospital continued to prosper and grow. Emergency medical services were established, always within the context of its mission to promote and improve the health status of patients and surrounding community. Nason Hospital has always maintained a reputation for giving high-quality healthcare.

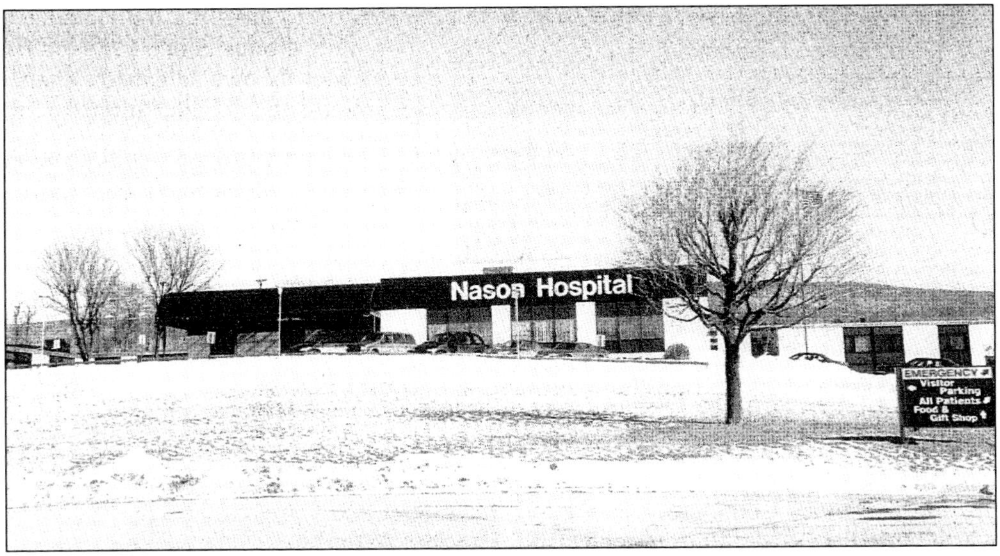

Patient population grew and necessitated the expansion of Nason Hospital. In 1959, it was decided to establish a new hospital centrally located to the area it served. A 10-acre site was purchased from Clare S. Kauffman on Route 36. Situated on a gentle slope, it would be adequate for the new building, provide ample room for future expansion, and afford pleasant surroundings with picturesque views. The new Nason Hospital was dedicated on January 21, 1961. Since its inception, the hospital has responded to advances in medical technology.

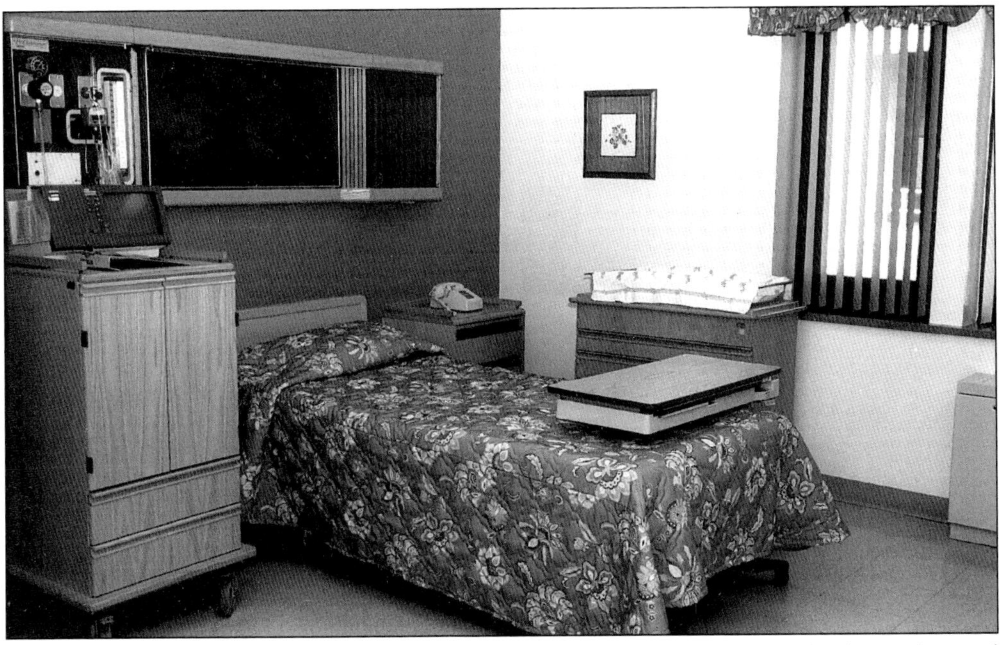

The challenges of progressive medicine and modernized procedures were met by the professional staff. In 1971, a new wing provided an ambulatory care program and the advancement of support services. A new medical office building was added, and a gift shop and snack bar became part of the complex. The auxiliary promotes the welfare of the facility through service to the hospital and patients. The highest level of efficiency and economy are maintained at Nason Hospital.

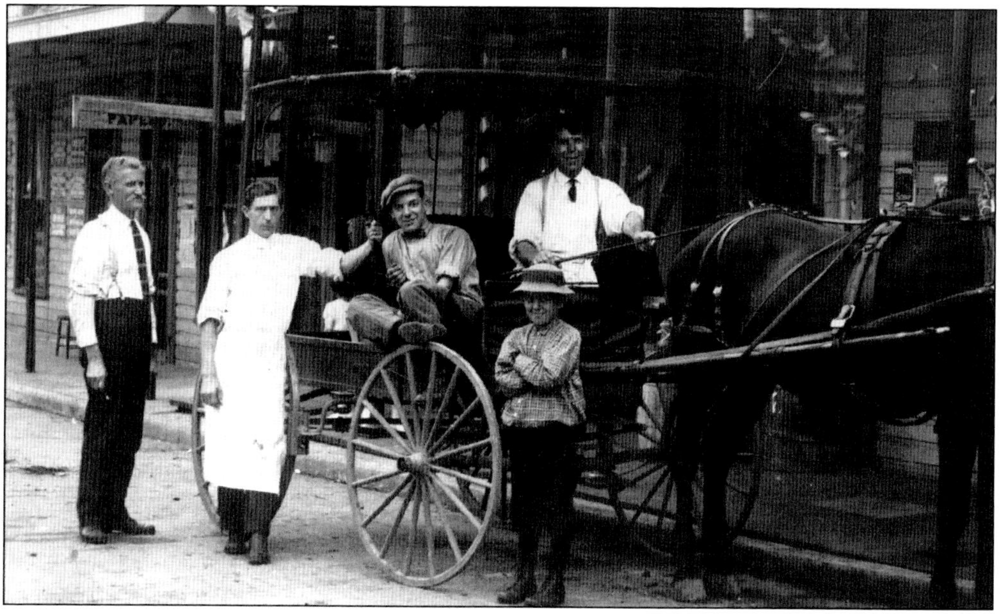

J.P. Martin's general store on Main Street was a scene of activity. It had been the Edward Hair Pharmacy. In 1908, it was taken over by J.P. Martin, a prominent businessman and teacher in the area. Adam Heuston holds the reins, and J.P. Martin (left) supervises as the delivery lads prepare to make their rounds throughout the cove. Clarence Albright is the smiling lad sitting in the wagon.

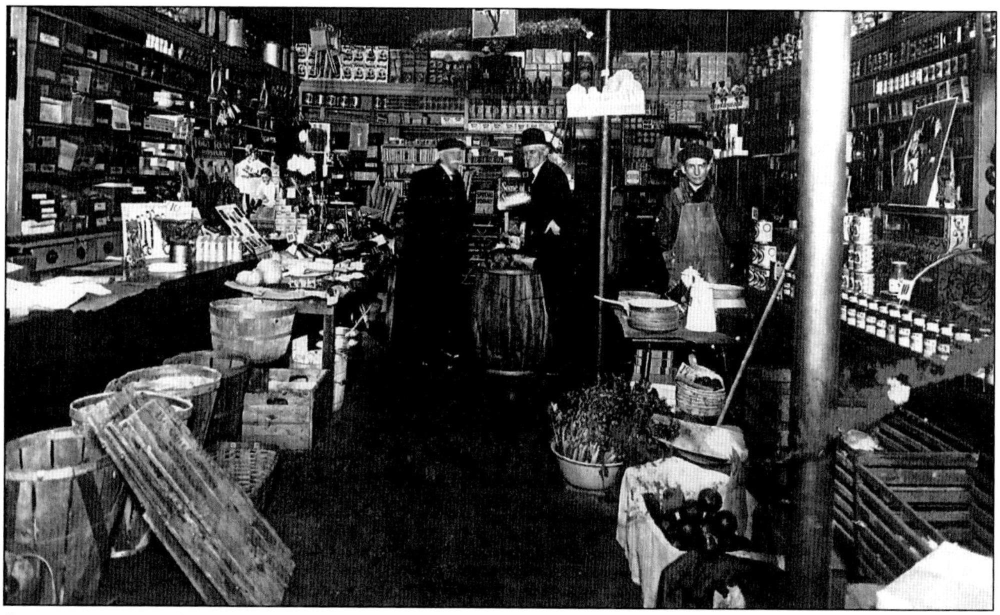

"Meet Your Neighbors at Martins" became a familiar slogan in Roaring Spring. The interior of J.P. Martin's general store was an emporium of necessities. He operated three stores at different times. In 1919, Martin divided his work with his son, Paul. In later years, a five-and-dime store was opened on the second floor. Martin was active in community affairs, the borough council, and the school board. Note the clerks in the left background and the old-fashioned cash register in the right foreground.

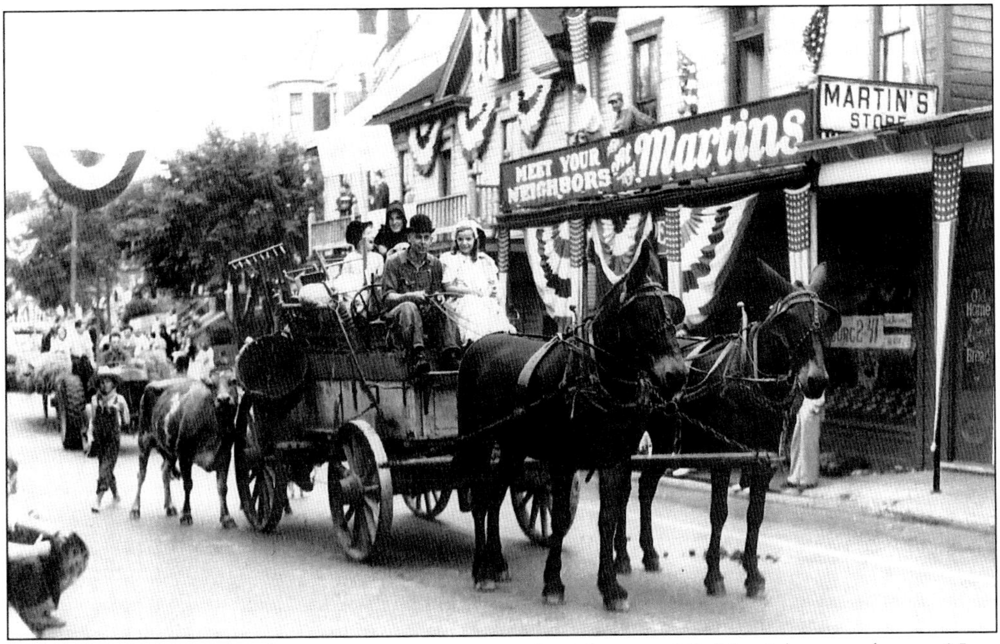

The Fern Kauffman family, in an anniversary parade, rides past J.P. Martin's general store. Note the cow that accompanies the family. This is indicative of the numerous dairy farms in this area. J.P. Martin's store was an exceptionally modern establishment. Note also that the dusty, unpaved road did not deter the festivities. The parade routes were always decorated with bunting. Tractors follow the wagon. The entire family turned out complete with equipment.

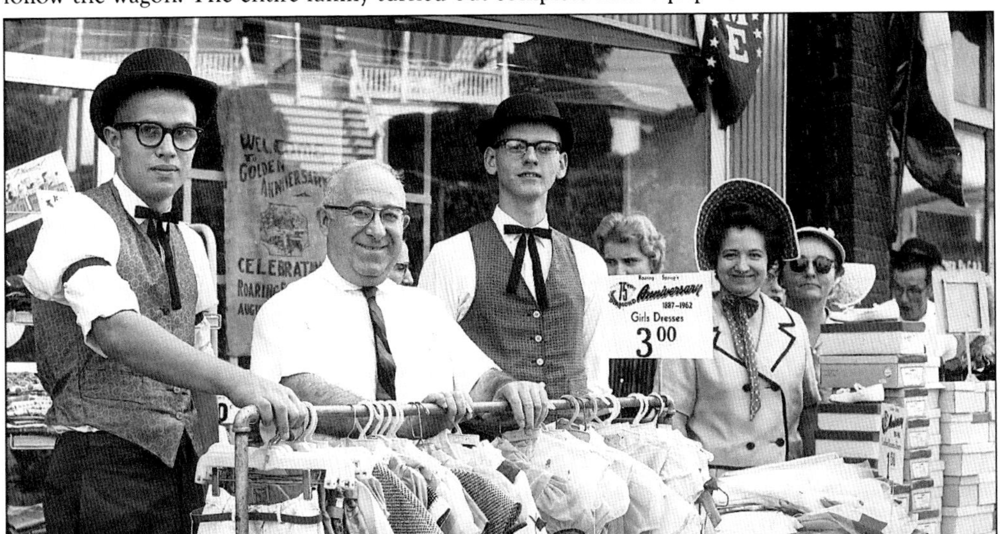

Sidewalk sales were an attraction during the golden anniversary celebrations. William Klevens (center) was the son of a retailer. His father, Louis, operated a store in Claysburg. William Klevens's clothing store was on Main Street for many years. His clerks were Raymond Thompson and Joe Zimmerman. Good service and good merchandise created credibility. In this view, shoppers are ready to devour bargains. Does anyone recall when girls dresses were $3 apiece?

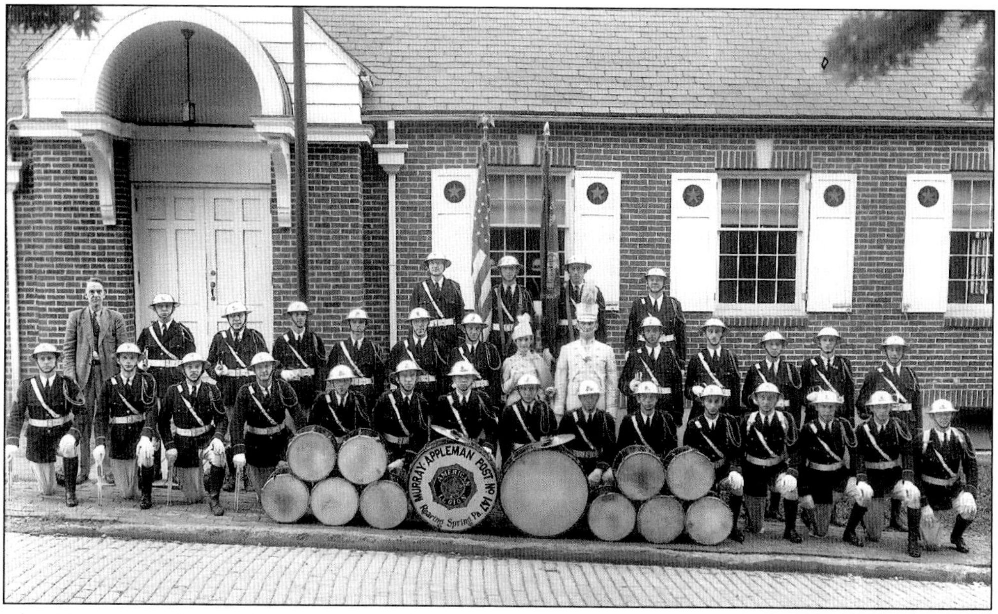

The Murray-Appleman Drum and Bugle Corps was formed in 1931 as part of the American Legion Post 147. It was named in memory of two men who gave their lives on the battlefield. The legion was formed by veterans of World War I. The Drum and Bugle Corps rehearsed through the first year and then stepped into competition. They became prominent in central Pennsylvania and were sought after for their musical ability. They won the Pennsylvania Class B Championship for three consecutive years.

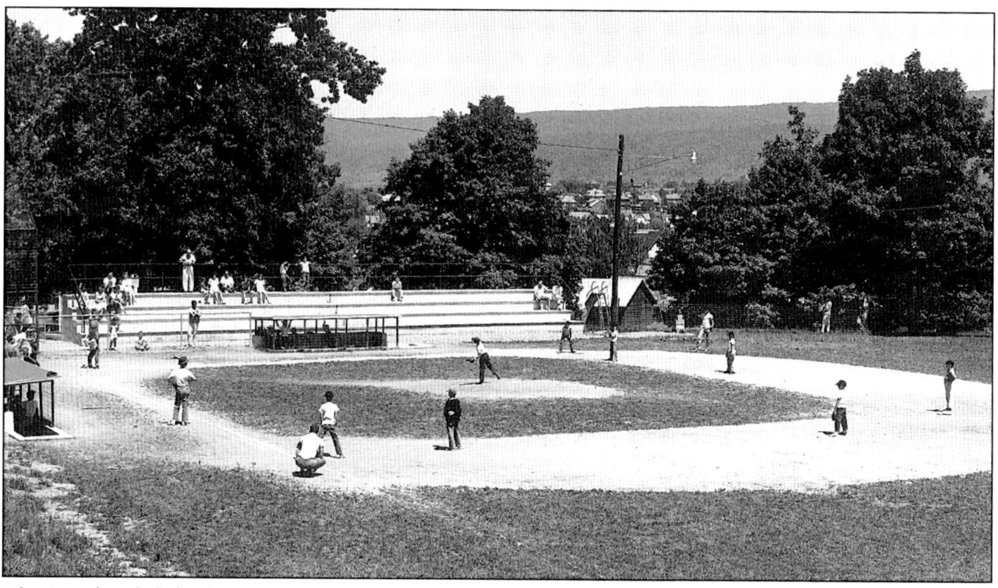

The Lion's Club laid out the Little League ball field in 1962. Located near the WMCA building, it was equipped with lights and an electric scoreboard. In 1952, the Lions Club was formed in Roaring Spring. From its inception, the club is dedicated to improving the community. The Lions have sponsored such activities as the Lions Minstrel Time, the Apple Blossom Festival, the Annual Roaring Spring Homecoming Celebration, quarterly ox roasts, and a traveling playhouse for the benefit of youngsters.

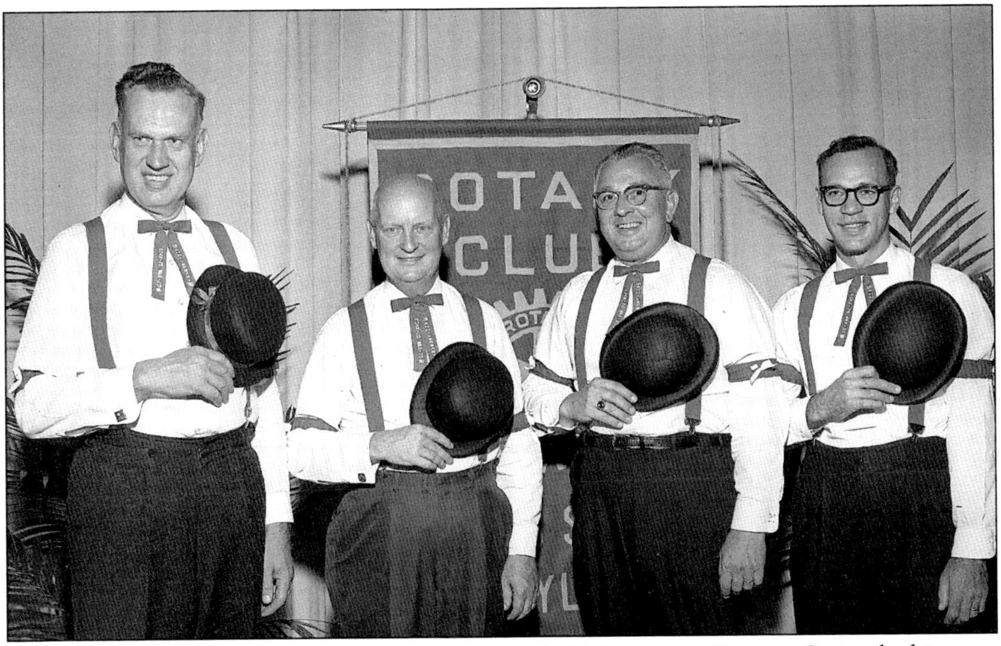

Barbershop quartets were very prominent in the early 20th century. Roaring Spring had its own quartet, made up of businessmen who performed on various occasions. Their renditions were enjoyed by all. From left to right are Barrel Mock, who had a dry-cleaning establishment; Merrill "Hop" Rough, an insurance agent; Vance Myers, a purchasing agent for the Appleton Paper Company; and Merle Hess, an insurance agent.

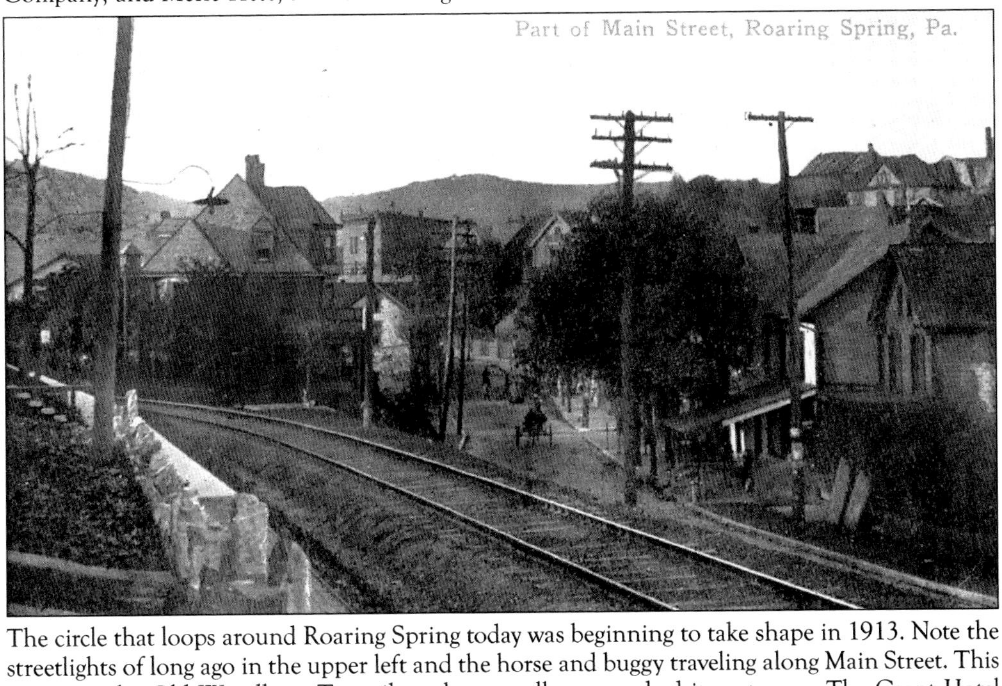

The circle that loops around Roaring Spring today was beginning to take shape in 1913. Note the streetlights of long ago in the upper left and the horse and buggy traveling along Main Street. This was once the Old Woodbury Turnpike, where a toll gate marked its entrance. The Grant Hotel is in the foreground. In 1894, electricity was introduced into town, and the era of the kerosene lamps phased into history.

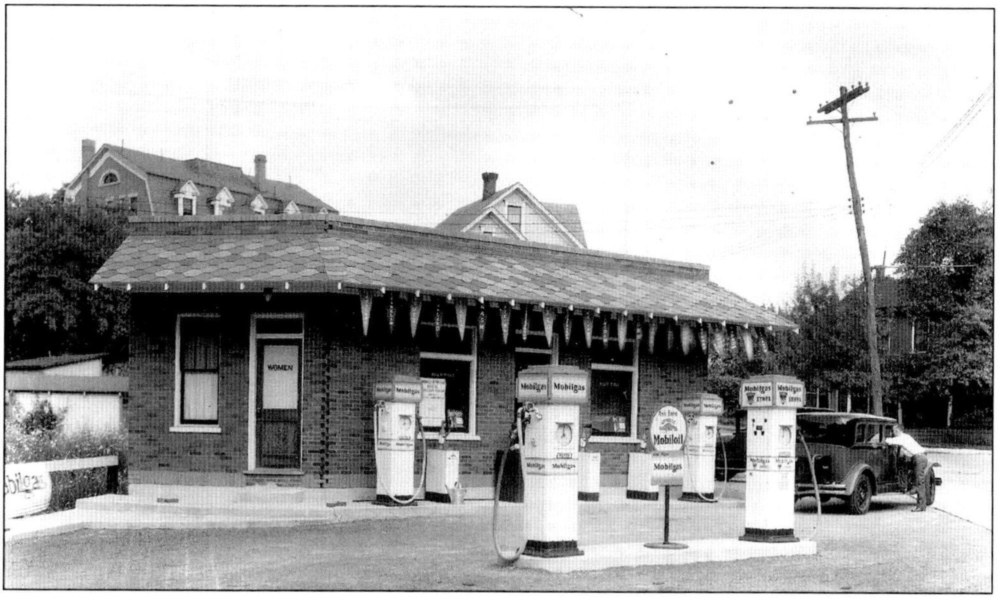

Service stations kept pace with automobiles. This Mobil gas station was among the first in Roaring Spring. It advertises Kelly's Tires, and the triangular flags advertise the various makes of cars. L & L Motors was the first service station in Roaring Spring. It was opened by Clarence Lauer in 1936, at which time he secured a dealership of Chrysler and Plymouth.

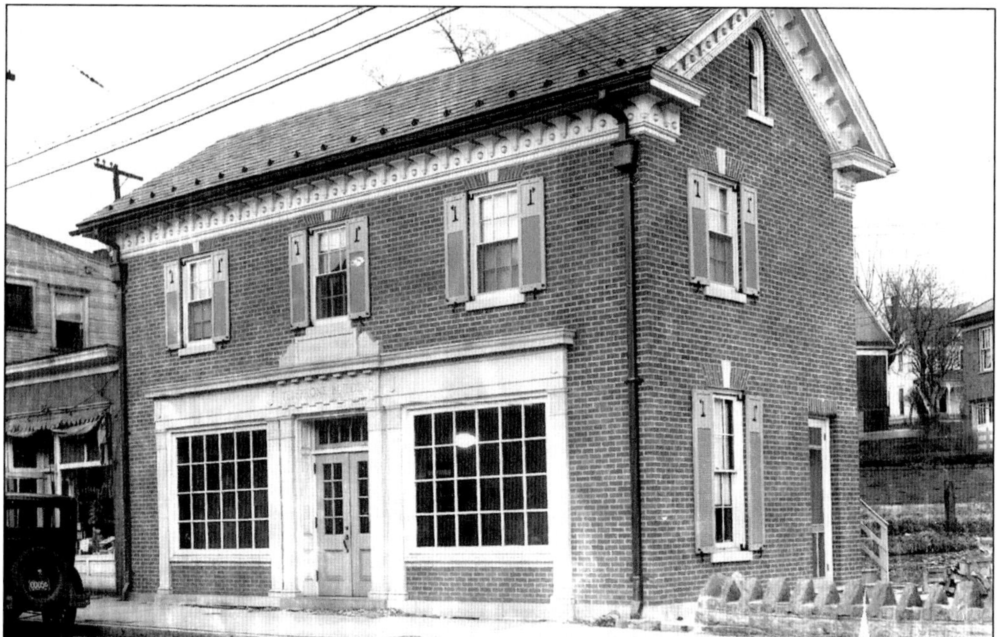

United Telephone of Pennsylvania is a predecessor of Morrison's Cove Telephone Company. It has served Roaring Spring since 1905. Telephone service first came to Roaring Spring in 1877, when the Altoona Telephone Company extended a line into town at the urging of the Morrison Bare and Cass Paper Company. In 1905, a switchboard capable of handling 100 lines was installed. It was located on the second floor of the bank building. Earliest customers paid $12 a year.

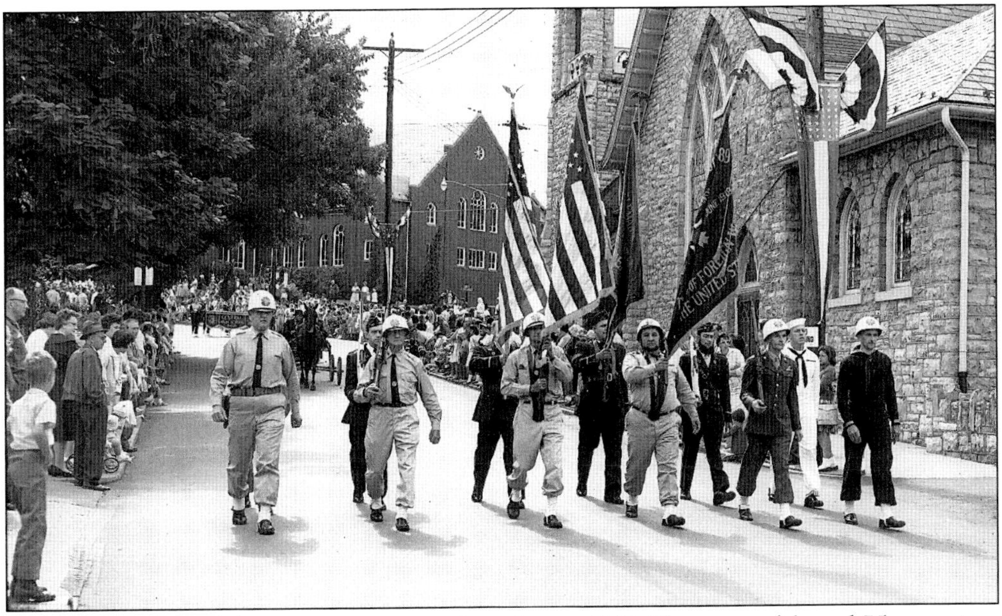

Parades were featured during anniversary week in August 1962. The town celebrated 75 years since its incorporation in 1887. The American Legion Drum and Bugle Corp is shown here. From left to right are the following: (front row) Tom Yingling, Robert Riley, Dick Myers (flag bearer), unidentified, and Eugene McKinney; (back row) David Long, Robert Kaufman, and Fred Herron (the sailor). The Church of God and the Methodist church are in the background.

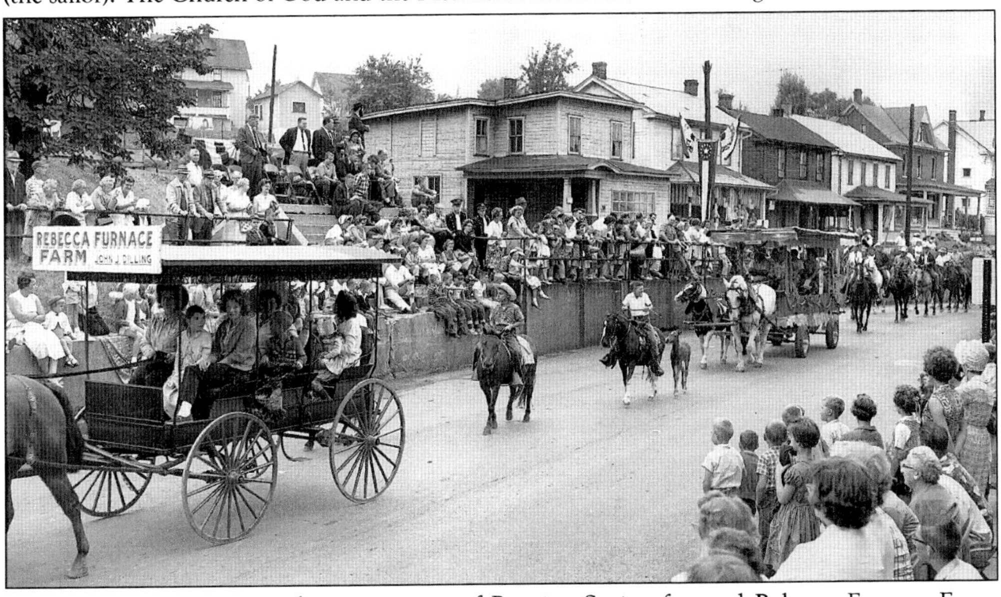

A parade commemorating the anniversary of Roaring Spring featured Rebecca Furnace Farm. The furnace was built by ironmaster Dr. Peter Shoenberger in 1817. Located in Huston Township along Clover Creek, it was the first furnace in southern Blair County. The furnace was named for Shoenberger's daughter and was supplied entirely of ore taken from Molasses Town and Milltown. Rebecca Furnace changed owners several times before it was dismantled in 1882. The coming of iron, mining, and smelting furnaces were a magnet for drawing the railroad into the area.

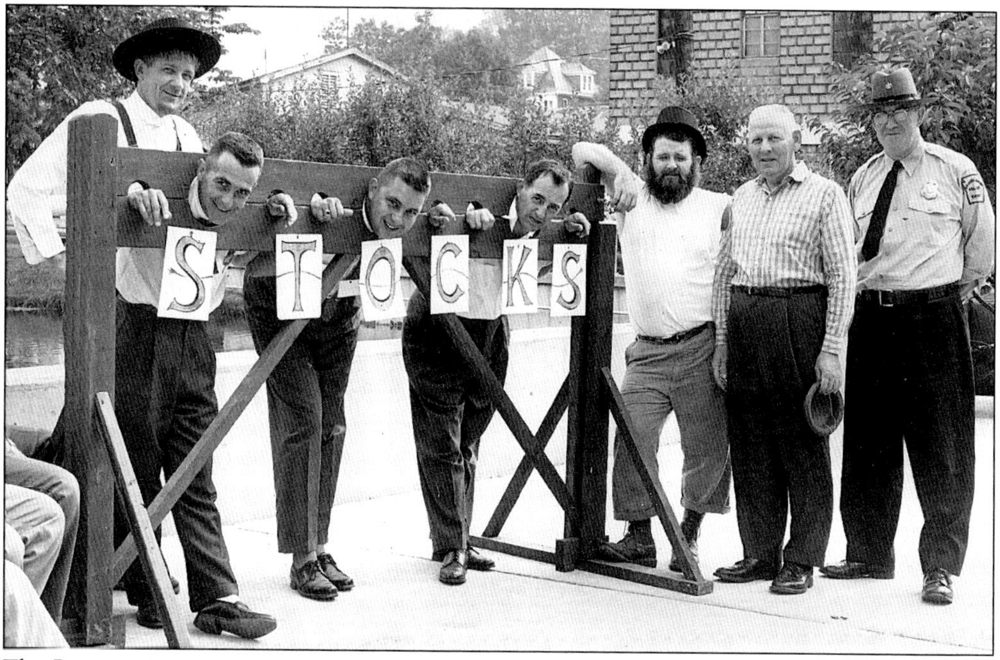

The Roaring Spring Festival provided amusement of various kinds. John Thompson looks on while three of his buddies—John Kaufman, Wilbur Hite, and Clarence "Coony" Wineland—are in the stockade. Joe Oakes; Joe Hendrick, mayor; and Joe Robinson, chief of police, are thankful that the era of stockades is over. The festival was held around the commons near the spring.

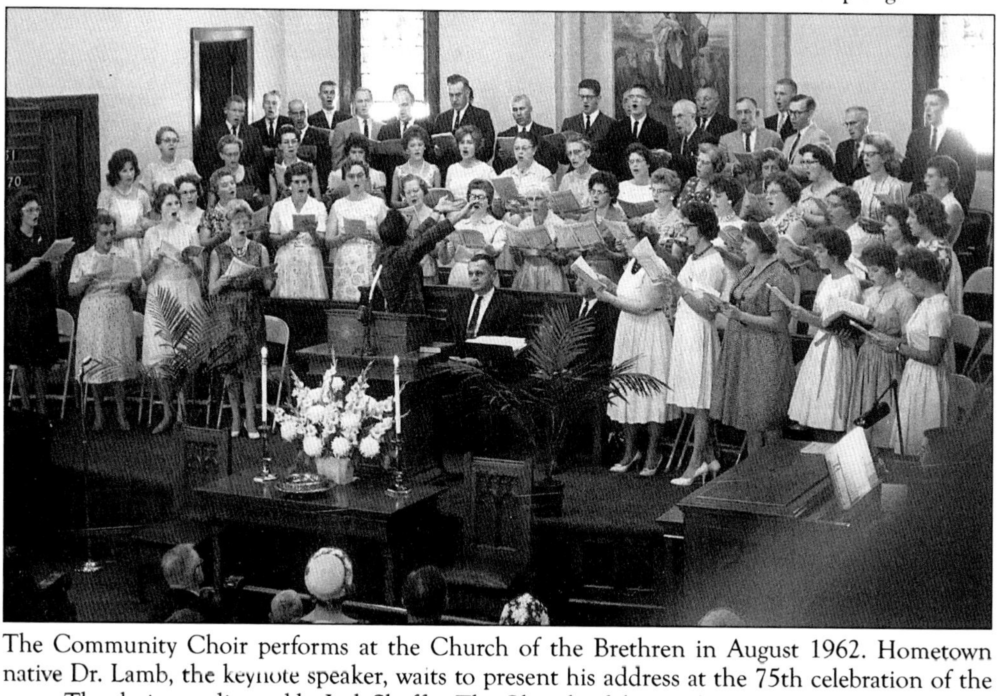

The Community Choir performs at the Church of the Brethren in August 1962. Hometown native Dr. Lamb, the keynote speaker, waits to present his address at the 75th celebration of the town. The choir was directed by Jack Shaffer. The Church of the Brethren dates back to 1755. The congregation was chiefly German Baptists and worshiped at various sites. In 1910, their church was built in the heart of town. It has been renovated several times.

Elaine Ake is crowned Miss Roaring Spring by former queen Mary Elizabeth Ground Good. She had been queen at the golden anniversary of the borough in 1937. The ceremony took place in Spring Park on August 14, 1962. The former queen is the daughter of Dr. Wilbert Ground and was a teacher in the Roaring Spring schools. Her father was the president of the Blair Medical Association in 1931 and chief surgeon at Nason Hospital in 1933.

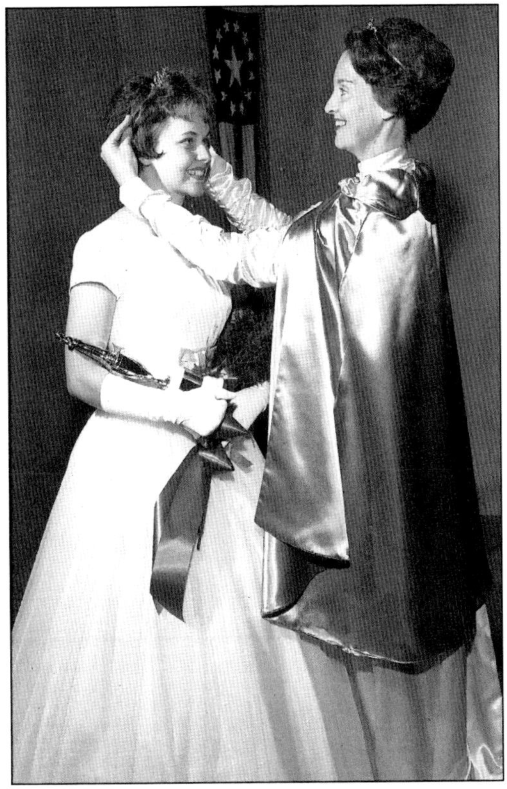

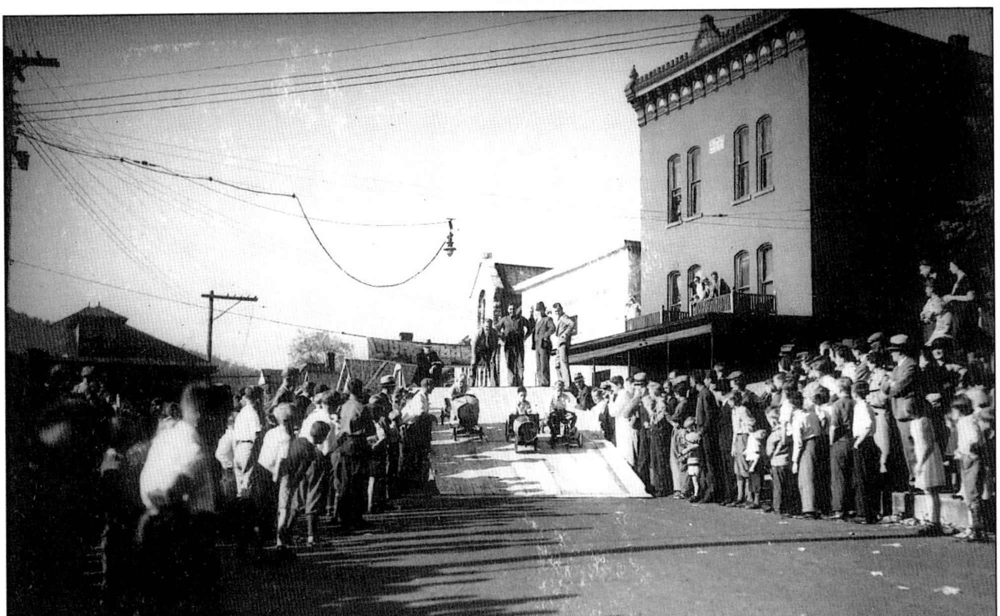

The soapbox derby was a spectacular event. The participants constructed their own vehicles. On August 15, 1937, spectators gathered to witness the contest. It was the golden anniversary of the incorporation of Roaring Spring. Celebrations continued all week. These boys had a head start in the race when they rolled down the ramp at Eldon's Point and proceeded south on Main Street.

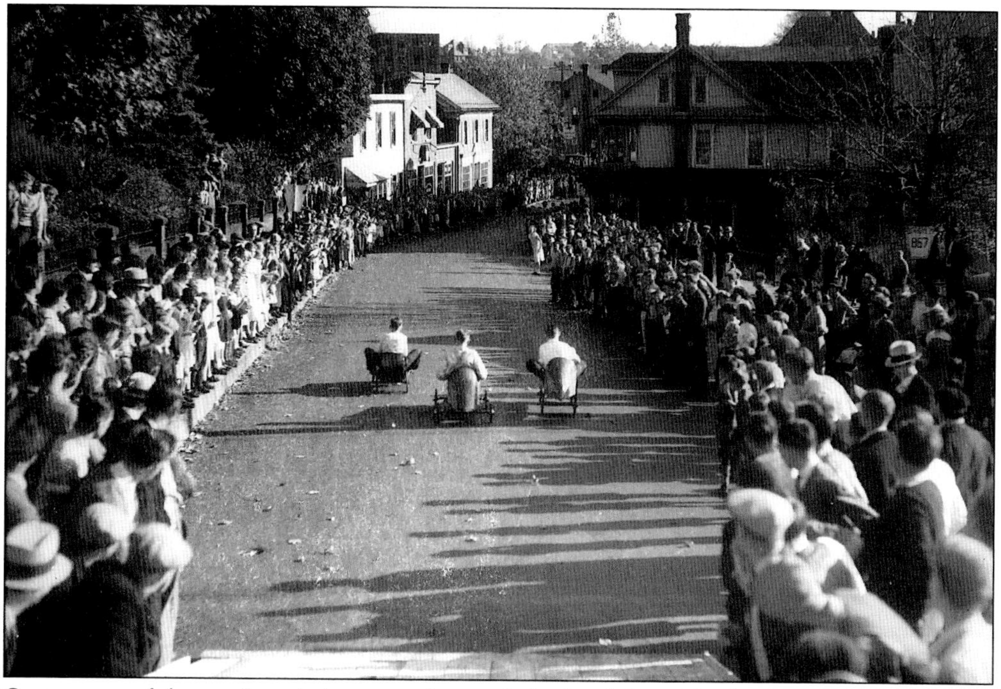

Contestants of the soapbox derby proceed toward the finish line. The background of this image includes Miller Appliance, the telephone exchange (in an era when few phones were in existence), the bank building, and Replogle's Coffee Shop. The event drew hundreds of observers. The festivities included further spectacular exhibits, such as doll, pet, and odd-hat exhibits.

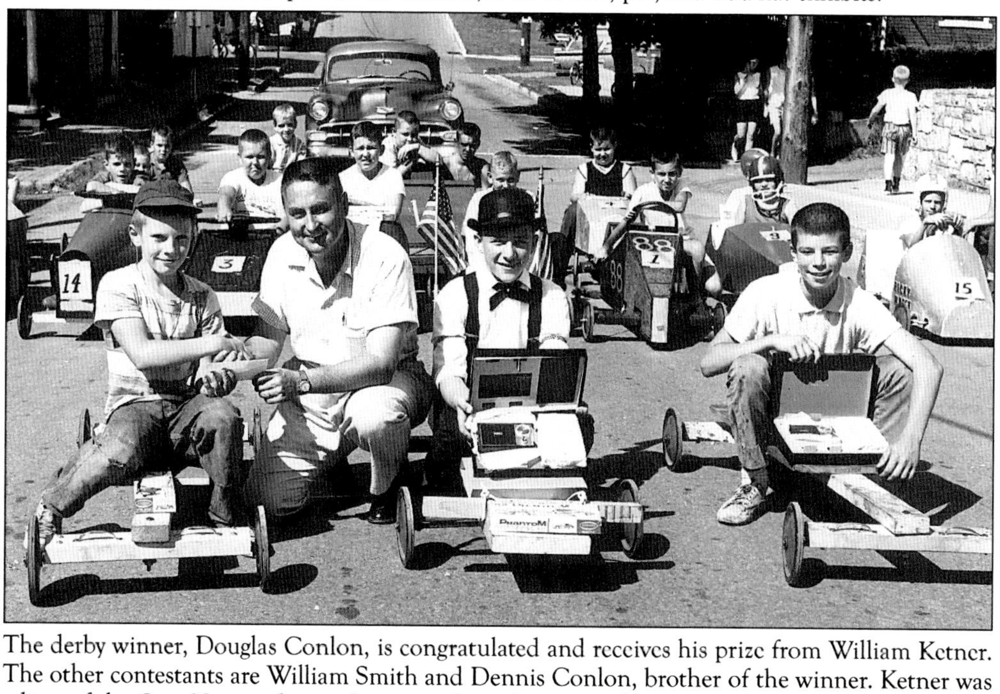

The derby winner, Douglas Conlon, is congratulated and receives his prize from William Ketner. The other contestants are William Smith and Dennis Conlon, brother of the winner. Ketner was editor of the *Cove News* and served as a combat pilot in World War II. He managed the Altoona station WVAM before founding his own radio station, WKMC, in the 1950s.

Six

THE HEART OF THE COVE

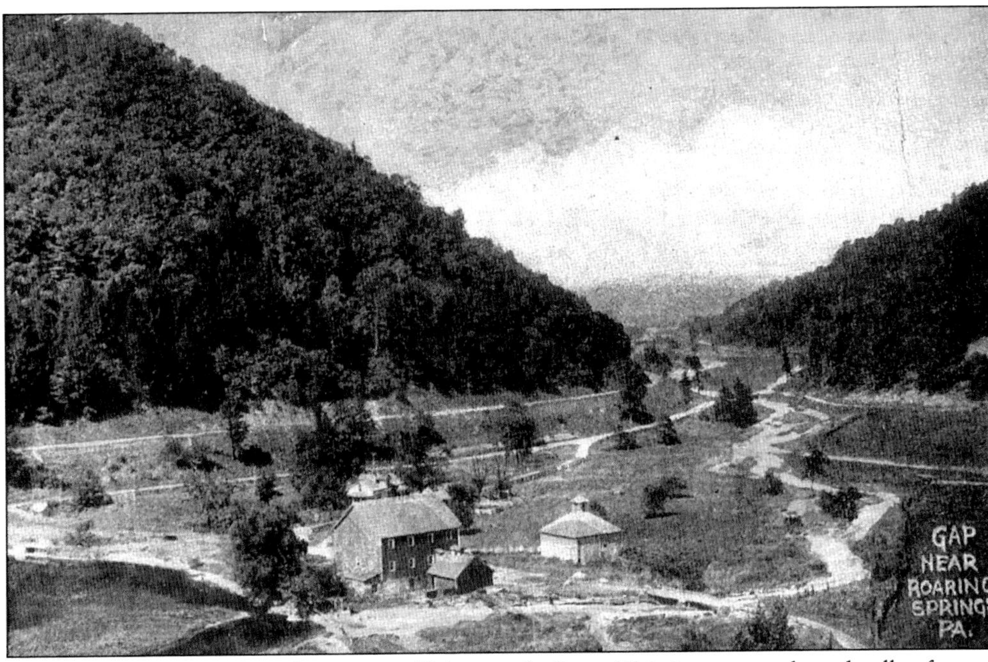

Martinsburg is situated in the center of Morrison's Cove. This is a canoe-shaped valley formed by three mountains: Dunnings Mountain to the west, Tussy Mountain to the east, and Lock Mountain to the north. These are all foothills of the Allegheny Mountains. The eight-mile valley was the chosen site for surveyor James Morrison when he was sent from Cumberland to check the land. Captivated by the rolling hills, the exotic, picturesque terrain, and the fertile land conducive for agriculture, Morrison returned here and brought a following with him. This scene marks the entrance to the cove.

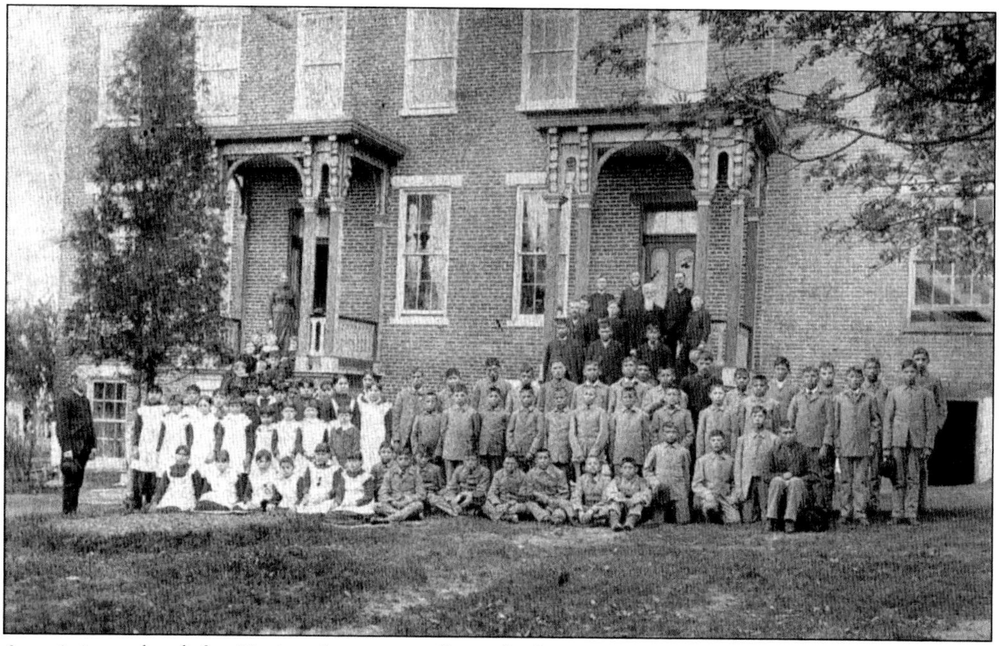

A training school for Native Americans flourished in Martinsburg in the late 1800s. It was conducted by Professor Bridenbaugh. Young men and women were brought to the cove from their tribal homes and were taught the arts and sciences of civilization along with industrial training. The school was authorized by the Federal Bureau of Indian Affairs and prospered at Martinsburg. It was located on East Allegheny Street. In this view, instructors grace the portico. Among them is Prof. Calvin Skyles, a harness maker who later took up ministry.

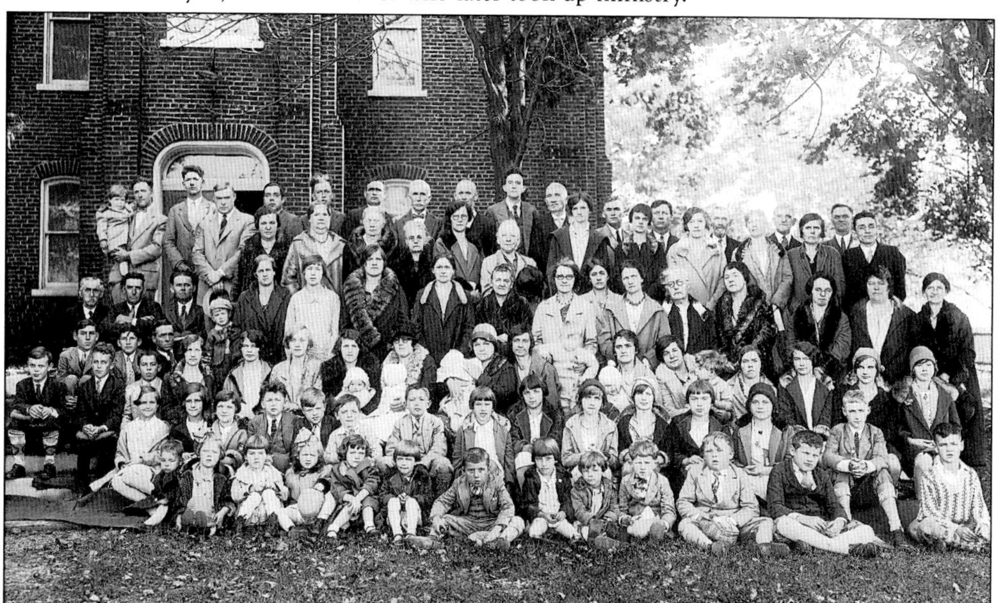

The congregation of the Salem Evangelical and Reformed Church assembles in this early 20th century photograph. The congregation was formed in 1832 as the Clover Creek Reformed Church. The chosen site was on the property of Nicholas and Margaret Fonse. It was the first church in the cove built by Lutheran and Reformed settlers who came from eastern Pennsylvania.

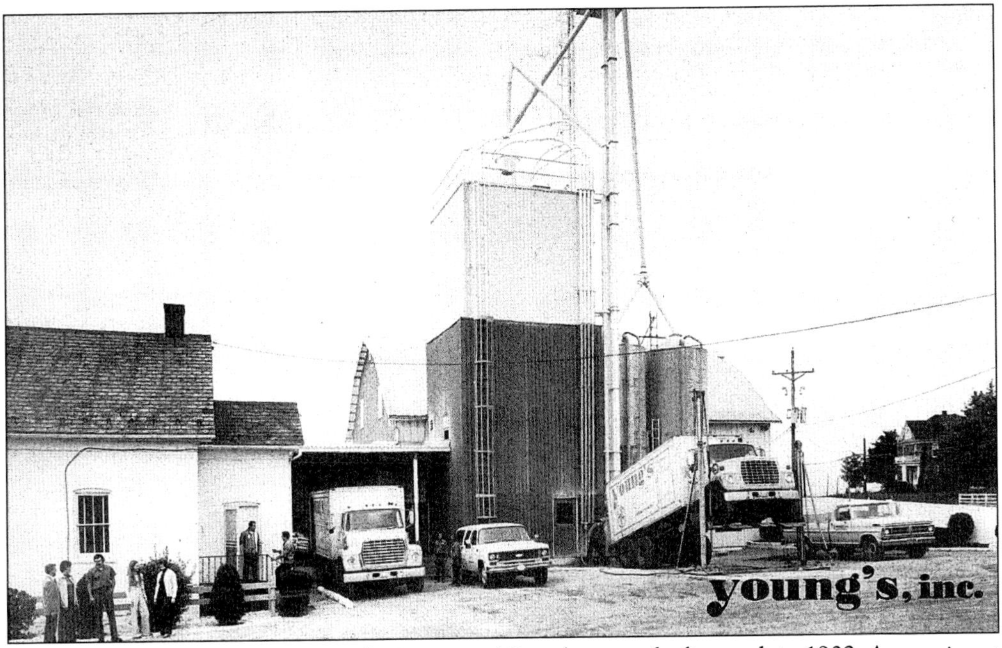

Dr. Thomas Young founded Young's Nutritional Supplements for livestock in 1902. A prominent veterinarian, he recognized the need of proper nutrition for livestock and became a pioneer in the field of animal health. He developed some of the earliest supplement formulas. Following his death in 1916, the firm was taken over by Frank Brown. Three generations of this family have owned, modernized, and expanded the company, which markets many products and has a staff of more than 100 employees. Products are sold through field representatives.

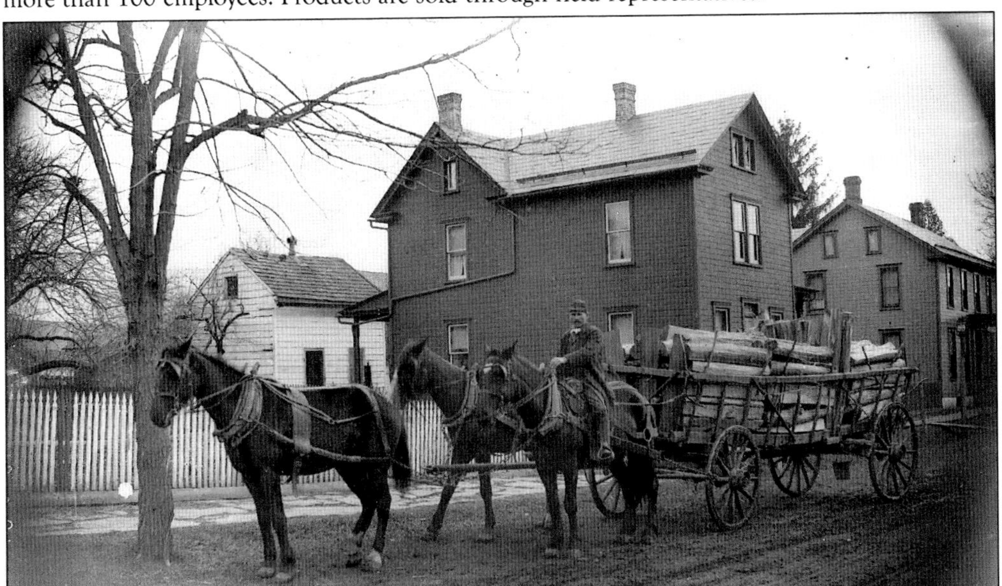

The land held an abundance of virgin forests. A three-horse team would deliver logs for dwellings, cabins, fence poles, mine props, furniture, barn raising, or any number of uses in pioneer times. The ideal conditions for timber production in the area created choice wood. Timber acreage was profuse throughout Morrison's Cove.

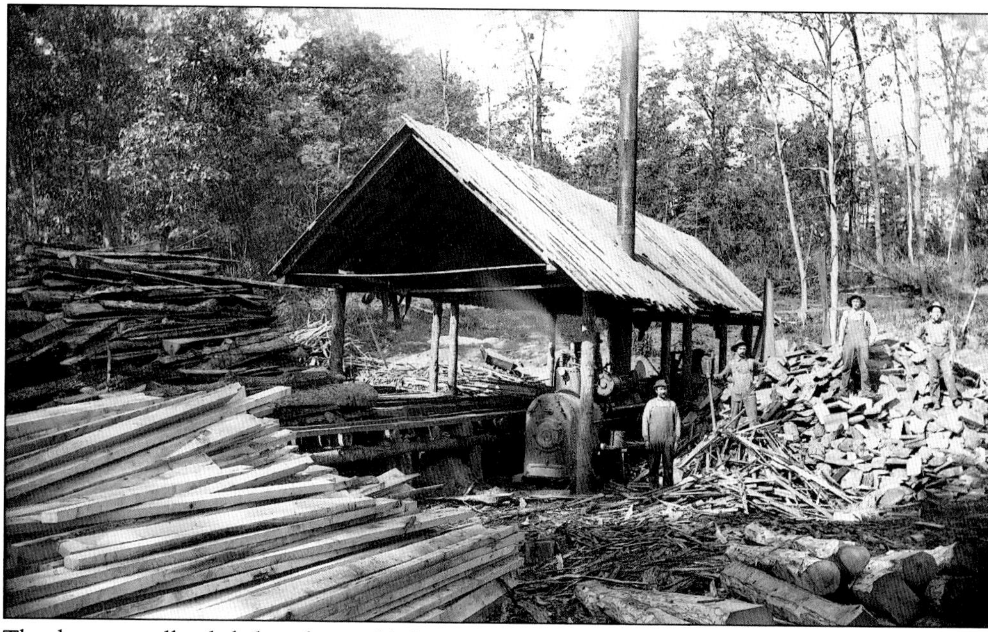

The dense woodlands led to the establishment of numerous sawmills. Lumber was plentiful and in demand, but to prepare it for use was a gigantic task. Tools were scarce, but with an ax and a crosscut saw, much timber was prepared for building. Sawmills were often built where they could manufacture lumber by waterpower.

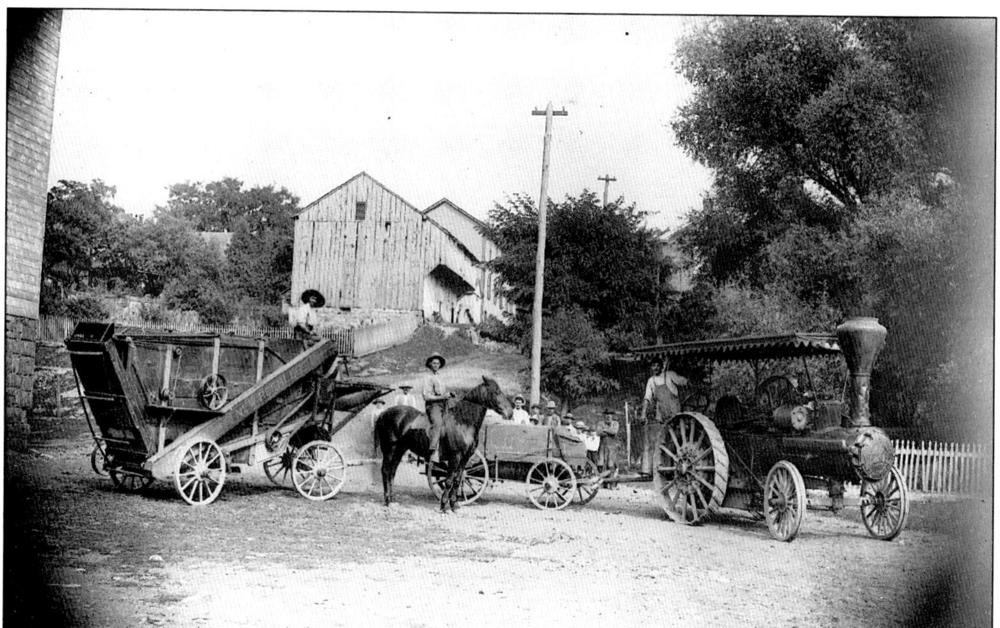

Steam tractors pulled heavy loads before the gasoline tractor came into service. The surrey protected the farmer and the machinery from the summer sun and winter snow. This small wagonload of people seems to be enjoying the wagon ride. The thrashing machine will be used for hay.

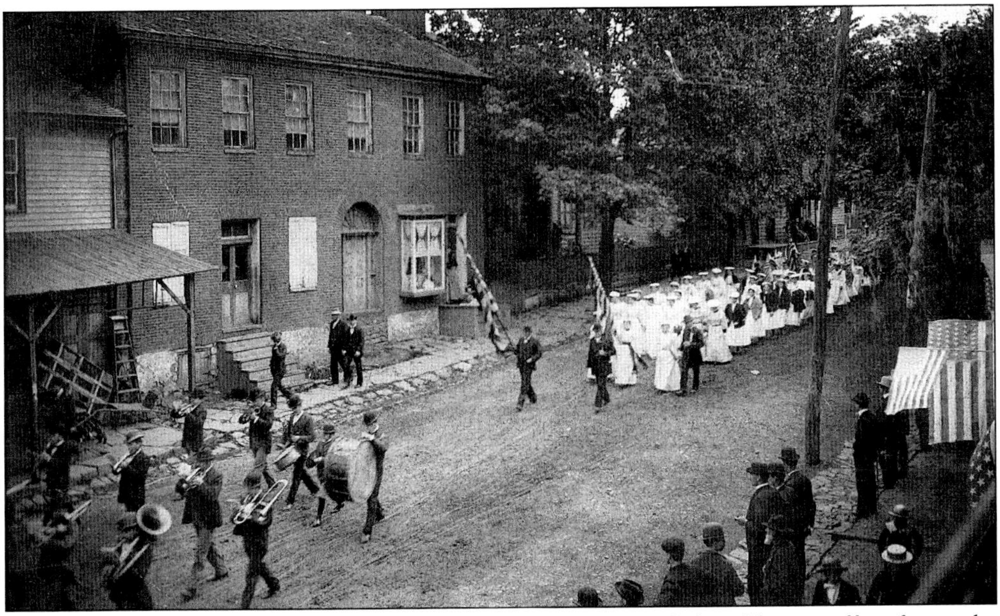

A parade marches along an unpaved Allegheny Street. Part of the old post office forms the background. The Goodwin building was owned by Joseph T. "Possy" Bolger. He was a barber who began as an apprentice to Joe Lantzer. In 1924, Bolger bought his employer's business and operated it successfully for many years. He sold the business to Richard Moore in 1974. The building was razed to make way for a new post office.

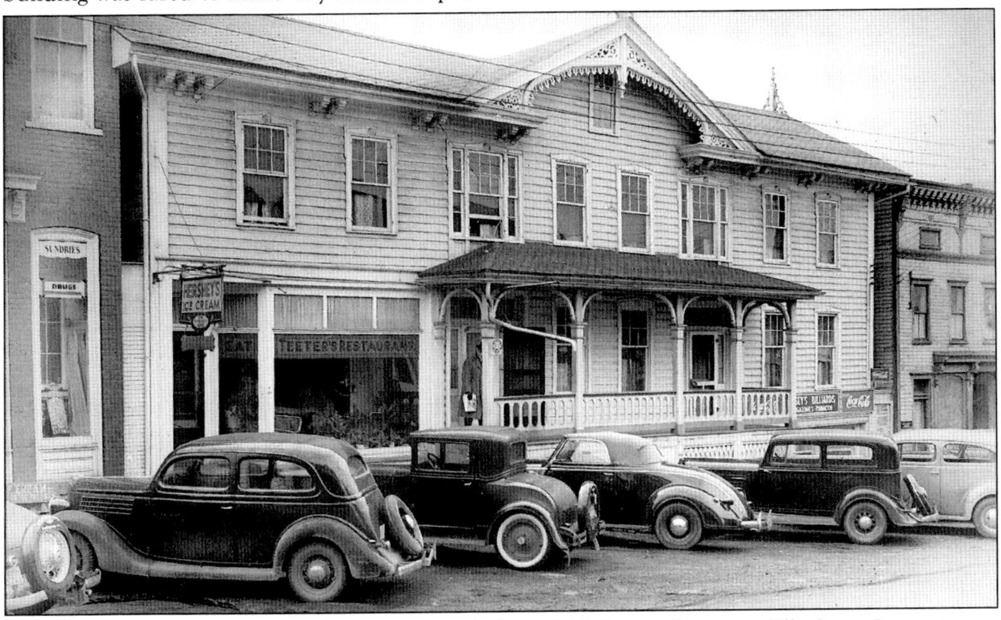

Teeter's Hotel was built by William F. Bridenthal in 1855. Located on east Allegheny Street, it was operated successfully by Bridenthal for 20 years. The hotel had many owners. In 1929, Frank and Mamie Teeter bought it from William Keim. Mamie Teeter gave it an outstanding reputation. She gave her personal attention to the kitchen. Menus came from the Pennsylvania Dutch cookbook and carried the savory appeal of that gourmet. Chicken and waffles were the Sunday specialty for many years. All meals were served in great abundance. William Teeter was a longtime fire chief.

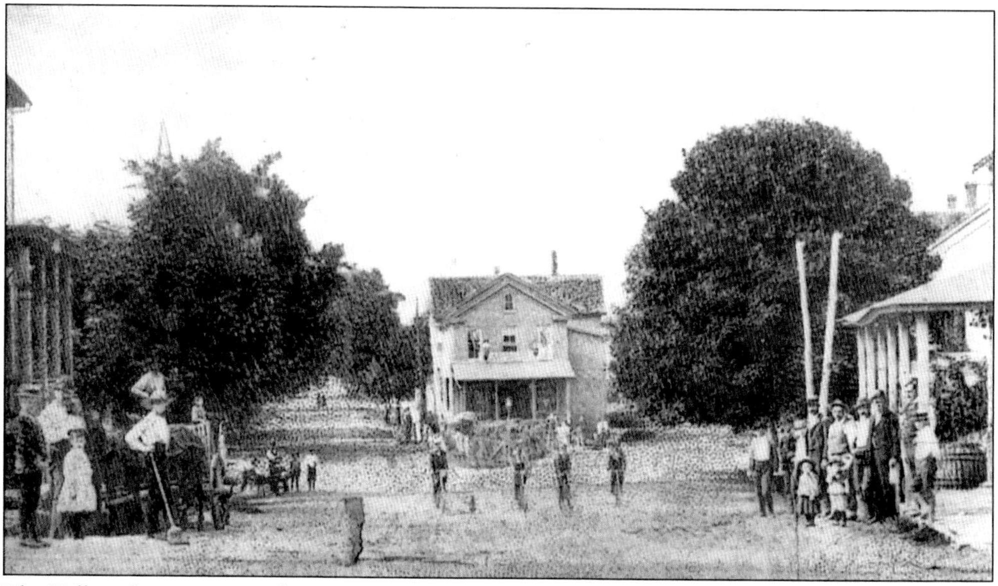

The Dilling Store is situated on a prominent triangular point of land between Market and Locust Streets. The building was constructed in the mid-19th century by Nehemiah Campbell. It later became a drugstore. In 1890, Bert Dilling opened it as a general store. His son J. Ealor Dilling took over in 1902 and continued the business until 1967. The third generation, John Dilling, later assumed ownership. J. Ealor Dilling was active in civic, business, and church affairs. He was a member of the First Brethren Church. Dilling Street is named for him.

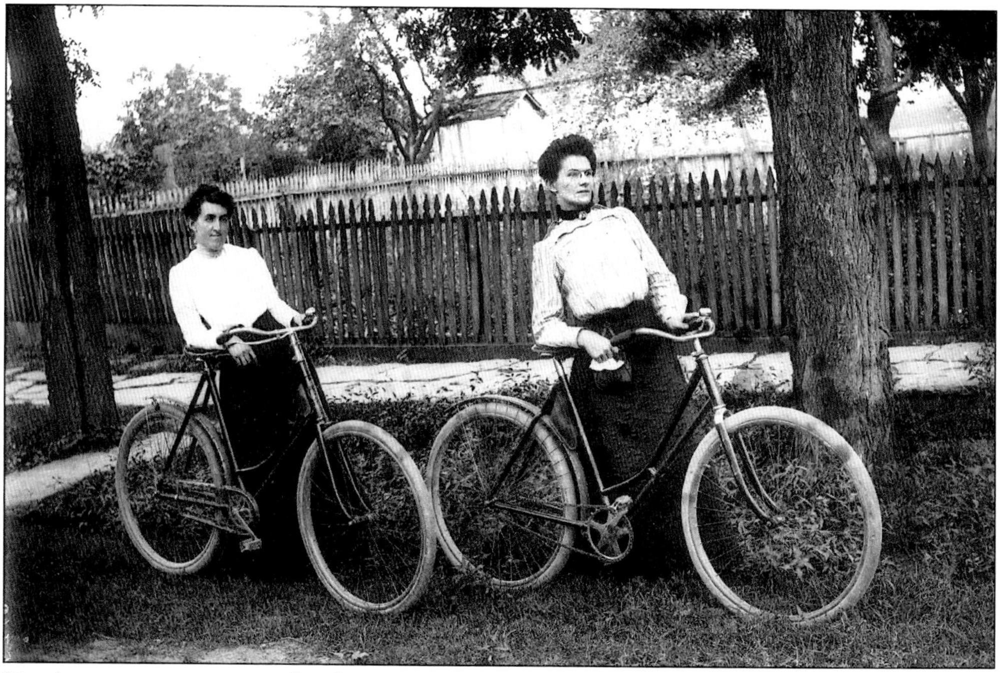

Bicycles were a common mode of transportation c. 1900. They were a necessity for many pioneers who resided in outlying districts. Distance often necessitated this form of conveyance. Bicycles were once as numerous as cars and became quite fashionable among women as well as men. They were used for commuting, sport, and fun.

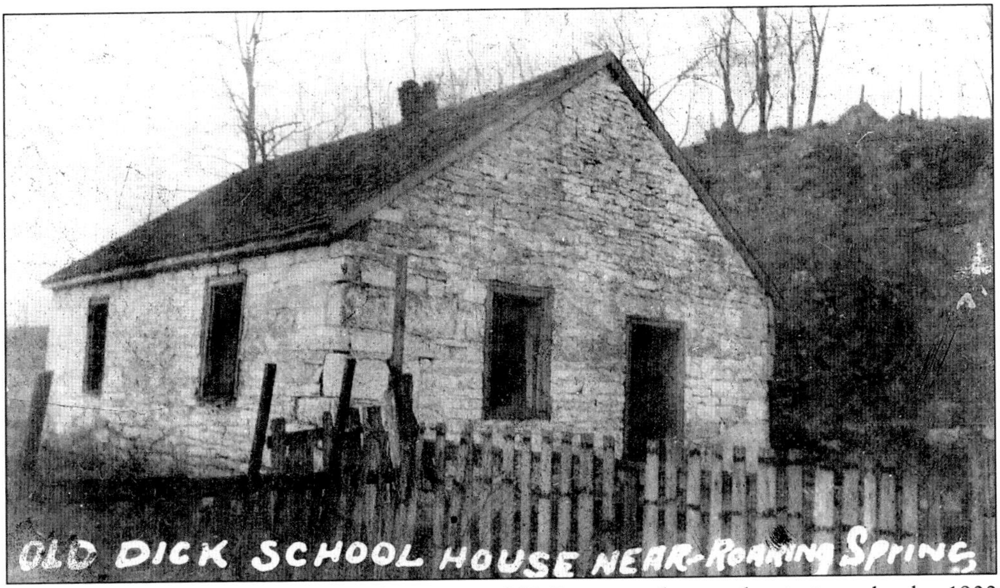

The Dick Schoolhouse was located along Route 867. It was used as a subscription school c. 1900 and then became a public school. It is the oldest remaining school building in Blair County. A meeting to arrange for the annual gathering at the Dick Schoolhouse was held on Friday, September 22, 1922, at 7:30 p.m. In the note on this penny postcard, Mattie Slick reminds A.A. Cowen of Roaring Spring about the meeting and hopes he and his folks will attend.

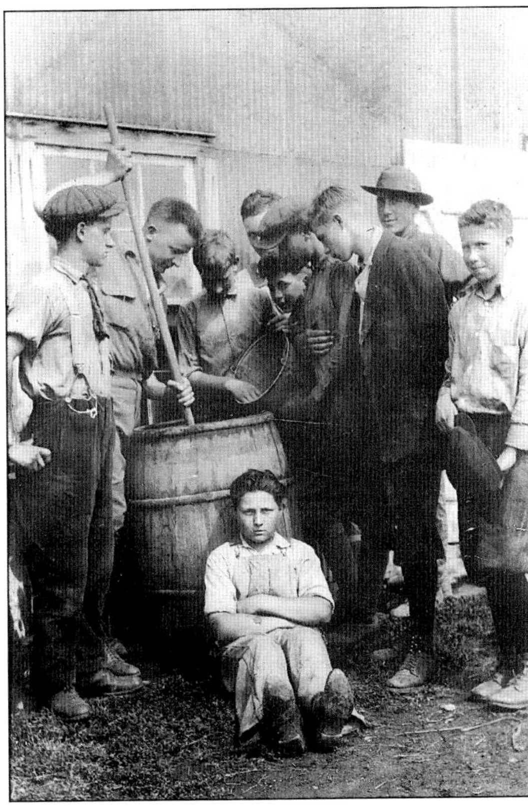

Lads gather at a rain barrel while on an educational hike. In June 1922, the 12 boys met at Allegheny Furnace and set out on a four-day excursion. F.F. Lininger, of the vocational high school, and A.S. Bernhart conducted the trip. They visited a market garden in Eldarado, a poultry farm in Juniata Gap, and a dairy farm in Pleasant Valley. They compared Guernsey cattle with many other species and then visited the Bush Mountain Hog Club. They were treated to a history of Blair County. A ball game followed each evening.

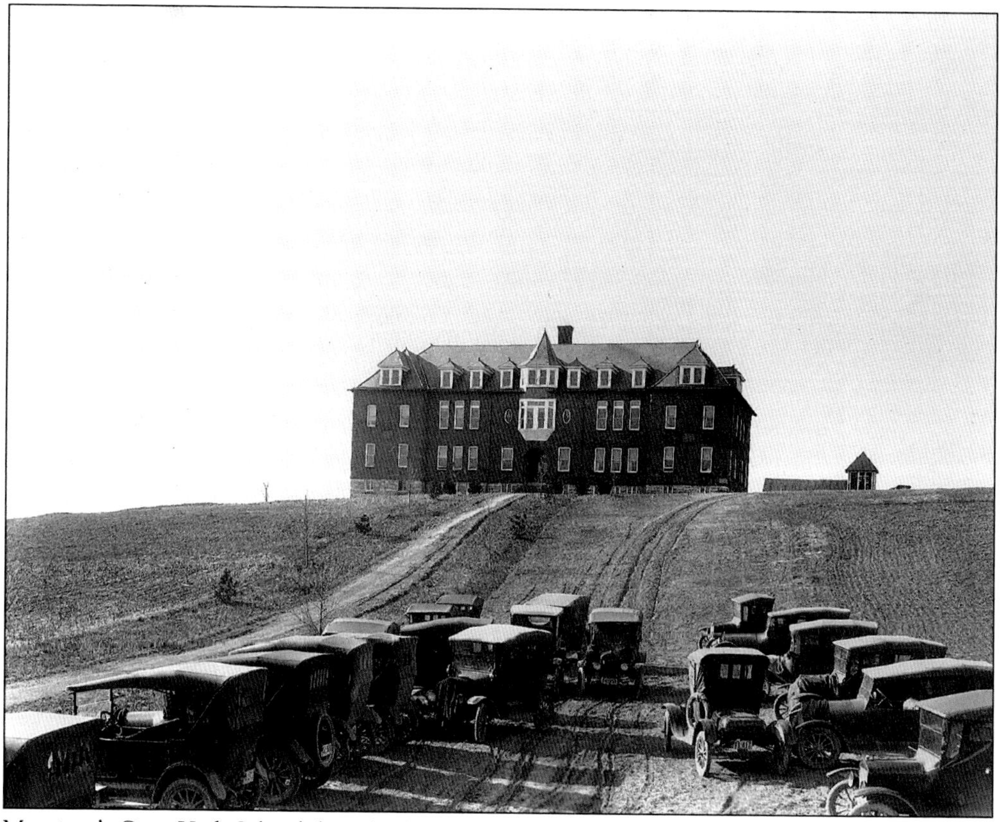

Morrison's Cove High School dates back to 1902, when ground was broken for the University of Southern Pennsylvania. The large stone building stood idle for years. Ownership with its 26 acres of campus passed to a Bellwood Bank. Edward E. Byers bought the property and opened a school for teachers. However, a secondary school was in great demand. In 1919, Byers opened the high school with 89 students. The cars belong to parents who came to attend Farmer's Week. Note that some of the cars are covered to keep the motor warm.

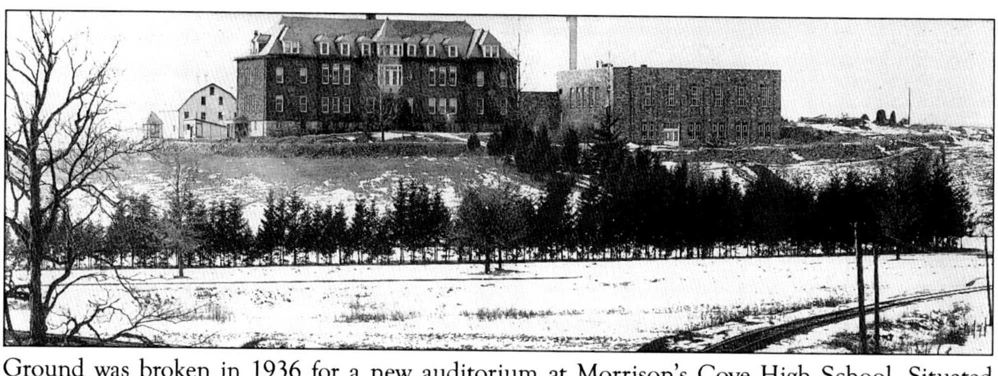

Ground was broken in 1936 for a new auditorium at Morrison's Cove High School. Situated near the main building, it was opened in September 1937 with a seating capacity of 800. The basement featured workrooms, lockers, showers, and a connection to the main building through corridors. One corridor was placed underground. Note the smokestack in the background and the barn on the left.

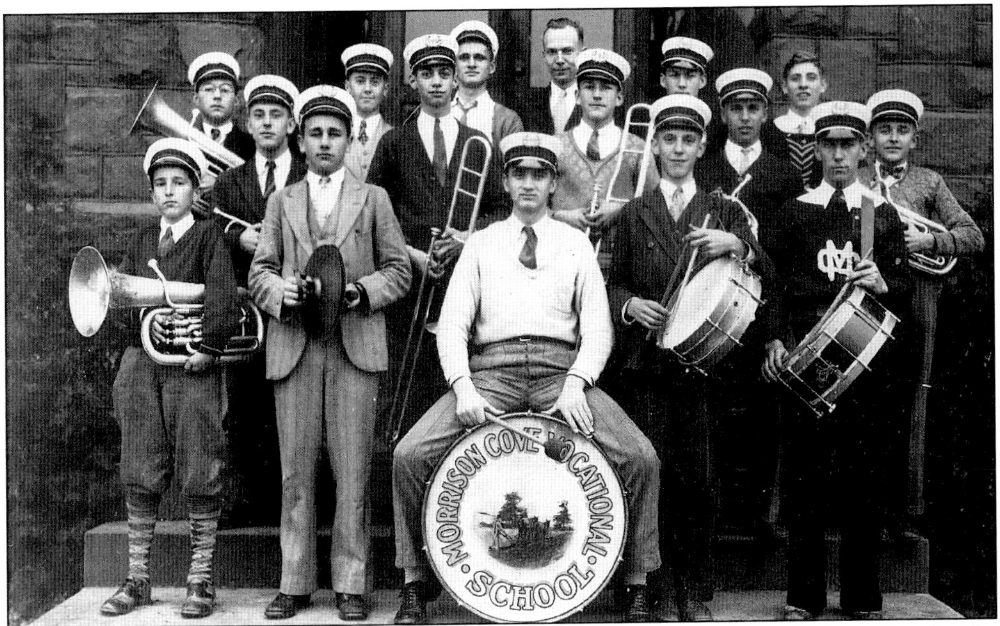

The orchestra was always ready to perform. This was especially evident in preparation for the annual Farmer's Week. One week each February, the students of Morrison's Cove High School had an opportunity to display their talents. All departments were represented. Singing, acting, performing on stage through music or entertainment, cooking, sewing, and shop for the boys were all part of the yearly demonstrations. Parents came to meet the teachers, and everyone had a role to play. The reward for the best in any given field was $5.

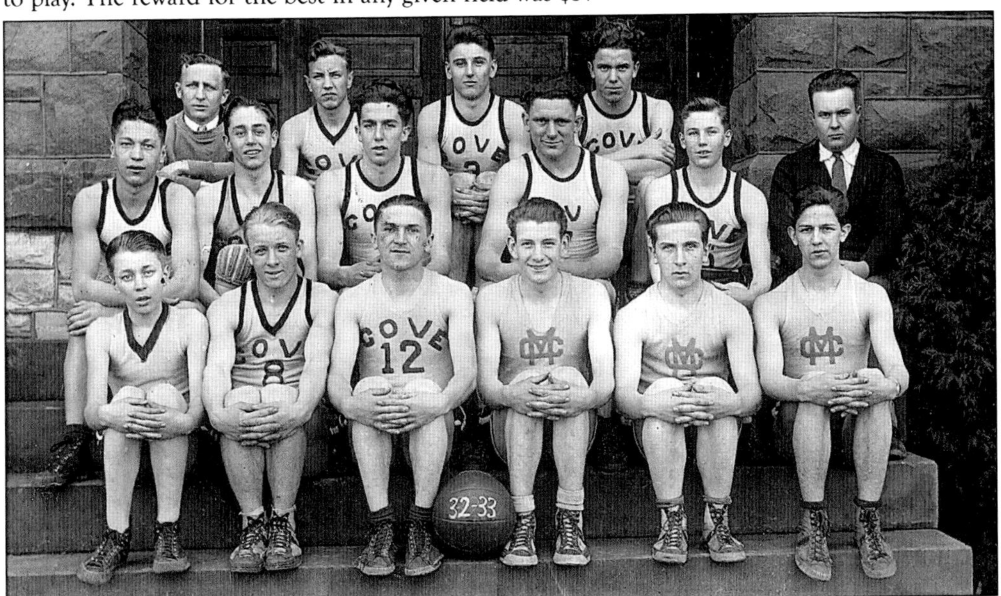

The basketball squad of 1932–1933 had a high standing in the Blair County Basketball League. Under the guidance of C.L. Provines, the coach, the interscholastic athletes achieved. The barn floor of the nearby Wyland farm served as the basketball court until the school gymnasium was complete. There was often rivalry among the neighboring Roaring Spring, Williamsburg, and Martinsburg teams.

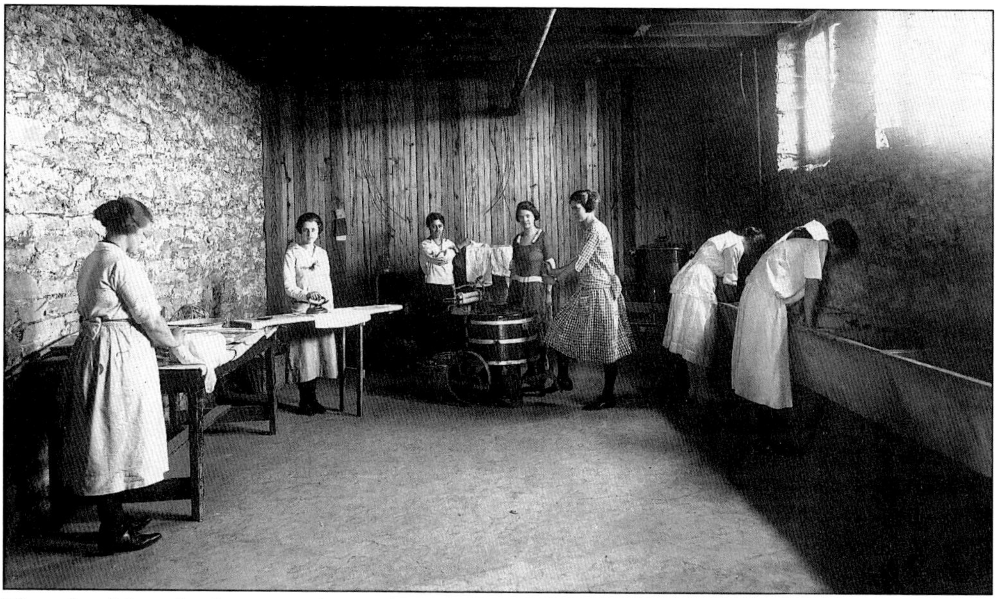

The school laundry became a busy place as Farmer's Week approached. In the right corner, a stove keeps the wash boiler hot. White clothes were boiled to keep them bright. Irons were heated on the stove. In this laundry, the washing machine was agitated by foot. The white wringer was attached to the tub and was then turned by hand. In 1922, electric washing machines were still in the future.

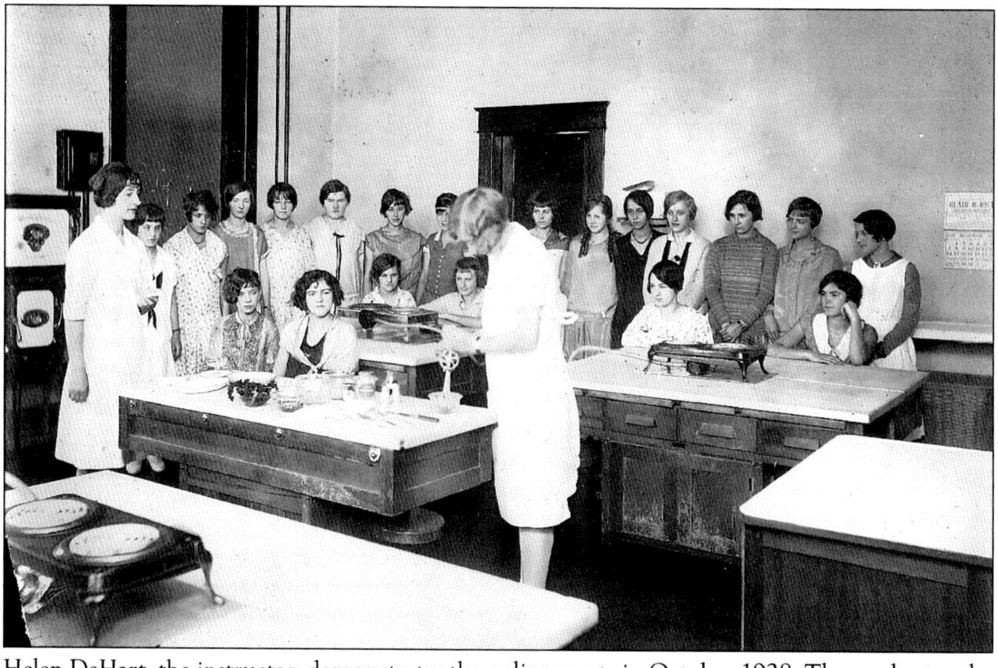

Helen DeHart, the instructor, demonstrates the culinary arts in October 1928. The egg beater she is using is the forerunner of the electric blender. A gas stove is on the left. Often, these stoves had a coal-burning section that sufficed for cooking in the wintertime. Note the hot plates used by the students. Refrigeration was not yet in most kitchens. The iceman would come around periodically to place a huge block of ice in the icebox.

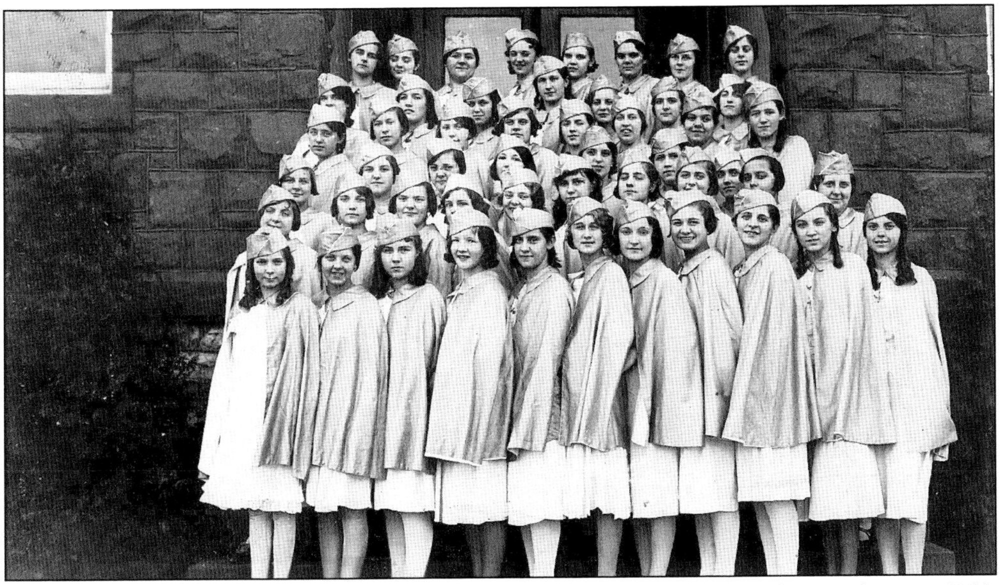

The school choir performs in uniform in January 1932. There were 50 members at the time. Fifth from the left in the second row is Wilma Guyer Mock, the mother of the current librarian, Joyce Mock Paden. Music and the fine arts were part of vocational school training. These were displayed during Farmer's Week, when parents and friends came to observe the students in action.

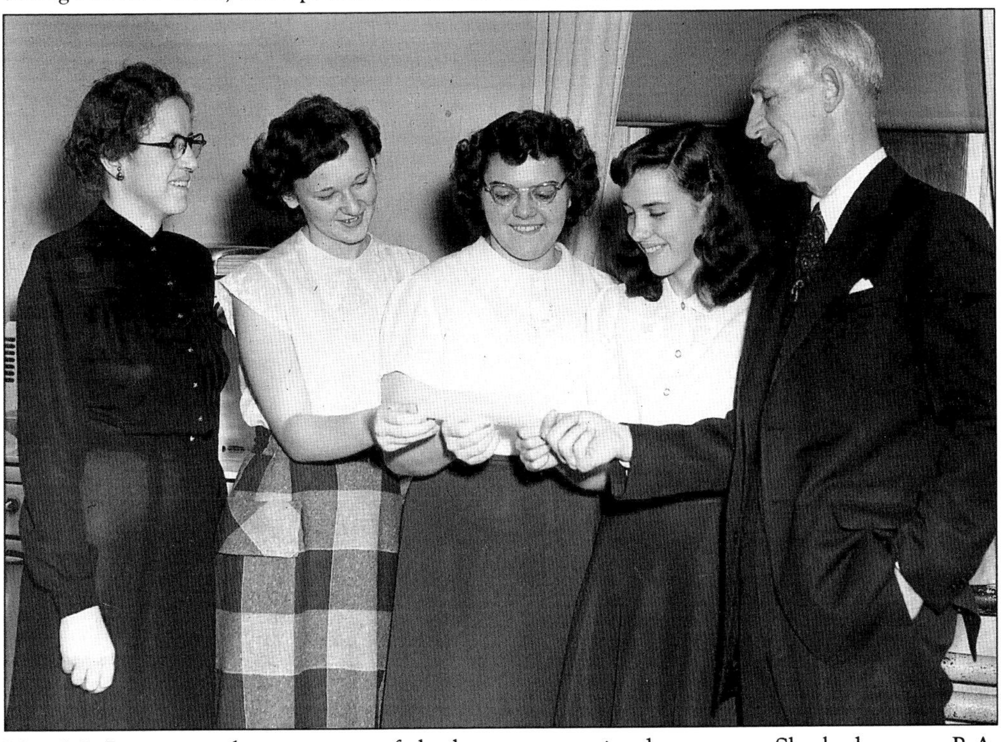

Mrs. L.J. Points was the instructor of the home economics department. She looks on as R.A. Matthews of Penelec distributes an award to three girls of Morrison's Cove High School. They won first place in the state in 1950. The girls are, from left to right, Betty Smith, Margaret Dilling, and Doris Stonerook.

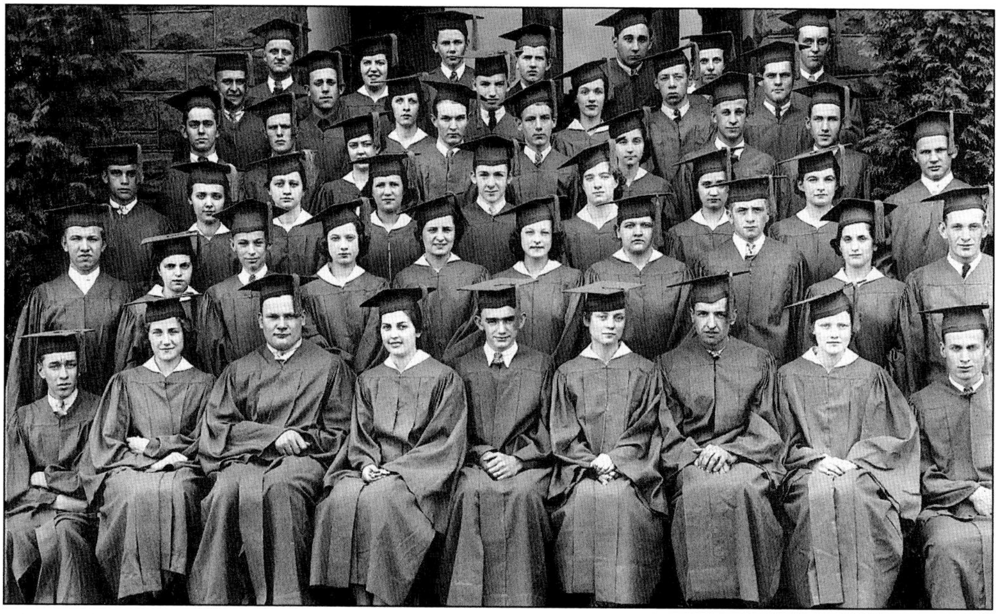

The graduates of 1936 celebrate a milestone in their young lives. Twenty-five of these students would return a half century later to celebrate their 50th anniversary and reminisce over their high-school days.

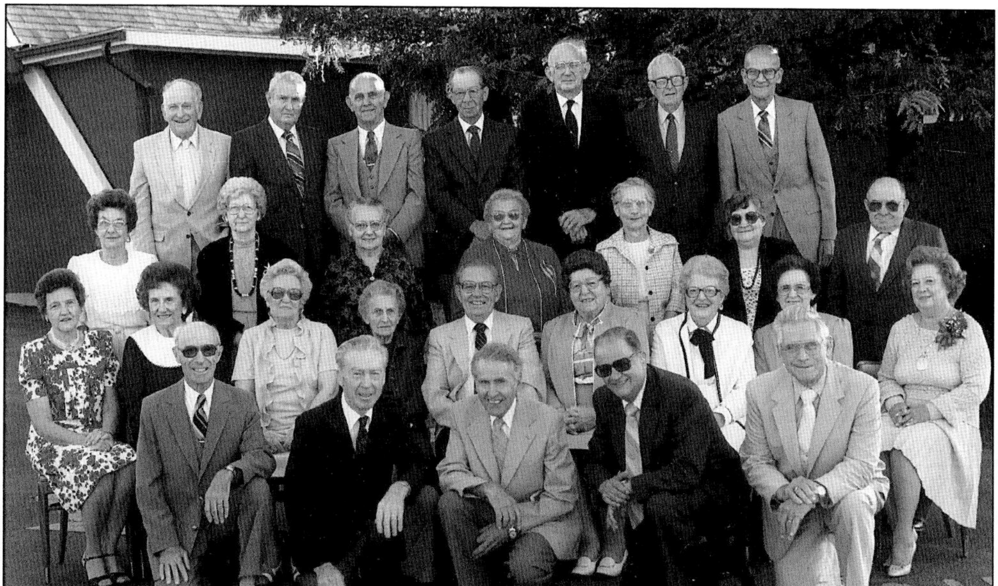

In August 1986, the Class of 1936 gathers for a reunion. From left to right are the following: (first row) Paul Leighty, Harold Shaw, Donald Horton, Clair Replogle, and Richard Brumburgh (second row) Rose Kyler Sell, Sara Replogle Ritchey, Romayne Keagy Gaston, Mary McKerihan (former teacher), Leon Kensigner (former teacher), Ella Ebersol (former teacher), Grace Shaw Shultz, Margaret Dodson Clarr, and Ada Knisley Pote; (third row) Jane Mentzer Bankert, Betty Langham Pittman, Florence Kauffman Miller, Ruth Hinton Gordon, Elad Kanode, Isabel Drake Dixon, and James Baker; (fourth row) Fred Wyland, Edward Guyer, Albert Gochnour, William Leighty, Dean Walter, Byron Gahagan, and David Metzker.

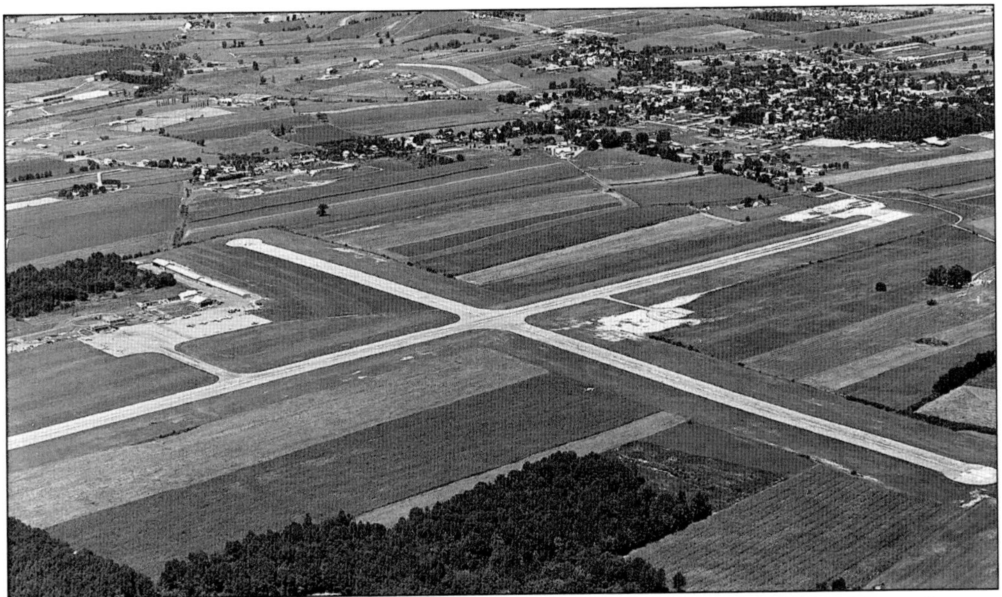

The runways of the Altoona–Blair County Airport were originally 3,700 and 4,400 feet–adequate at the time the airport was established. They were constructed of bituminous pavement on an aggregate base. The endings of each runway had a concrete circular turning button 150 feet in diameter. Huge crowds assembled at the airport in Martinsburg on October 22, 1938, to witness air maneuvers and hear the address given by Gov. George Earle. The airport was officially opened and was called the Cove Airport.

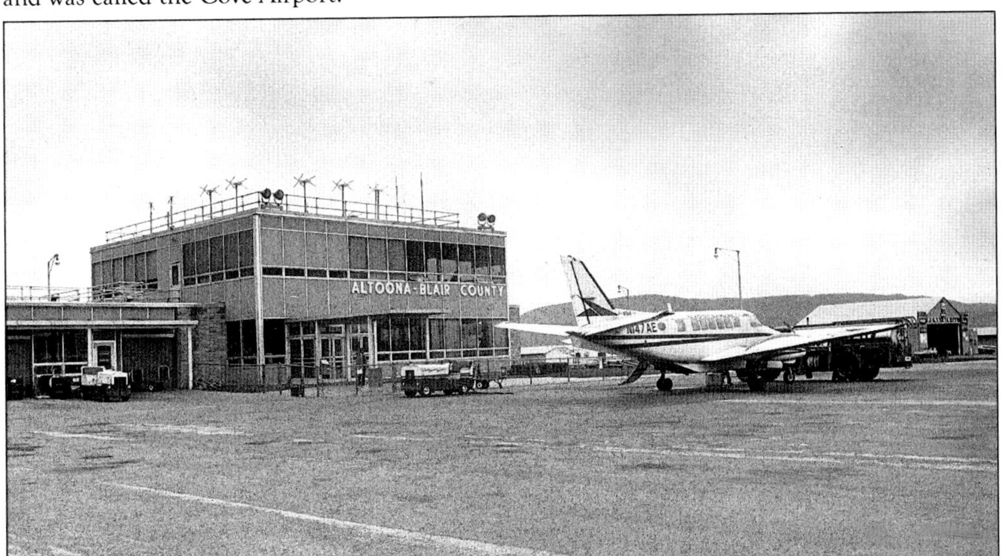

The building constructed in 1959 was a state-of-the-art facility at that time. The airport originated in Duncansville. The need for an emergency landing field and greater expansion led the Pennsylvania Board of Aeronautics to acquire land south of Martinsburg in 1936 and establish the airport in the heart of Morrison's Cove. It has undergone many changes. In 1944, it was leased by the City of Altoona and became the Altoona–Blair County Airport. The airport served many pilots who were caught in unexpected inclement weather or who encountered mechanical difficulties.

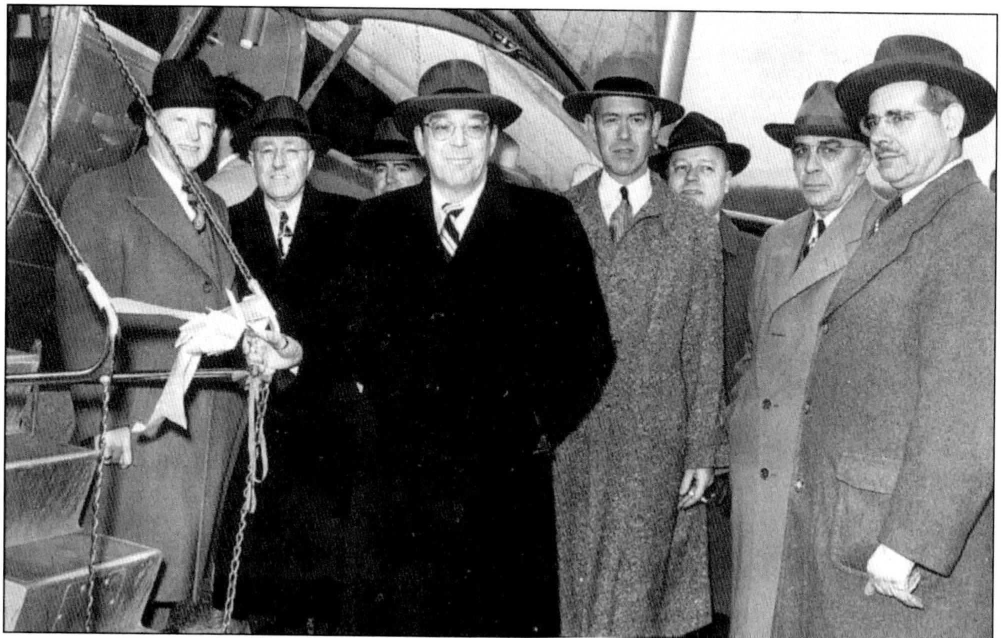

The inaugural program got under way with a ribbon-cutting ceremony at the Altoona–Blair County Airport on March 28, 1949. This marked the initial flight of American Airlines passenger service. The participants are Edgar C. Magill, Milton S. Emeigh, J. Lester Laughlin, William S. Eardley, Forrest L. Bartholomew, G. Stanley Ruth, Herbert S. Bolger, and Martin Goodman.

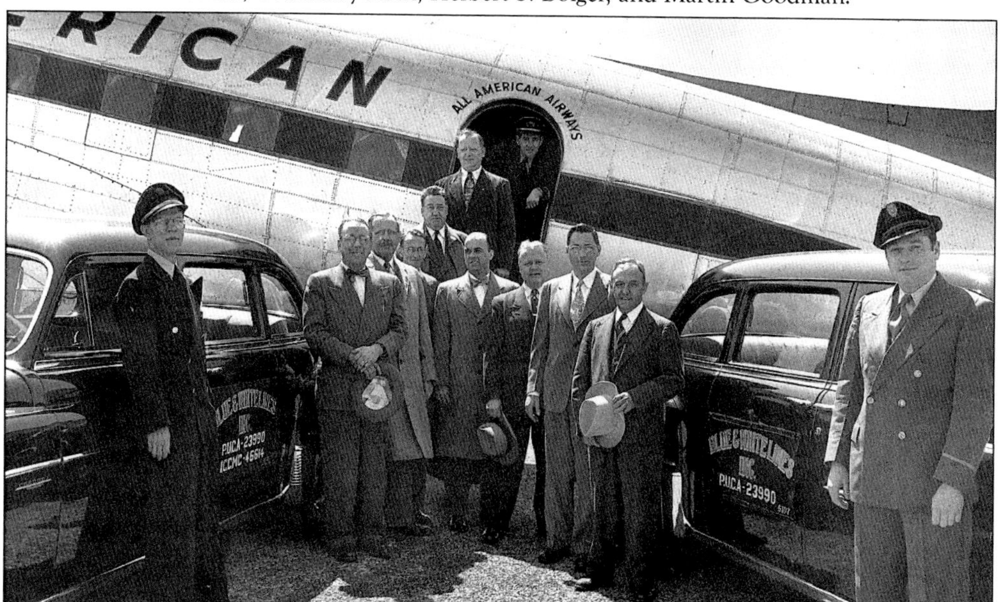

This group was among the first to take advantage of the new airport. In 1936, a small terminal building was constructed and was situated in the picturesque valley that affords unusual views of the rich surrounding farmland. American Airlines and Allegheny Airlines were among the first to service the area. Allegheny Airlines began commercial passenger service in 1949. The Blue and White Lines was a taxi service to the Penn Alto Hotel in Altoona. The airport occupies 89.6 acres in Cove Valley.

This airmail envelope was aboard an experimental pick up 63 years ago. It was on the first airmail flight leaving the area. The document carries the postmark of 10:30 a.m. on July 2, 1939. The canceled airmail stamp cost 6¢. The historic document recently made its way back from Chicago. It was gladly received by Charles Pillar, manager of the Altoona–Blair County Airport. The initial venture of the envelope transpired during an era of early commercial aviation.

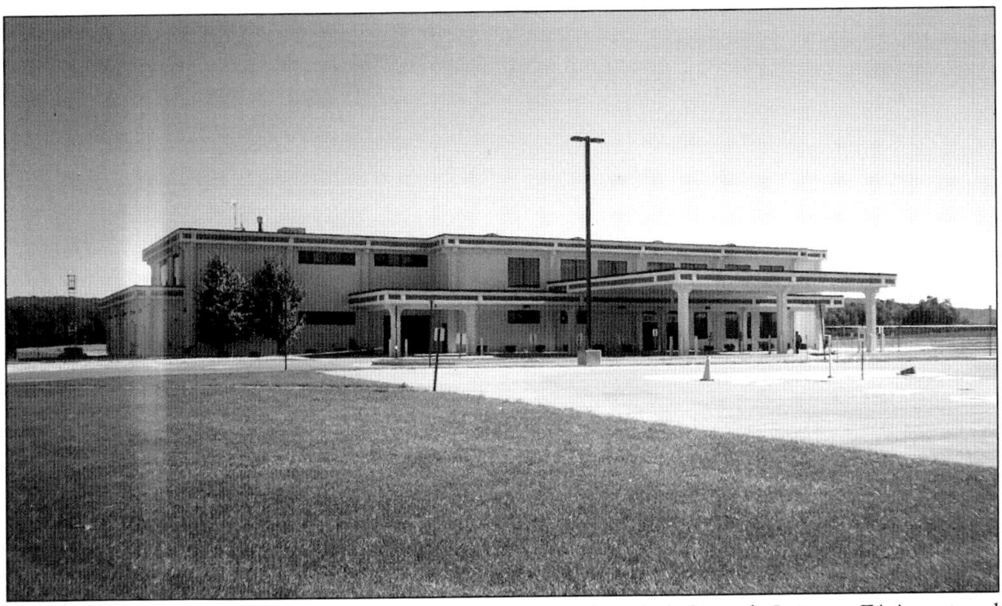

In October 1996, a $5 million terminal was completed and dedicated. It is an FAA regional automated flight service station. The airport services many passenger flights between Pittsburgh and Martinsburg daily. It occupies 89.6 acres in Cove Valley and includes a restaurant known as Kitty Hawk.

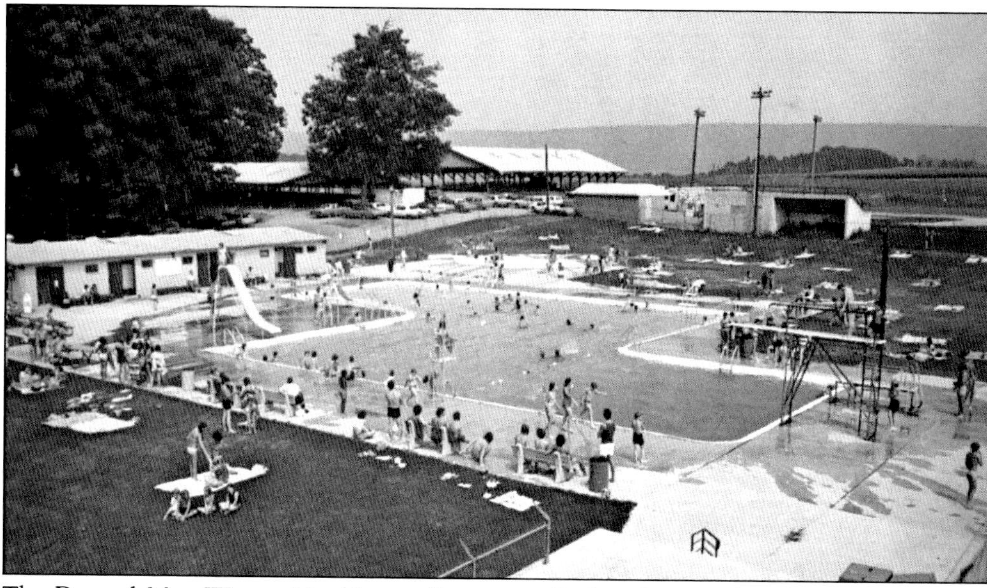

The Dr. and Mrs. Warren Hershberger Swimming Pool in Memorial Park was dedicated on May 30, 1966. The Hershbergers were prominent citizens whose ancestors date back to before the Revolutionary War. John Dilling was president of the park association and helped make the park a reality. The street is named for him. The most significant program held in the park was the Wedding of the Roads, which celebrated the formal opening of Piney Creek and Clover Creek Roads when they were macadamized in 1931.

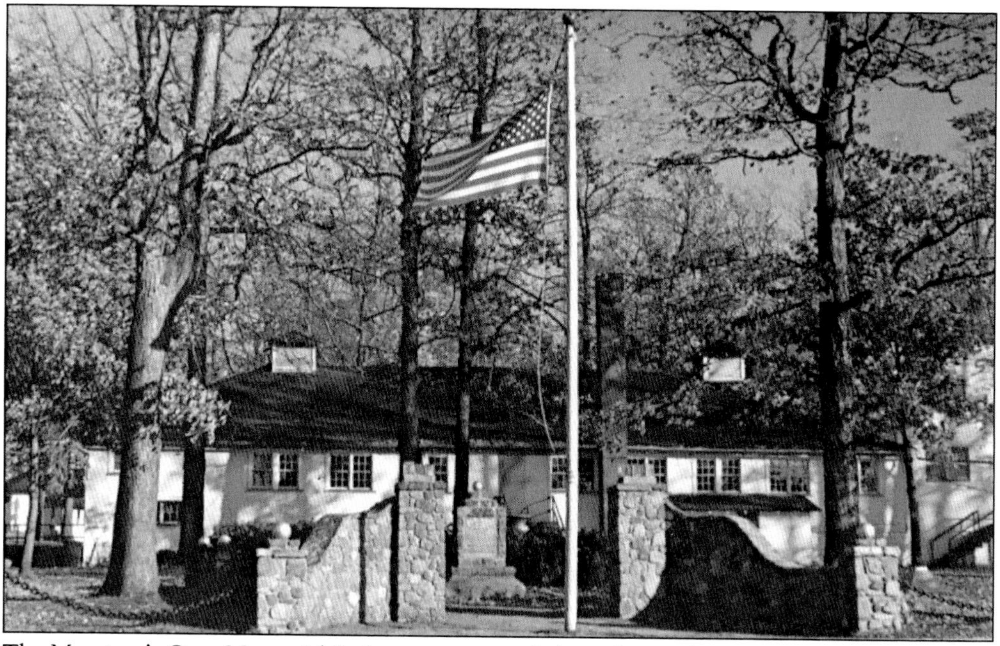

The Morrison's Cove Memorial Park entrance was dedicated on July 4, 1934. It was constructed in memory of the Morrison's Cove servicemen. The stone is from the Gettysburg battlefield, the chain from the USS *Dever* battleship, and the cannonballs from Wellsville, New York. A new building replaces the white structure. Martinsburg has always had a grove. Assemblies met in the shade of the old oaks. The property was purchased from Mary Ashcom in 1922.

Seven

Where the Mountains Meet

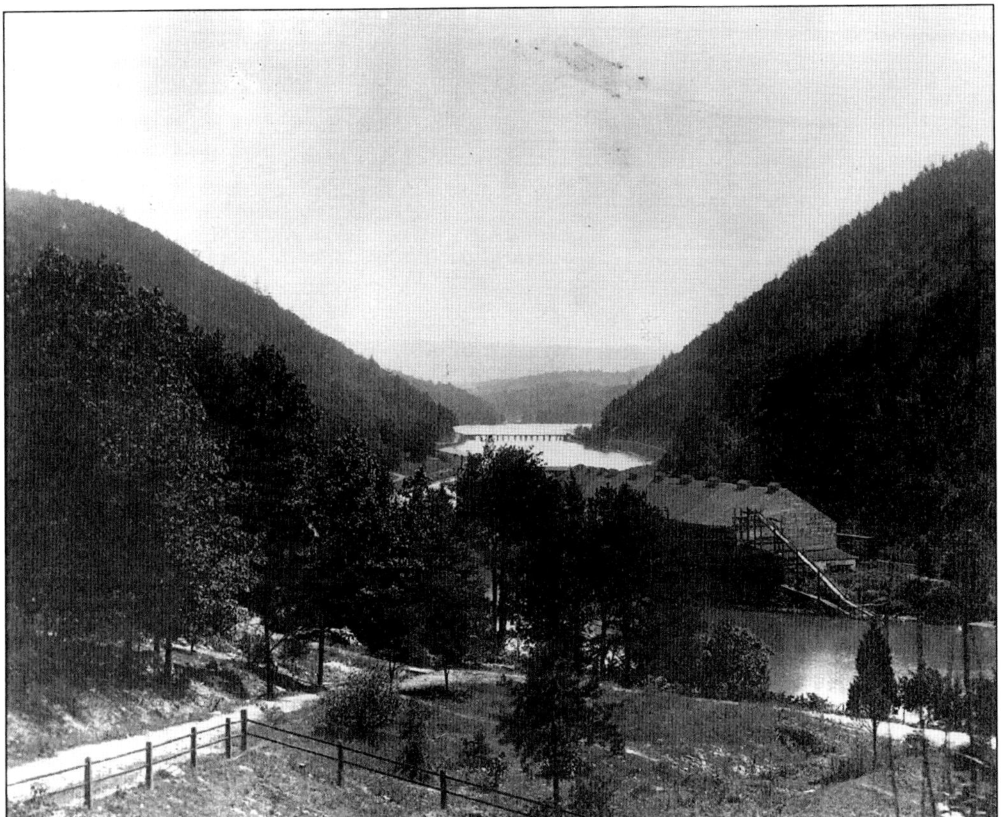

The gap is a natural, picturesque wonder. It is formed by Brush and Lock Mountains, which rise on either side. The Juniata River flows through the gap toward Three Mile Dam. Note the icehouse for the railroad in the right foreground. Barricading the water was necessary to service the icehouse. The scene is taken from the heights of Point View in the Ganister area.

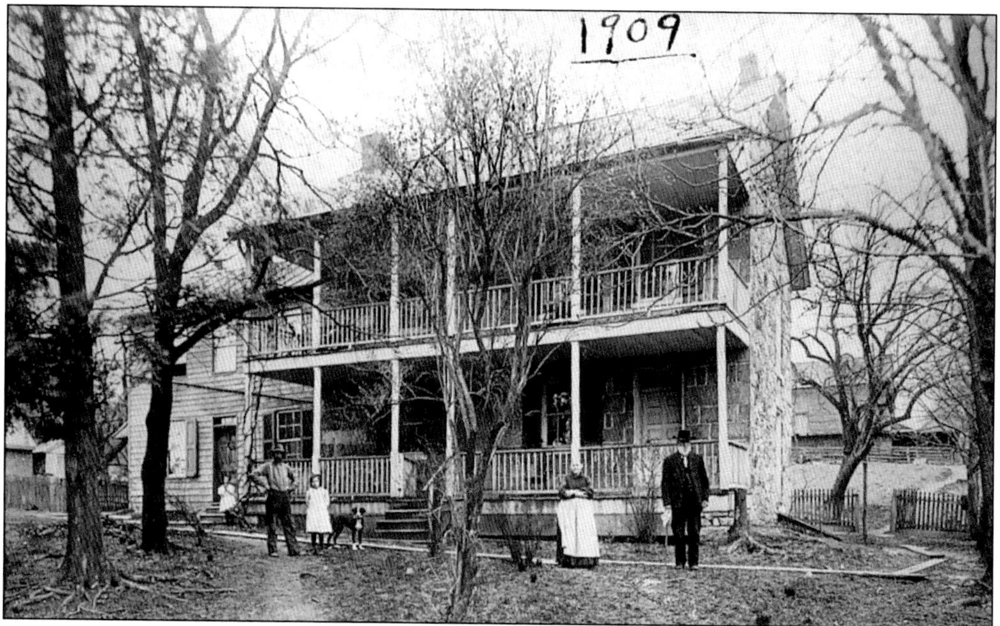

The scenic beauty and abundant spring waters of the Williamsburg area were attractive to Jacob Ake in 1790. It was his chosen site for a settlement. He bought 600 acres and established his family on the north side of the Juniata River. His early gristmills derived power from the big spring. He had his holdings surveyed and then established a school. He donated land for churches and always had the welfare of the village in mind. Originally called Aketown, the area was renamed for Jacob Ake's son William.

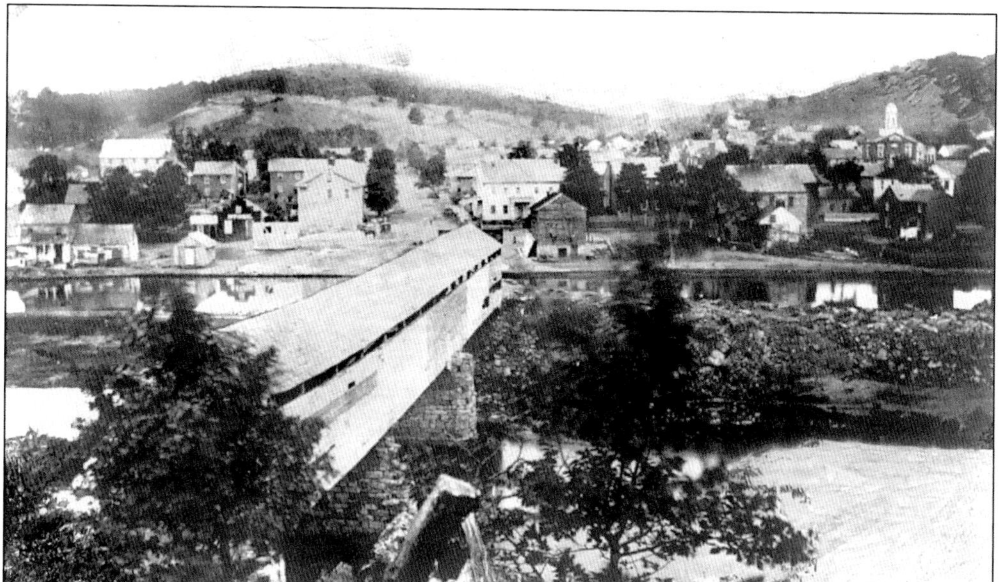

The covered bridge was the first to span the Juniata River at this site. It was one of the earliest bridges in Williamsburg. The scene faces Williamsburg from what would later be the Blair County Children's Home. Note the original Lutheran church in the upper right. The bridge was built prior to 1850 and served the hamlet until 1873, when a steel one was constructed. The town grew rapidly and, by 1818, 34 houses dotted the already magnificent landscape.

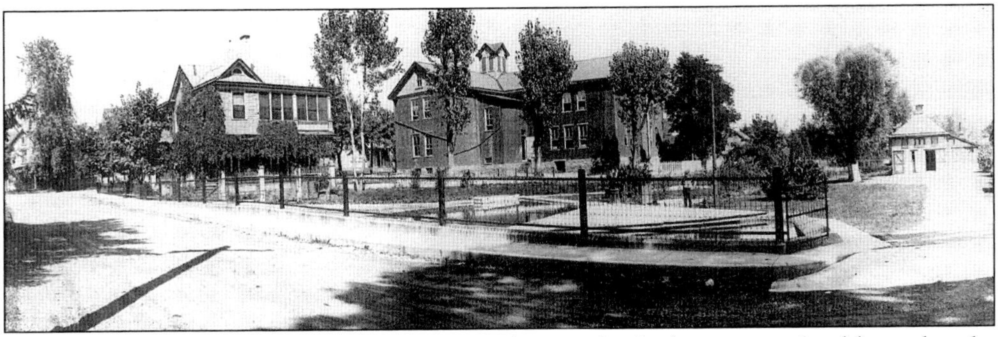

The clubhouse at Big Spring stood beside an eight-room brick elementary school located at the southern end of High Street. The building served as a meeting place for early settlers and later became a bed-and-breakfast facility.

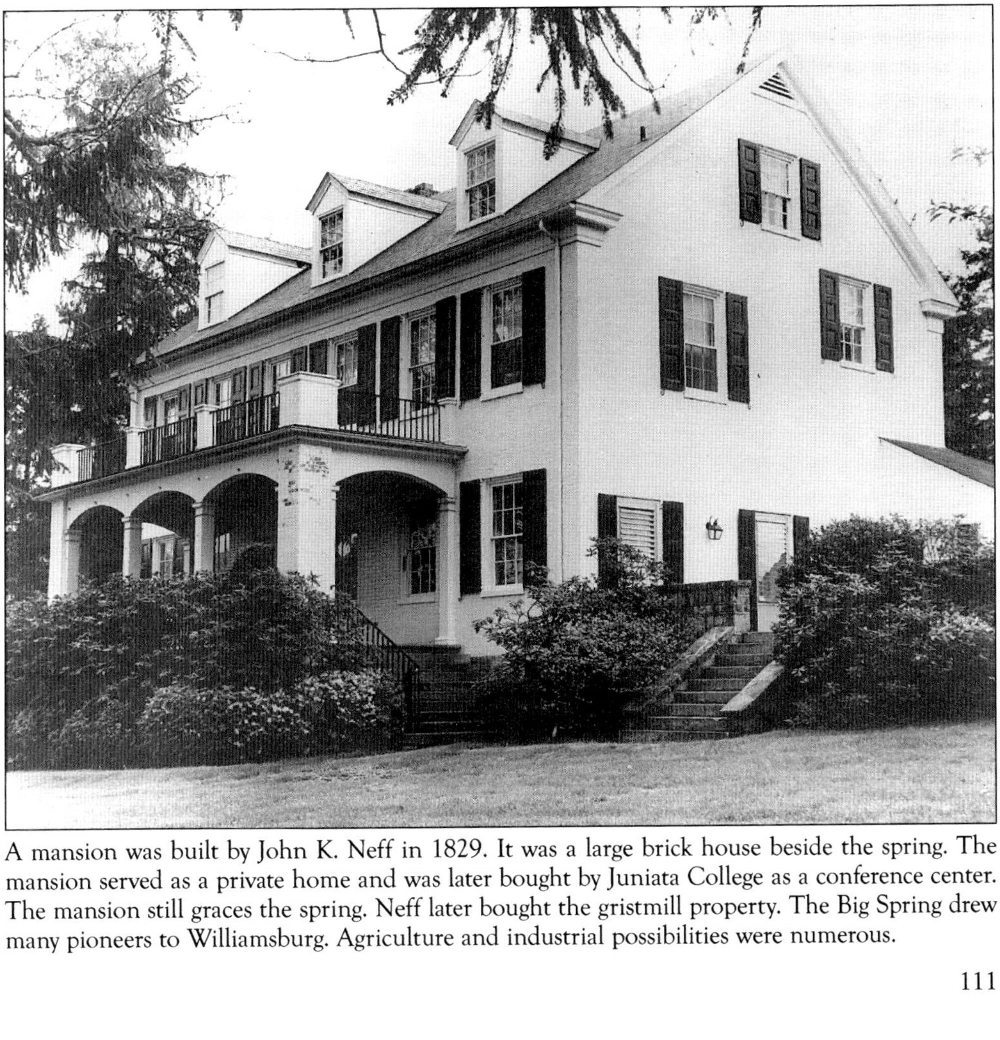

A mansion was built by John K. Neff in 1829. It was a large brick house beside the spring. The mansion served as a private home and was later bought by Juniata College as a conference center. The mansion still graces the spring. Neff later bought the gristmill property. The Big Spring drew many pioneers to Williamsburg. Agriculture and industrial possibilities were numerous.

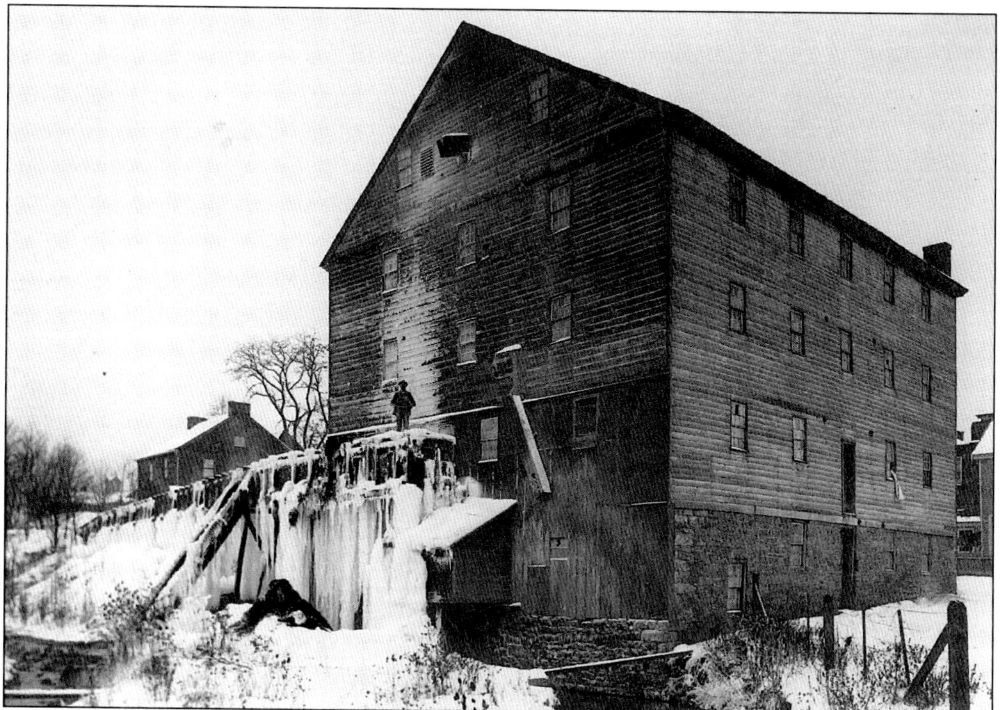

This gristmill,-with its double waterwheel, was located on Second Street in Williamsburg. Such thick ice is typical of mountain regions in midwinter. In its heyday, the gristmill was a vital source of food for the hamlet dwellers. The original direction of the water in the race from Big Spring to the waterwheels was eventually changed.

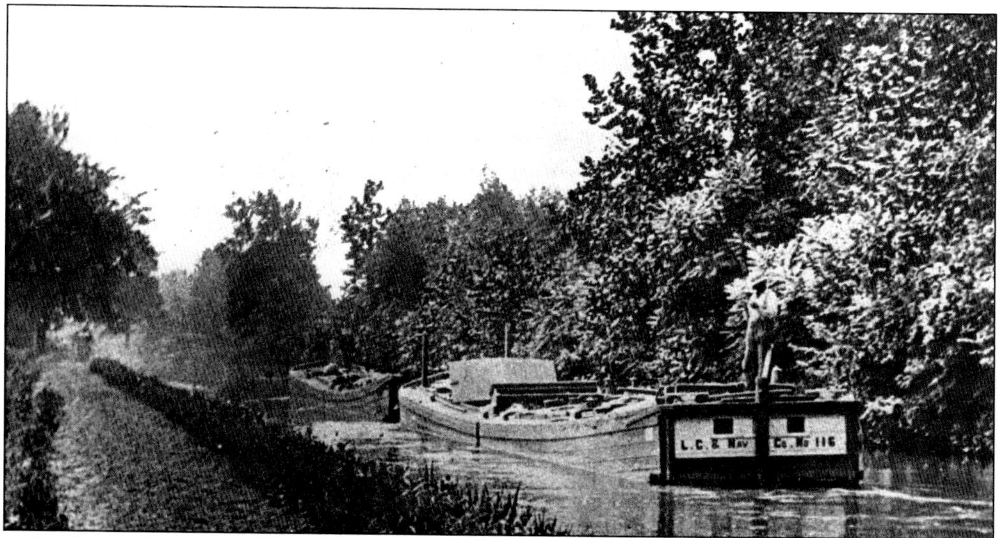

Packard boats came up the canal from the east and connected with Hollidaysburg. Here, they would be loaded on to the Old Portage Railroad for the trip over the Allegheny Mountains. Note the split in the center of each boat. Most canal craft could be separated in the middle when they reached the mountains in order to be transported on to the rail cars of the inclined planes. The canal of 1832 lured passengers by offering a journey of only three and a half days from Philadelphia to Pittsburgh.

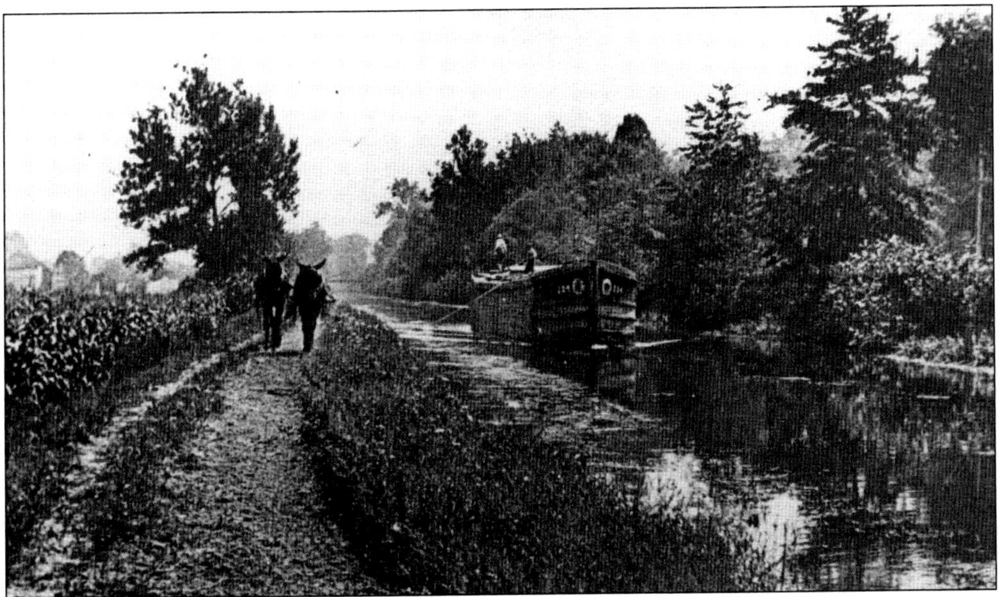

The mules and towline are on the path, with the tender behind. Other mules rested in the stable on board and were switched at regular intervals. The idea of a canal route over the mountain emerged from a meeting of the Board of Canal Commissioners in 1824. An all-water route would have necessitated a four-mile tunnel through the Allegheny Mountains. The Old Portage Railroad, with its 10 inclines, was the more feasible route in 1832.

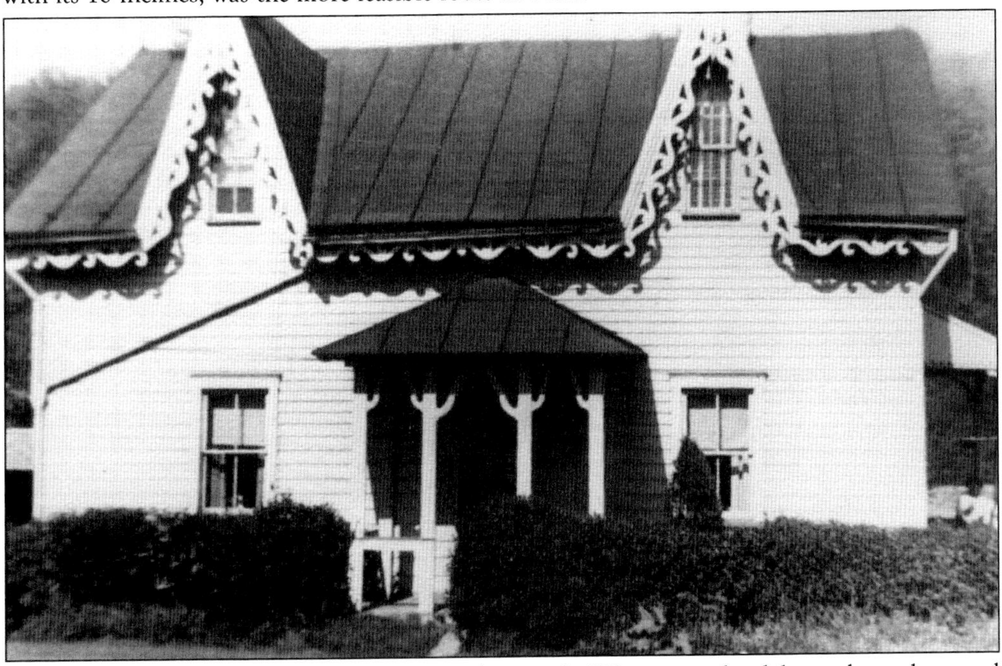

The lock tender's house was located near the canal. When a packard boat along the canal approached a lock, the steersman sounded a horn and the lock master prepared the lock for the boat to pass through. There were four dams and 15 locks between Williamsburg and Hollidaysburg. Later, this site became the drainage basins for Penelec. The house was last occupied by the Joseph Cramer family.

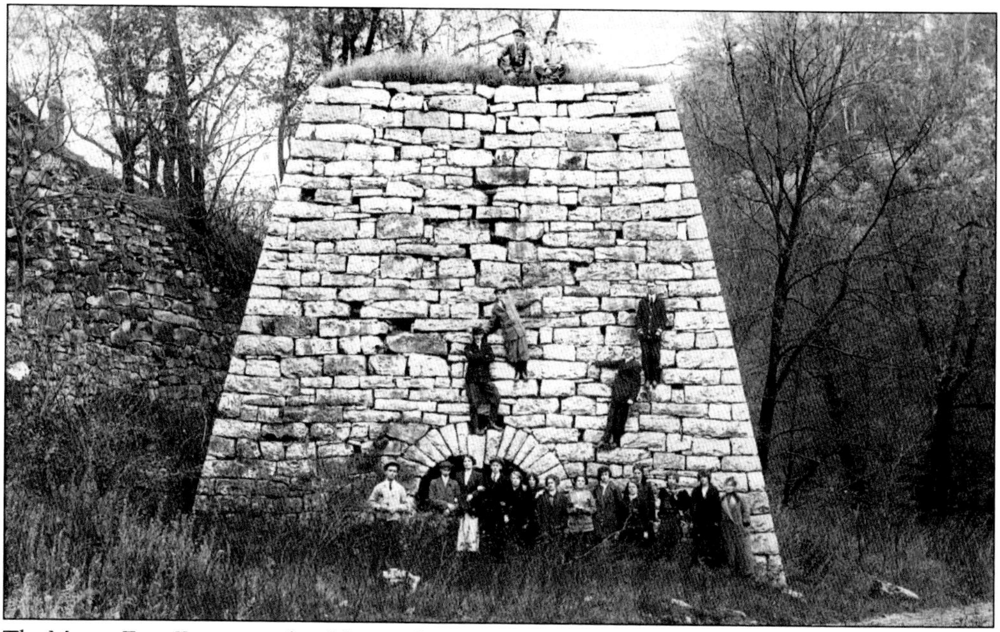

The Mount Etna Furnace is the oldest in the county. Built in 1808 by John Cannon, David Steward, and a Mr. Moore, it reached its peak during the Civil War. In 1849, Etna Furnace turned out 1,000 tons of pig iron with 100 employees and produced 600 tons of blossom iron with 30 employees. The remains of the furnace lingered on after its closing in 1877. The truncated pyramid has been restored. It is now a complete and nostalgic monument of the past.

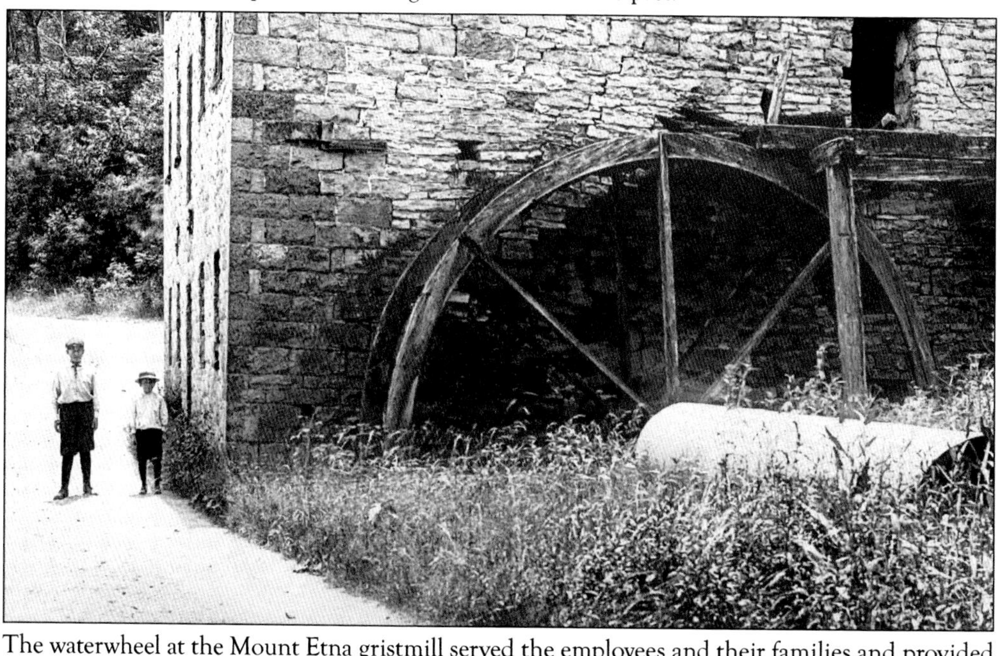

The waterwheel at the Mount Etna gristmill served the employees and their families and provided water for the forge. The forge was once an industrial site for the preparation of limestone used in the iron industry. In 1823, David Steward, ancestor of the famous Jimmy Steward, became the sole owner. He was followed by other owners. It was located in Catherine Township. A settlement clustered around the site that was long known as Mount Etna.

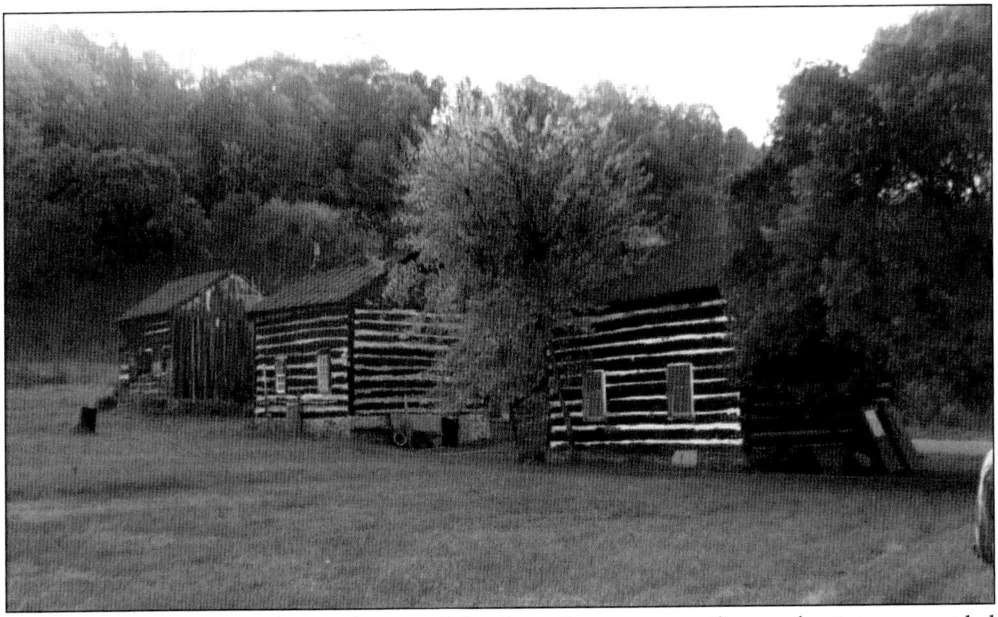

Cabins were erected for the employees of the forge. Ironmasters of an early vintage provided shelter for their employees by erecting these small cabins. Owners managed their establishments like the feudal mansions of Europe. Employees lived in these cabins and were dependent on their masters for the necessities of life. All purchases were made at the company store, including food, clothing, and medicine.

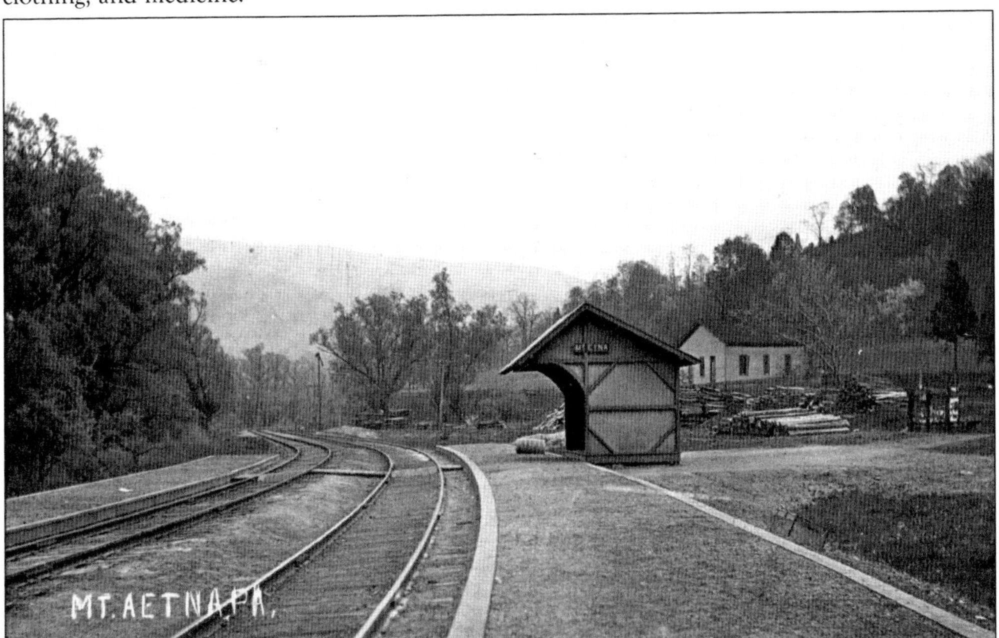

Mount Etna grew to a large and diversified settlement of more than 20,000 acres. The population soared and the settlement evolved into a town with its own small railroad station. The one-room schoolhouse at Mount Etna stands in the background. Although it has been more than 120 years since Mount Etna was an active furnace, many of the buildings have survived the ravages of time.

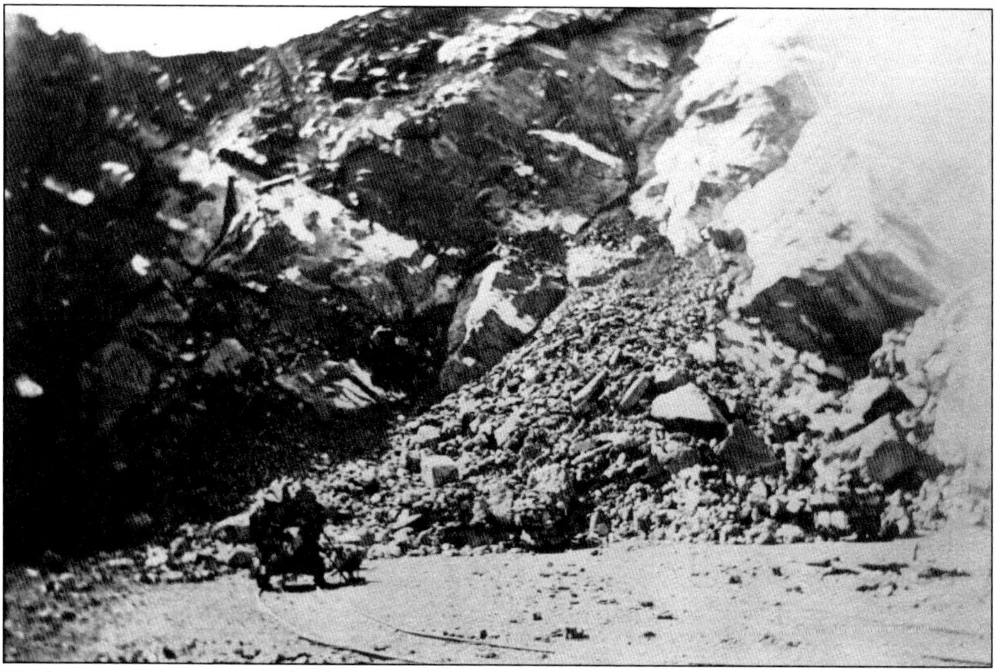

Ten limestone quarries were built along Tussy and Lock Mountains. Limestone was very prevalent in the area. The quarries employed 2,000 men. Iron ore of Blair County is fossil ore estimated to be 400 million years old. Pockets of ore and limestone are scattered in the mountains throughout the county.

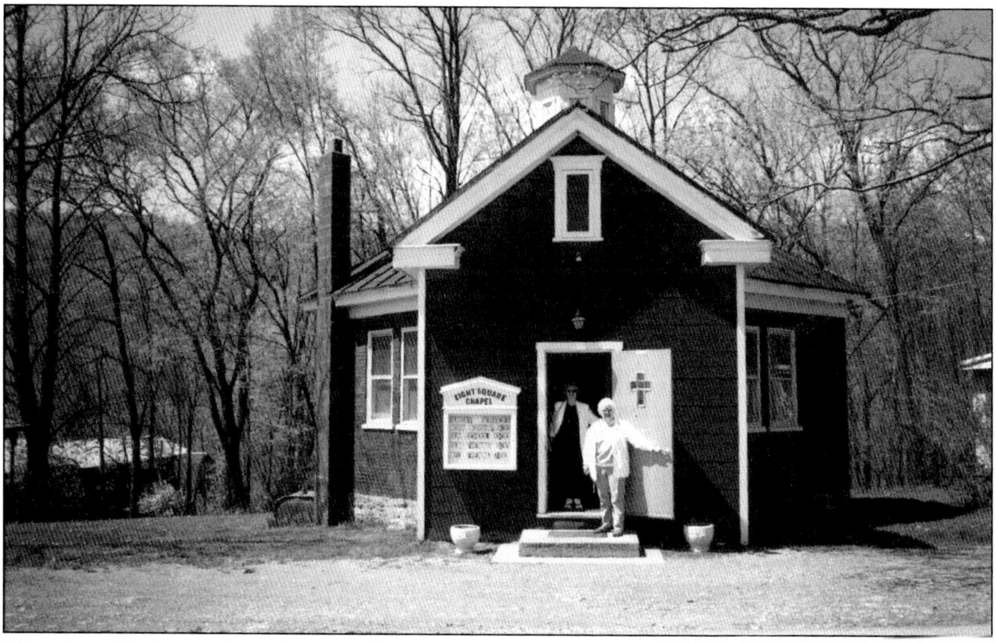

The eight-sided chapel was built on Piney Road in 1834. For many years, it served as the Good School. The Brethern of Christ Chapel was established here in 1942. Octagonal buildings were so constructed to eliminate acute angles and economize on space. The eight-sided building continues to grace the landscape.

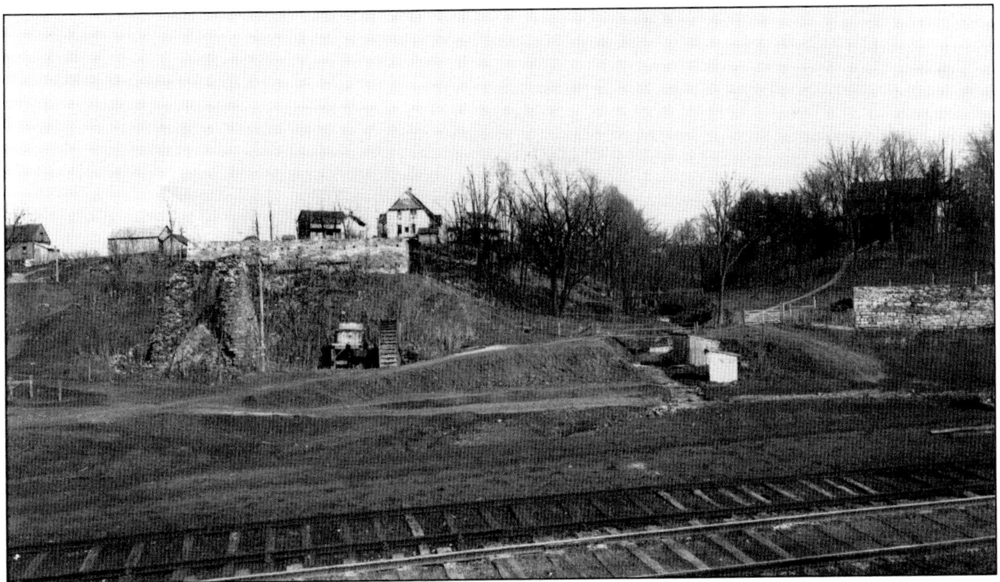

John Royer was the ironmaster of Cove Forge. He owned tracts of land on Tussy Mountain along Williamsburg's Sky Line Drive. He employed many men at the site. In 1815, he and his brother purchased land in Piney Creek, where they had the natural ingredients for the manufacture of pig iron. Ore, limestone, waterpower, and fuel were found in abundance. They made the best-quality cannonballs for the Union army during the Civil War.

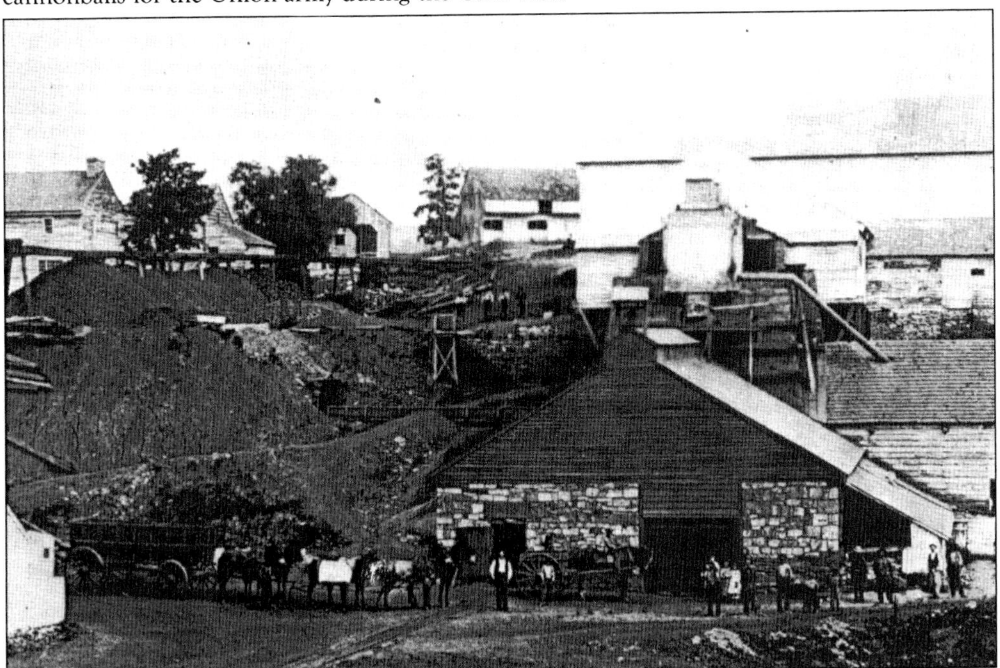

The Royer brothers established a small village known as Springfield. They built a furnace adjoining the ore veins and a limestone quarry. The little village was complete with cottages for employees, a store, sawmill, gristmill, and many necessities of a plantation. His furnace was built into the side of a hill so that ore, limestone, charcoal, and flux could be placed into the furnace at the top. This created a glowing spectacle at night.

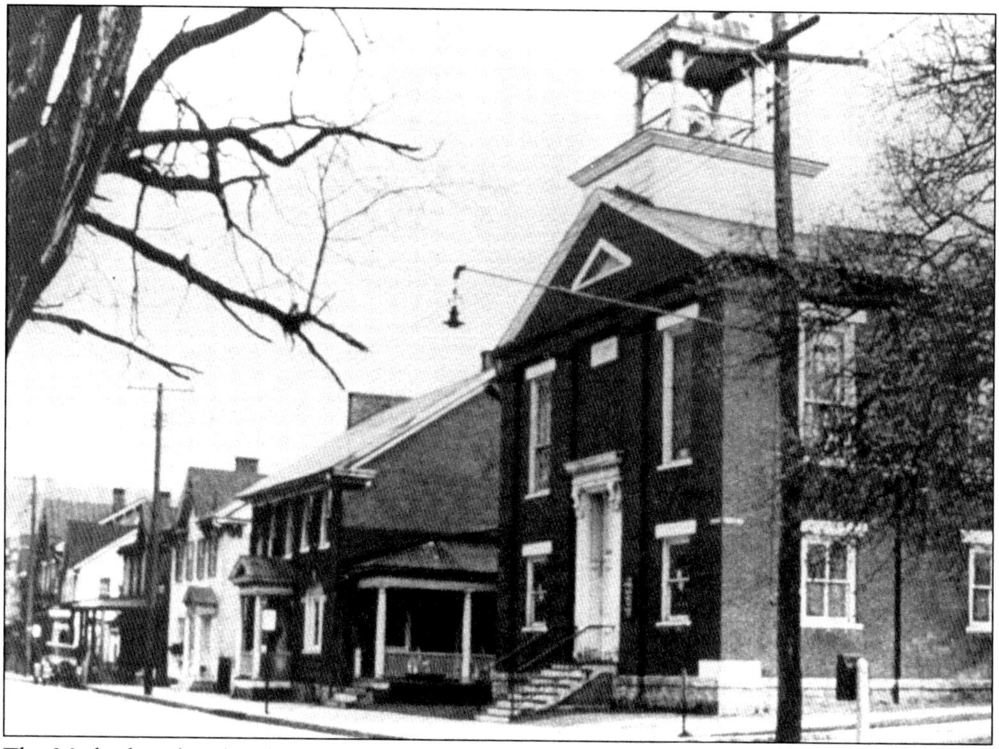

The Methodist church, Fluke's General Store, Kellers House, and the parsonage were located on Second Street *c.* 1900. The Methodist congregation dates back to 1792, when circuit riders brought the faith to the settlement. The founding father, Jacob Ake, was a Catholic who permitted the Methodist congregation to have meetings in his home. Ake donated property for the church on Second Street. The new Methodist church was built in 1951.

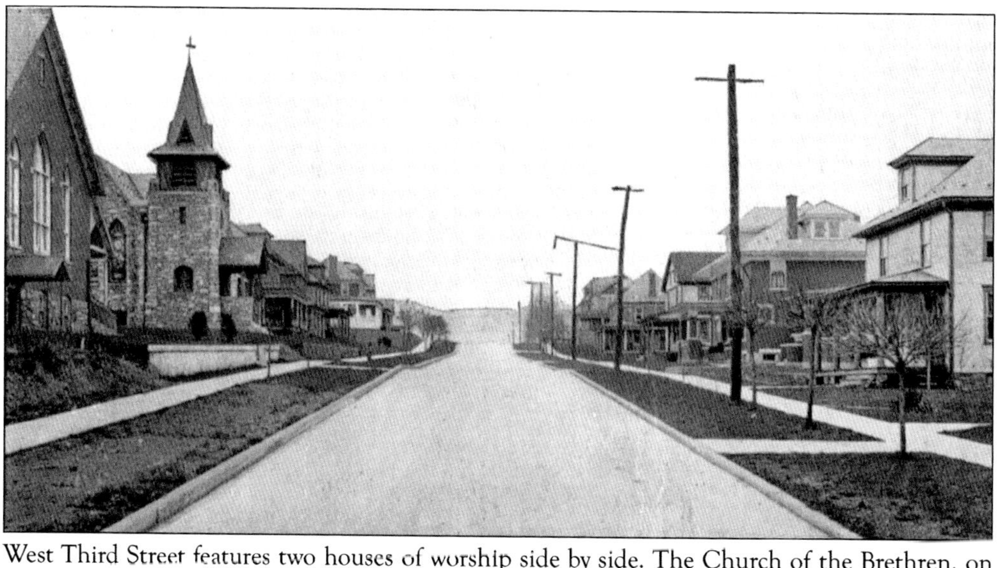

West Third Street features two houses of worship side by side. The Church of the Brethren, on the extreme left, is followed by the gray stone Reformed church, now known as Trinity Church of Christ. Third Street was paved with cement in 1914. The Williamsburg High School also stands on Third Street.

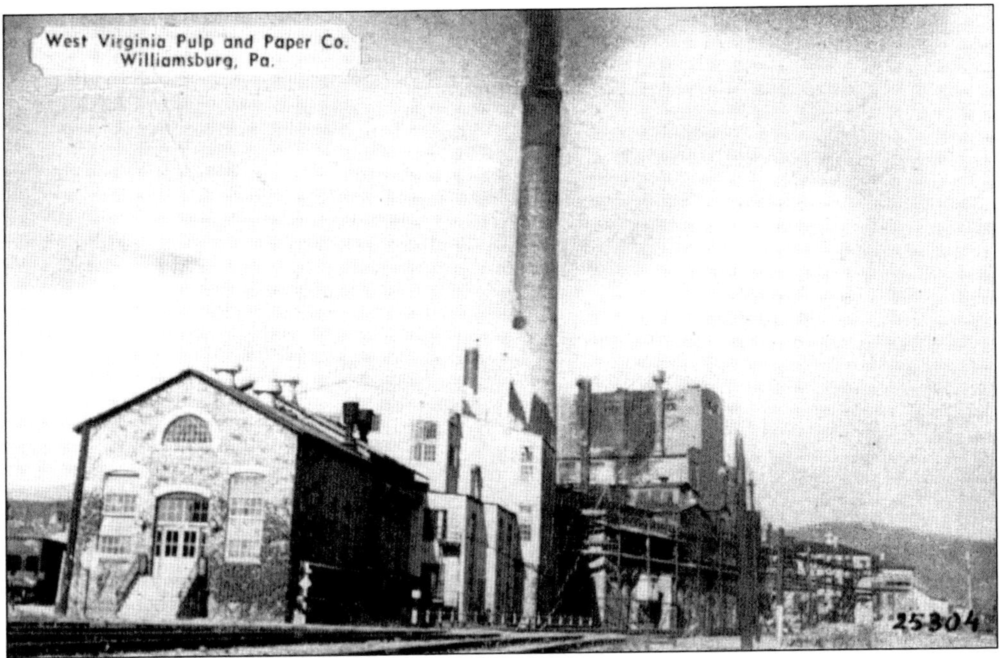

A paper mill was established in Williamsburg early in the 20th century. With the financial help of hometown celebrity Charles Schwab, the business got underway and the cornerstone was laid in 1903. The mill was powered from the Big Spring. Books and blank books were turned out here. The generating plant for the mill is on the left. It was closed in 1975. Fortunately, the town had previously acquired an envelope factory that gave employment to many former mill workers.

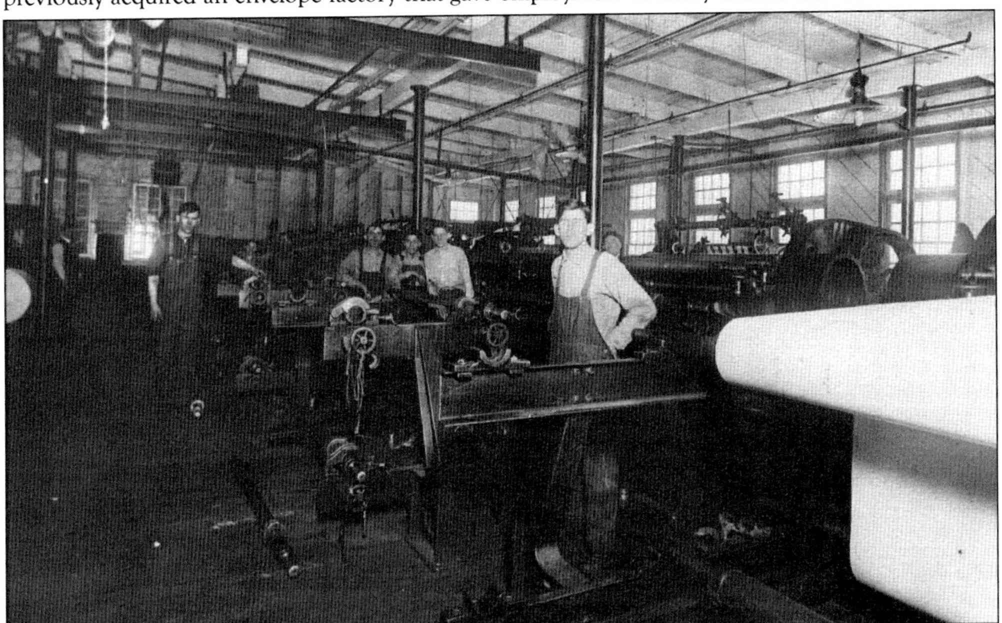

This is the finishing room of the paper mill in 1930. The mill turned out a high-quality lithograph paper. Lengths of wood were placed in the jaws of a giant steel chopper. This began the process of changing wood pulp into paper. The Williamsburg plant consolidated with the West Virginia Pulp and Paper Company.

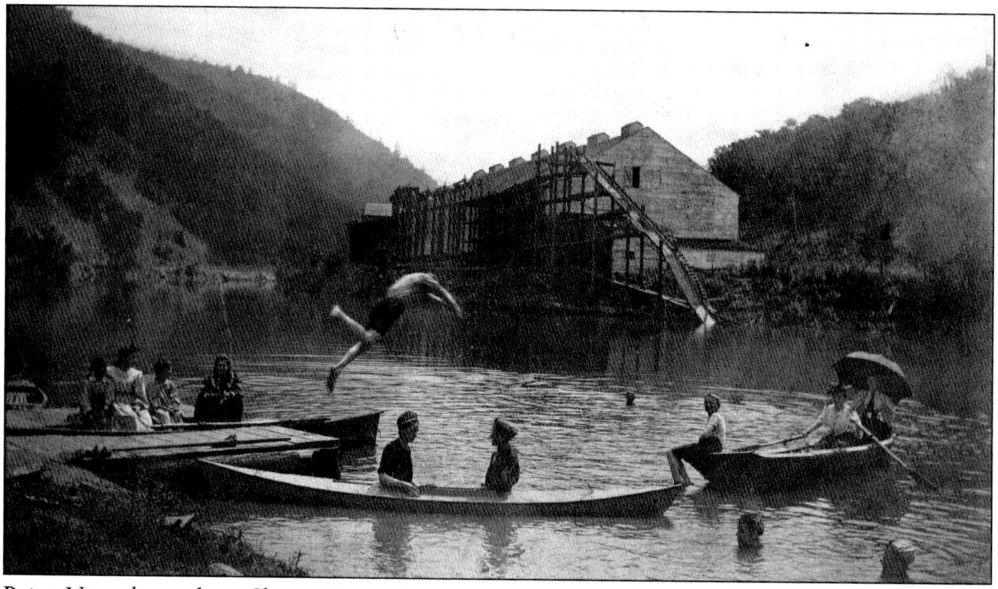

Point View, located on Short Mountain, was inviting on a hot summer day. The Frankstown branch of the Juniata River flowed through the settlement, and youngsters were quick to seize an opportunity for water frolicks. The railroad icehouse in the background was located between the river and the dam. When ice was ready for harvest, it was cut into strips, pulled up on an elevator, and stored in the icehouse for the following summer's cold storage. Some ice was cut into blocks for home delivery.

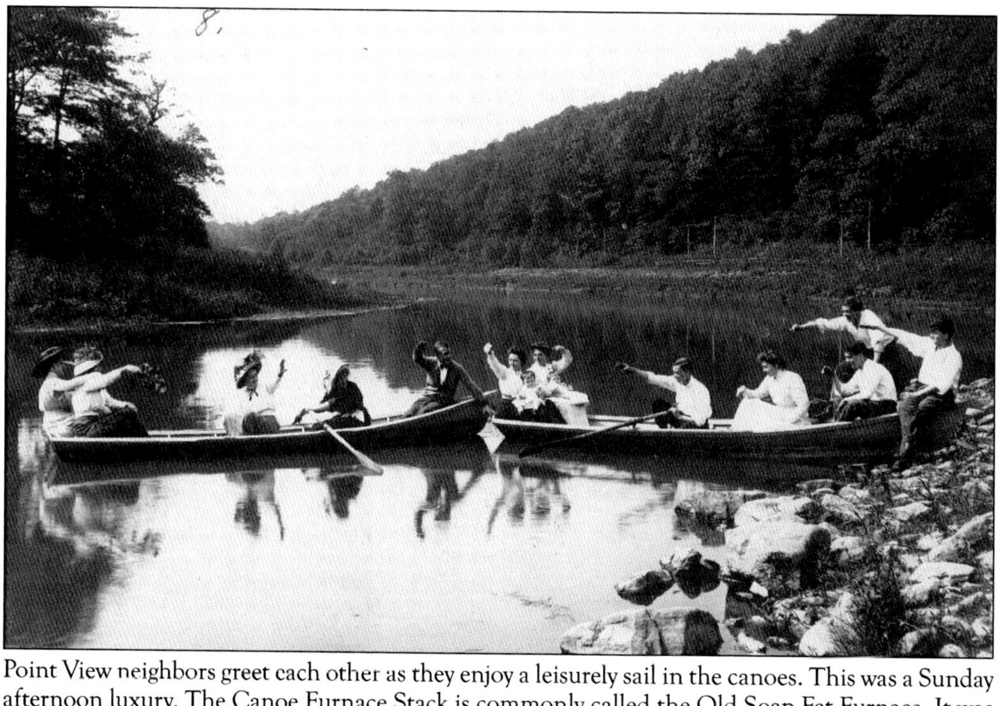

Point View neighbors greet each other as they enjoy a leisurely sail in the canoes. This was a Sunday afternoon luxury. The Canoe Furnace Stack is commonly called the Old Soap Fat Furnace. It was built at Point View by Henry Sparge in 1830. This area became an exclusive resort. By the time Point View became prominent as a summer resort, the furnace had phased into history.

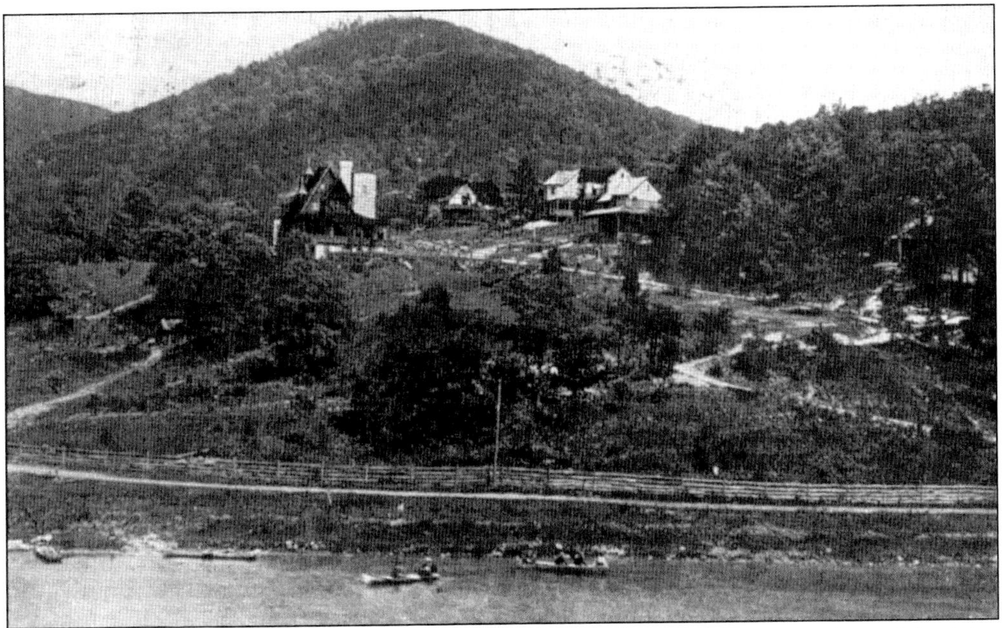

Point View Cottages were built as a community project in 1897. Wealthy patrons formed the Point View Association and built their dwellings on the picturesque mountain overlooking the gap with its icehouse, railroad, and areas for swimming and canoeing. This is a 1904 photograph of the "cottages" at Point View. Waddington House is the one resembling a castle.

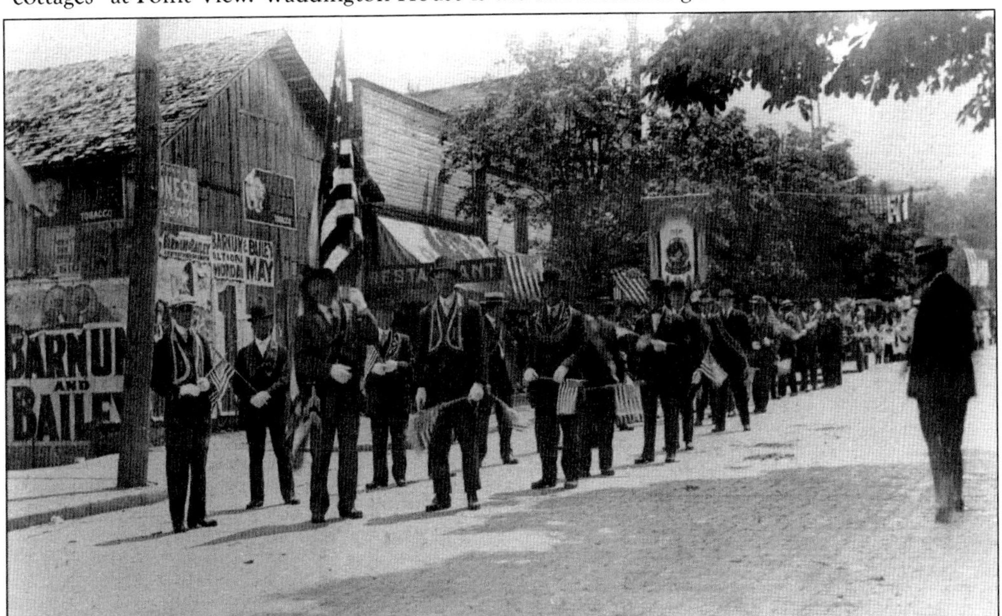

In 1915, the Army of the Republic parade gets under way on High Street. This organization was formed in 1888 with 16 charter members to encourage enlistment in military service. Membership declined and the organization phased out before World War I. The restaurant in the background later became Veteran's Park. The building advertising the Barnum and Bailey circus and Polar Bear tobacco is that of Louis Sottie's shoe store.

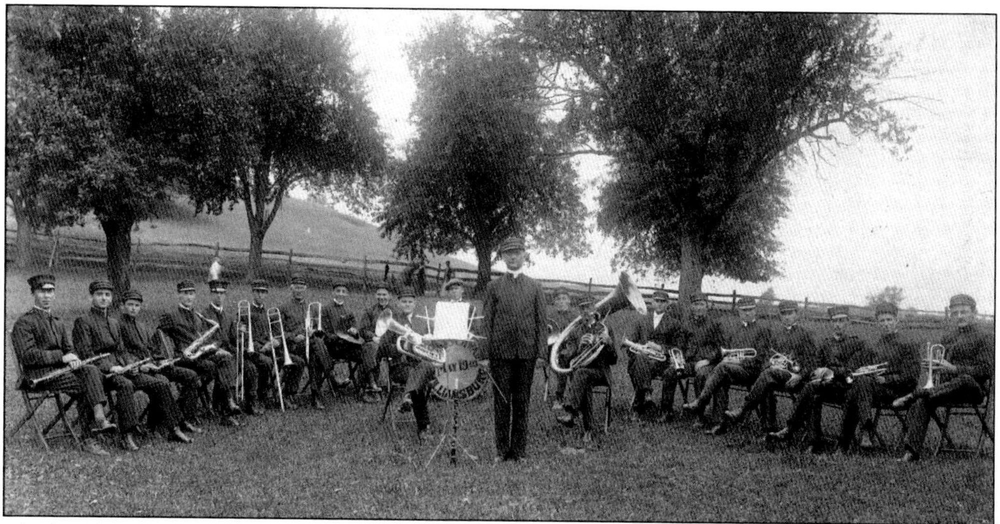

The band dedicated to Charles Schwab performed in a concert on May 19, 1903. Schwab's family loved music and instilled it in their children. Charles took music lessons from the Sisters of Mercy. The family relocated to Loretto when his father, John, could no longer work in a woolen factory. Charles was born in Williamsburg in 1862. His honored position as president of U.S. Steel and Bethlehem Steel did not deter him from remembering his hometown and humble beginnings.

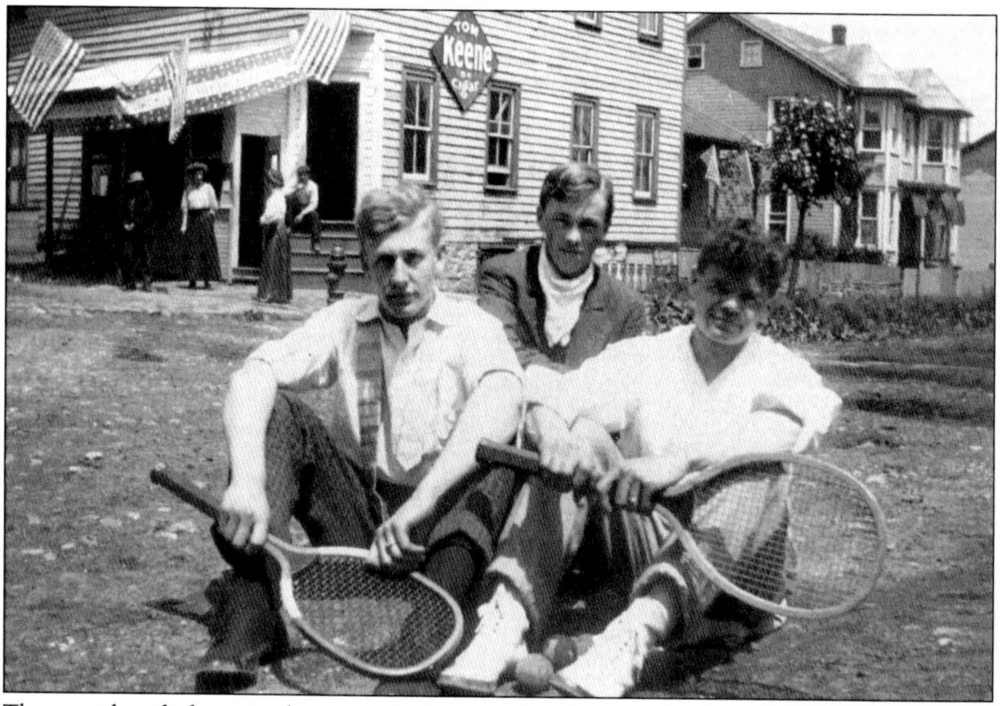

Three unidentified tennis players rest in front of the Maize Hotel. The hotel was located on the corner of High and West Second Streets during the canal era. It was a prominent hostelry after the Civil War. The building was once the home of Charles Schwab, the steel magnate. His father, John Schwab, was proprietor of the Maize Hotel for several years. The site is now occupied by an Exxon service station.

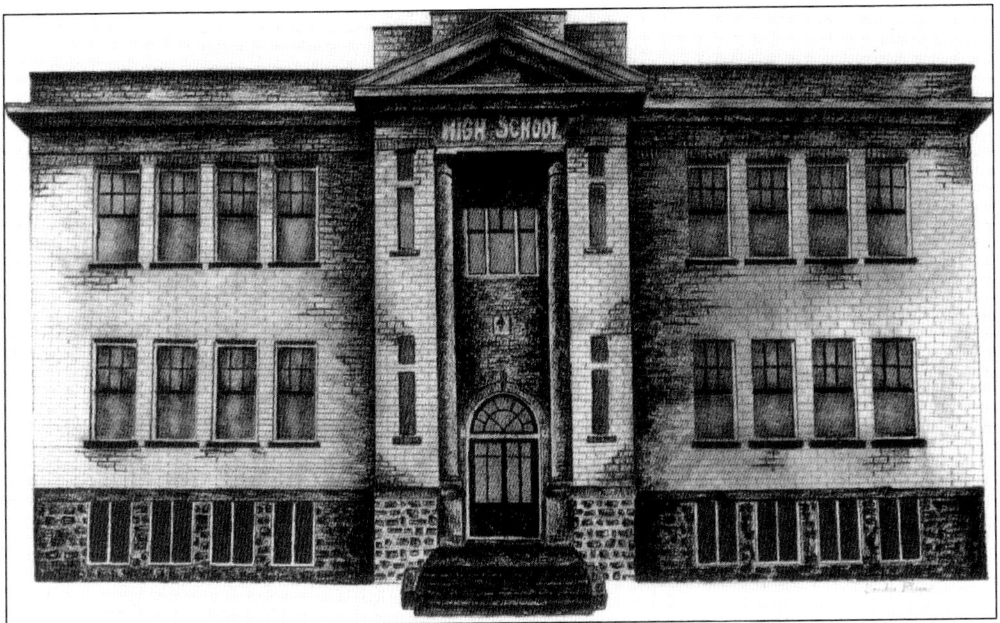

The earliest-known secondary education in Williamsburg was at the Williamsburg Academy, which opened in 1847. It was a two-year course that flourished for many years. The initial construction of the present school building took place in 1918. Two years later, the facility became a four-year high school. Additions were built. In 1936, the gymnasium was finished and, later, a third addition was completed. This school grew in leaps and bounds.

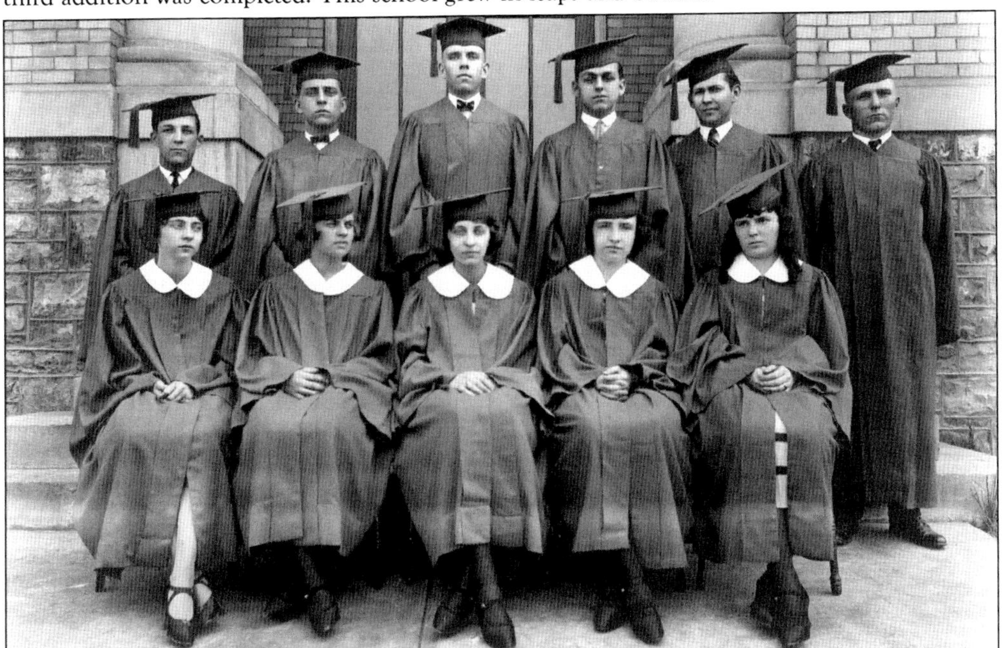

The graduating class of 1923 was the first to complete four years in the Williamsburg High School. Pictured from left to right are the following: (front row) Martha Patterson, Dorothy Norris, Catherine Metz, Marjorie Patterson, and Marjorie Stoner; (back row) James McMahon, George Beckman, Claud Reisch, Raymond Stoner, Lester Parks, and Marshal Dunn.

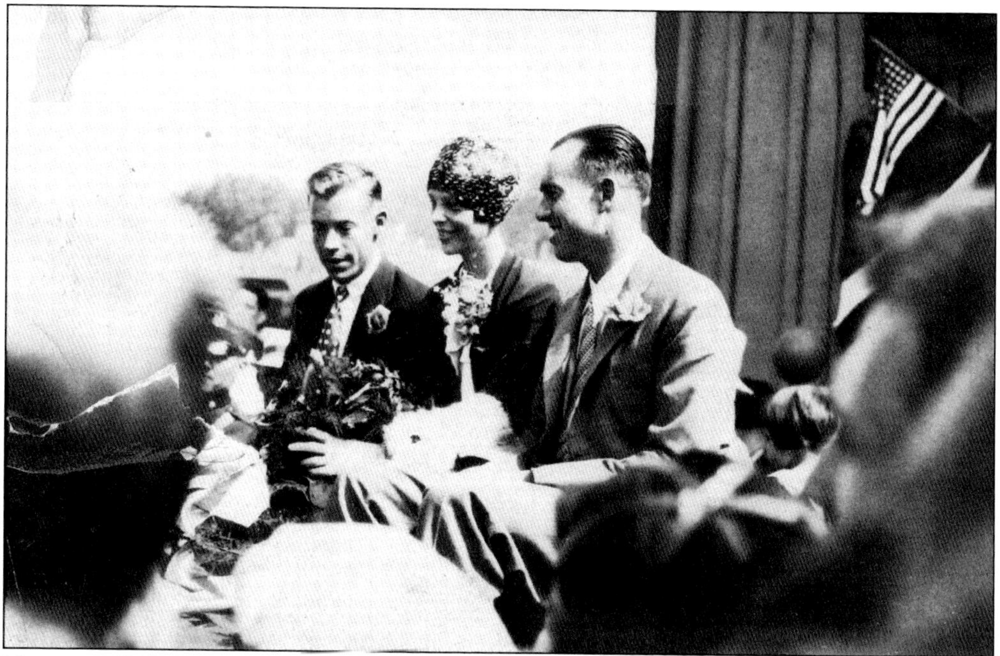

Native son Wilbur Stultz (left), Amelia Earhart, and Louis Gordon enjoy a parade in their honor. They made a historic flight across the Atlantic Ocean on July 28, 1928. The trio made the Atlantic crossing in a small biplane named *Friendship* from Newfoundland to Wales in 20 hours and 40 minutes. Stultz was a skilled pilot. The venture was significant because several passengers were aboard, one of whom was a woman.

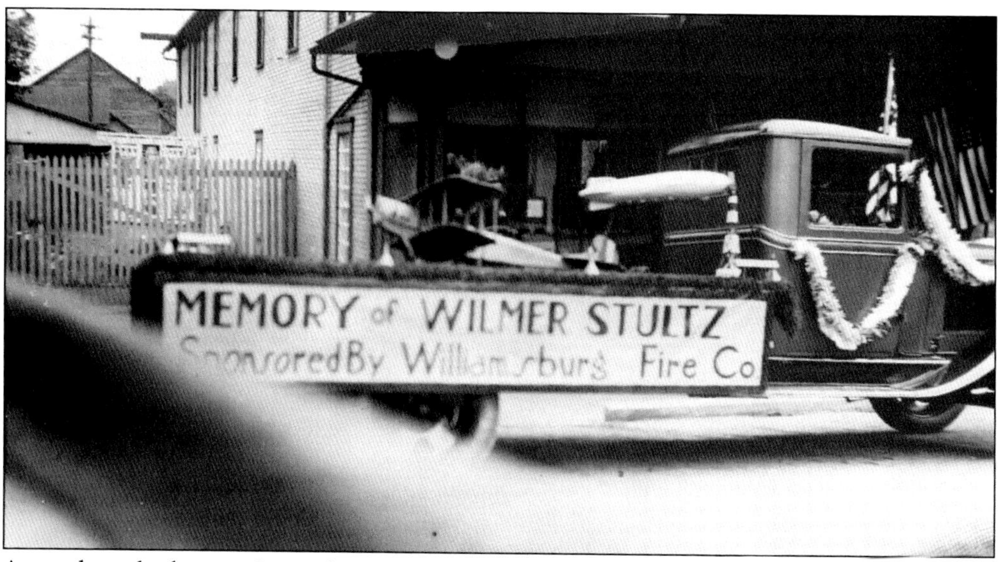

A parade took place on September 1, 1932, in memory of Wilmer Stutz. Sponsored by the fire department, this float featured a replica of his aircraft. It is passing in front of Metz's hardware store on the corner of Second and Spring Streets. Wilbur Stultz was killed in an accident on Roosevelt Field, Long Island, on July 1, 1929.

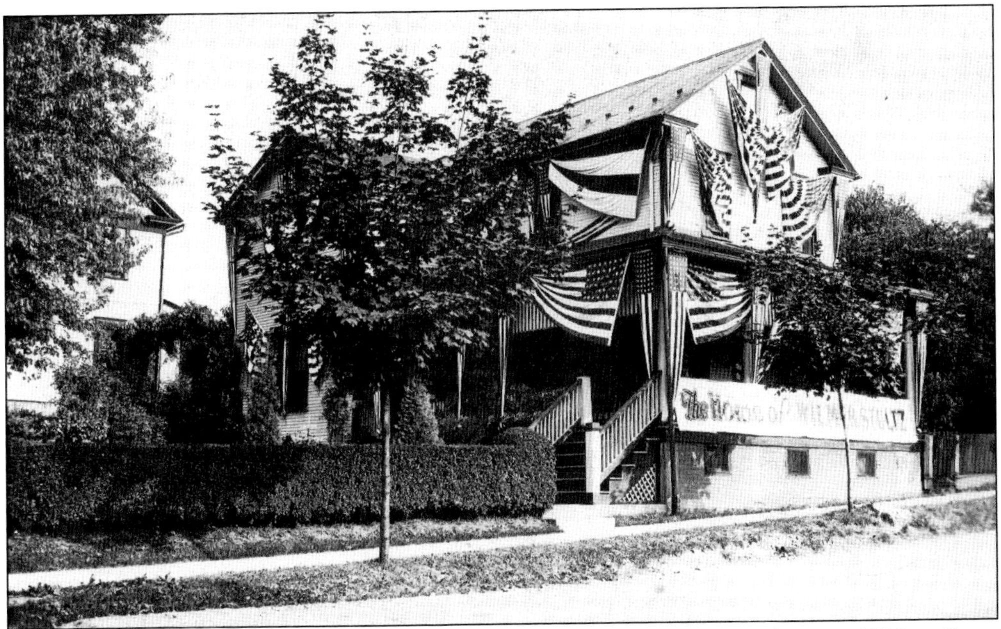

The home of Wilbur Stutz was decorated for the patriotic occasion. He was born in 1900 on Piney Creek Road. The three travelers had shared numerous honors. Louis Gordon was the mechanic, and Stultz was among the best aviators of his day. Amelia Earhart sent a telegram to Pres. Calvin Coolidge in order to tell him that the success of the mission was due to the competence of Stultz.

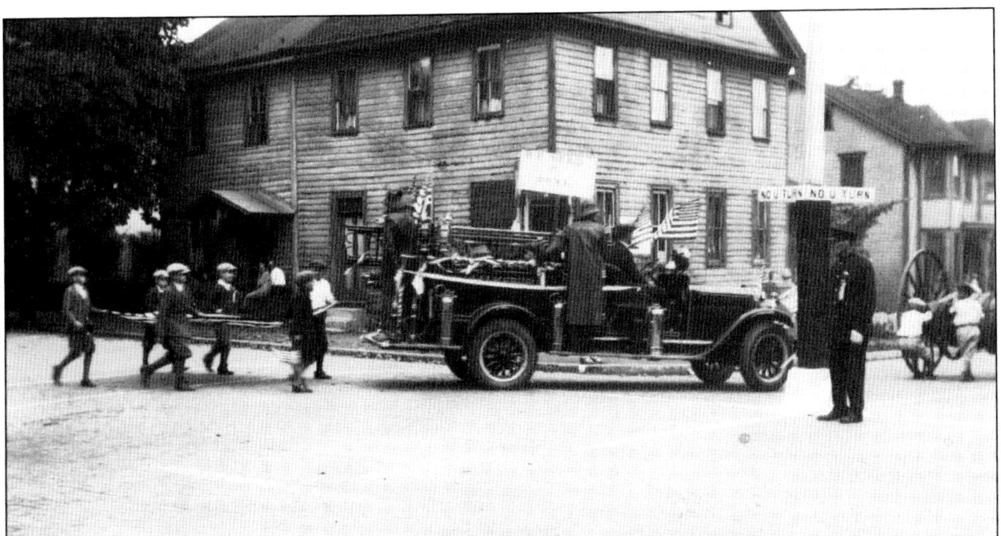

The parade is turning the corner at High and West Second Streets in front of the Maize Hotel. This was once the home of steel magnate Charles Schwab. The flag is carried behind the fire truck by a group of Boy Scouts. The town greeted its heroic son, and Williamsburg has always kept his memory alive.

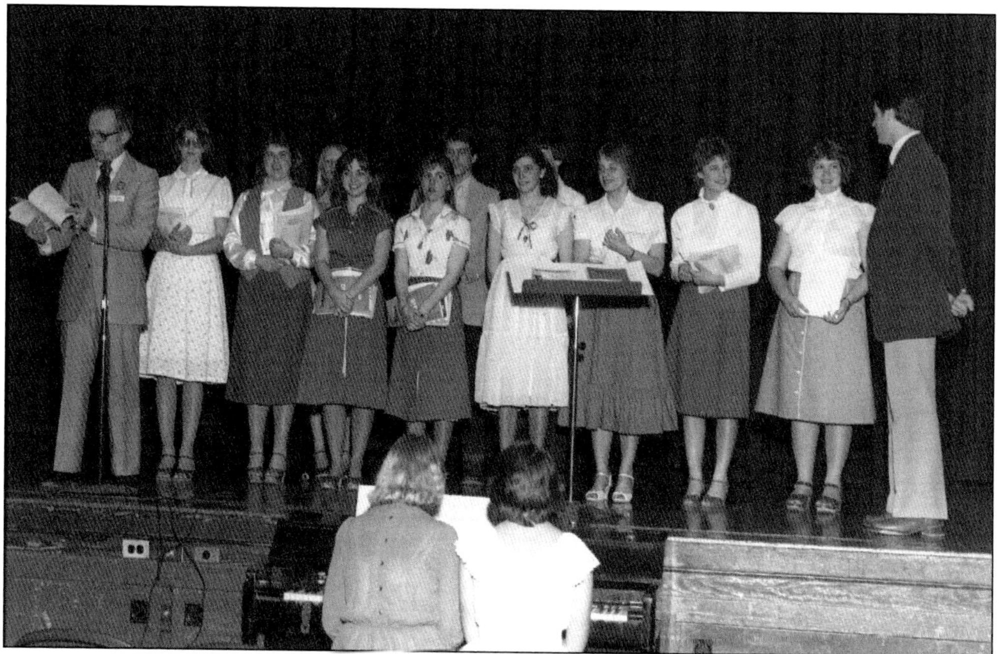

A choir performed for Heritage Night, April 14, 1982, honoring the 300th birthday of Pennsylvania. The welcome address was given by William Cramer. The vocal ensemble is shown here. They are, from left to right, as follows: (front row) Trine Sollenberger, Joan Battenfield, Wendi Creighton, Maureen Edwards, Mary L. Leidy, Karyn England, and Cindy Brubaker; (back row) Noel Heller, Michael White, and Charles Brua. John Gallace was the director, and the pianists were Joleen Kertz and Penny Campbell.

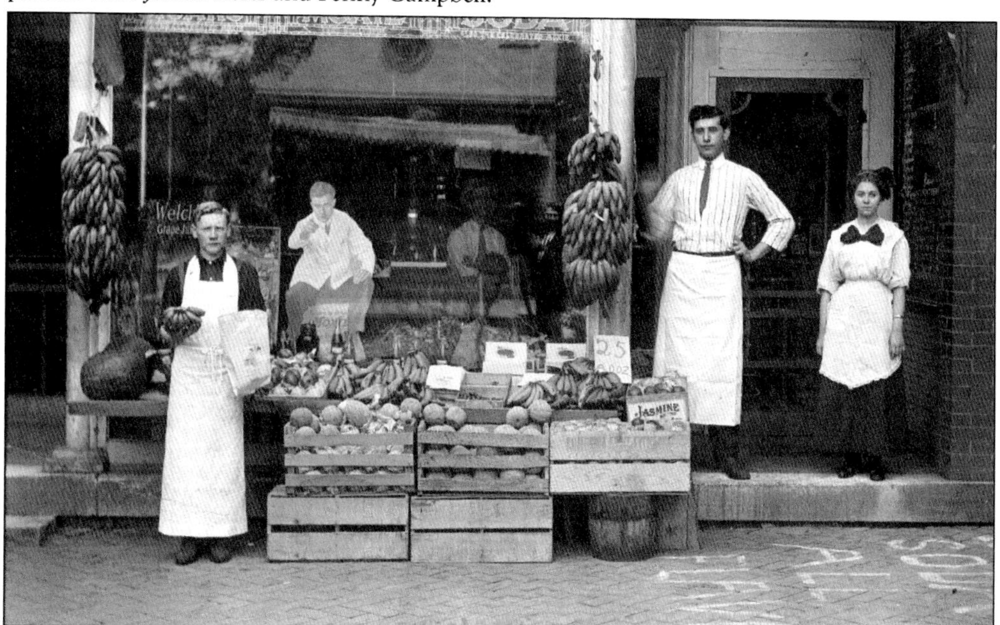

Wilt Store was an early establishment in Williamsburg. Does anyone remember when bananas were 25¢ a dozen? All flavors of soda were advertised in the road. Welches grape juice stands in the window.

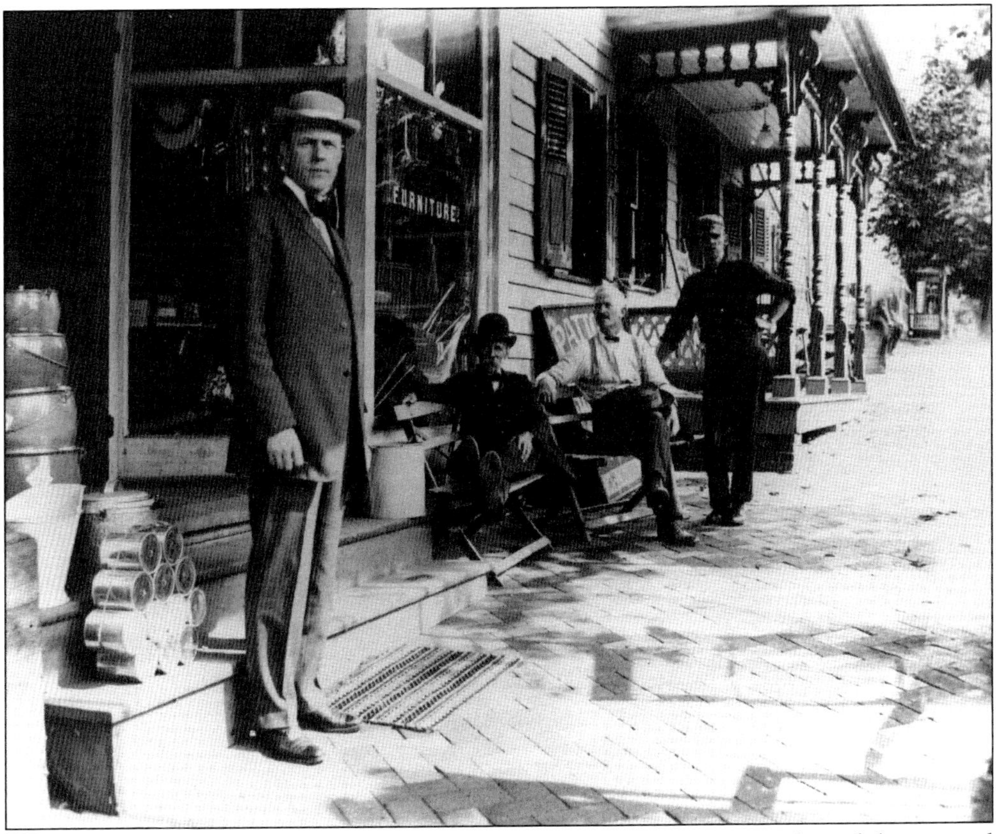

Garvin's Furniture Store was located on East Second Street. The owner was a funeral director and casket maker. He also owned a drugstore on High Street. "Dink" Garvin was his son. In the early days of merchandising, merchants took on several professions and seemed to manage them all.

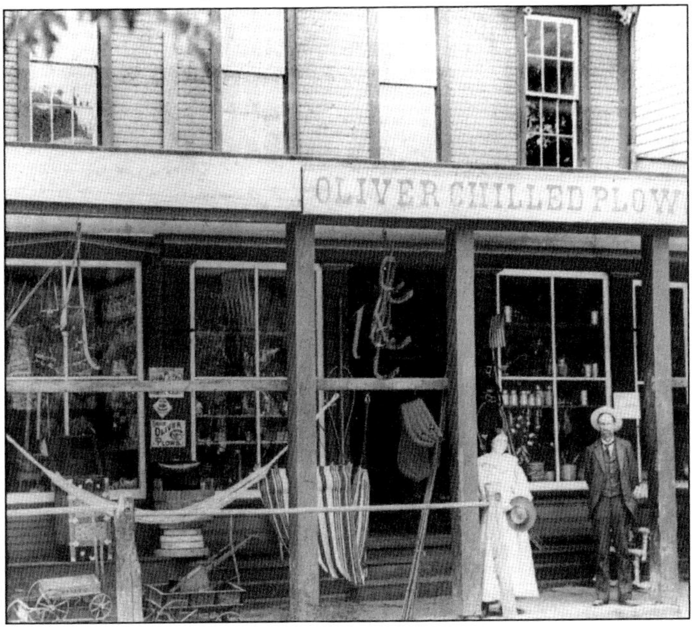

Edward Fluke's store was a turn-of-the-century establishment that sold the necessary items of the day, from hardware to general merchandise. Customers would use the hitching posts and rails across the front for hitching horses and wagons. The sign advertises Oliver's Chilled Plows (horse-drawn plows). Two different hammocks are displayed, along with children's wagons, a vintage washtub, a wind-up Victrola, and lanterns.

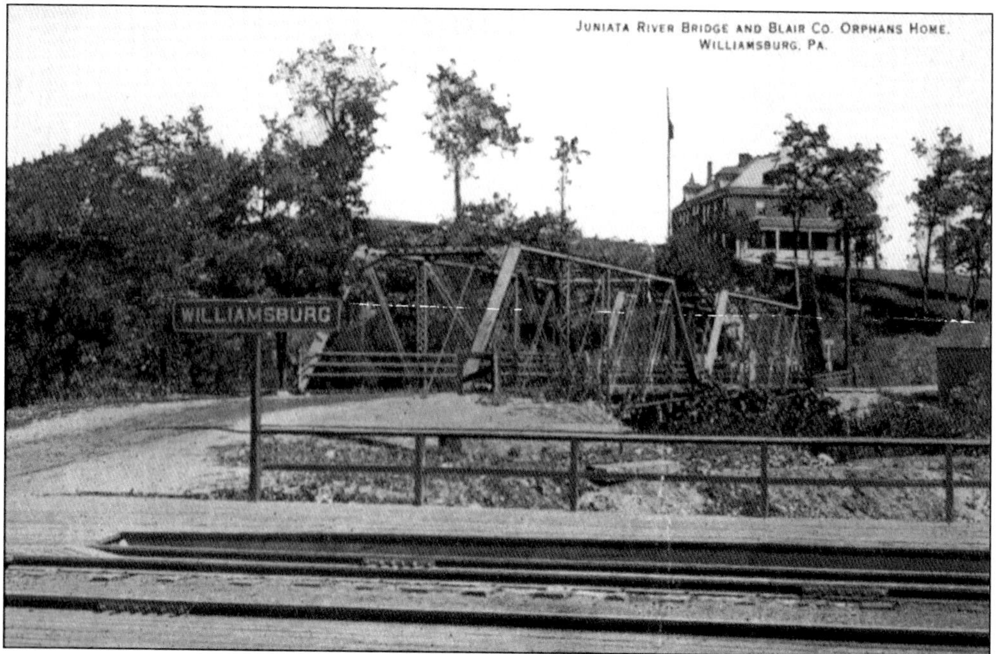

The steel bridge replaced the covered bridge of an earlier era. It was washed out in the flood of 1936. The Blair County Children's Home, in the background, was opened c. 1900. Proprietors of Dean's Theater treated these youngsters to free matinees on Saturdays when Gene Autrey and Shirley Temple were featured. Ruth Grassmeyer was pianist during the era of silent movies. An addition was built onto the home, which later became the Church of God. The old section was destroyed by fire in 1975.

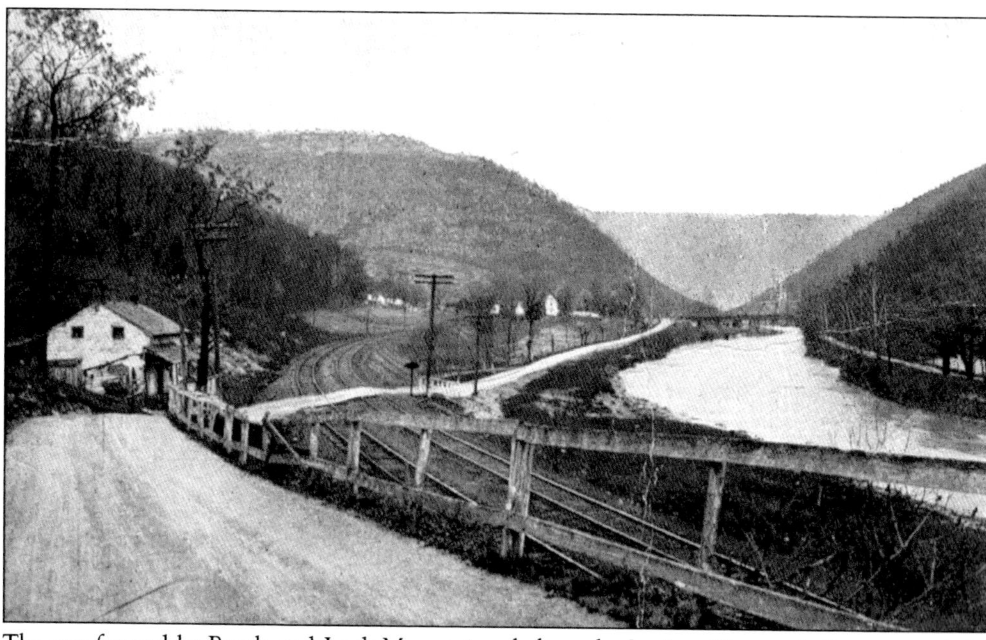

The gap formed by Brush and Lock Mountains shelters the Juniata River as it flows toward the Three Mile Dam. The Frankstown branch of the railroad accompanies the river, and the road links the main highway with Williamsburg.